Satirizing Modernism

Satirizing Modernism

Aesthetic Autonomy, Romanticism, and the Avant-Garde

Emmett Stinson

BLOOMSBURY ACADEMIC
LONDON • NEW YORK • OXFORD • NEW DELHI • SYDNEY

BLOOMSBURY ACADEMIC
Bloomsbury Publishing Plc
50 Bedford Square, London, WC1B 3DP, UK
1385 Broadway, New York, NY 10018, USA

BLOOMSBURY, BLOOMSBURY ACADEMIC and the Diana logo
are trademarks of Bloomsbury Publishing Plc

First published in Great Britain 2017
Paperback edition published 2018

Cover design: Eleanor Rose
Cover image © Renee Pabon

Names: Stinson, Emmett, author.
Title: Satirizing modernism: aesthetic autonomy, romanticism, and the
avant-garde / Emmett Stinson.
Description: New York: Bloomsbury Academic, 2017. | Includes bibliographical
references and index. | Description based on print version record and CIP
data provided by publisher; resource not viewed.
Identifiers: LCCN 2016052086 (print) | LCCN 2017012617 (ebook) |
ISBN 9781501329098 (ePub) | ISBN 9781501329104 (ePDF) | ISBN
9781501329081 (hardcover)
Subjects: LCSH: Modernism (Literature) | Experimental fi ction–History and
criticism. | Satire–History and criticism. | Autonomy in literature. |
Avant-garde (Aesthetics) | Fiction–Technique.
Classification: LCC PN56.M54 (ebook) | LCC PN56.M54 S85 2017 (print) | DDC
809/.9112–dc23
LC record available at https://lccn.loc.gov/2016052086

ISBN: HB: 978-1-5013-2908-1
PB: 978-1-5013-4808-2
ePDF: 978-1-5013-2910-4
ePub: 978-1-5013-2909-8

Typeset by Deanta Global Publishing Services, Chennai, India

To find out more about our authors and books visit
www.bloomsbury.com and sign up for our newsletters.

For Jade, Evie, and Elias

Contents

Acknowledgments

I want to thank Professor Peter Otto and Associate Professor Justin Clemens for their extensive commentary on early versions of this manuscript. I would also like to thank Nick Heron, who provided invaluable advice on the introductory chapter, in particular. I would never have pursued a career as a literary academic if not for some excellent teachers of literature—Bobby Rue, Will Spears, Tad Roach, and John Austin—whose early instruction literally changed the course of my life. This book has also been written in memory of my undergraduate mentor, Dr. David Kadlec, a great teacher and researcher, who was always generous with his time and encouragement. Finally, I want to thank my wife, Jade, and our children, Evie and Elias. I could never have completed this book without their constant love and support.

Introduction: Autonomy, Satire, Romanticism, Avant-Garde

1 Autonomy

In a notorious episode of the television show *Seinfeld* (1989–98), the characters George Costanza and Jerry Seinfeld go to the headquarters of the major TV network NBC to pitch a show "about nothing."[1] When the executives attempt to glean some meaningful detail about the contents of the show, George becomes irate, insisting "No! No! No! Nothing happens!" On one level, his protestations serve as a tongue-in-cheek metacommentary on *Seinfeld's* quotidian plots about riding the subway, going to the cinema, or having dinner at a Chinese restaurant. But George and Jerry's anti-pitch for a show that would subvert the formal conventions of a situational comedy also appears to parody the aesthetic autonomy and formal experimentation usually associated with modernist works. Indeed, Costanza later defends his angry replies in the meeting by saying, "I, for one, am not going to compromise my artistic integrity"; while this claim is clearly ironic, given that George lacks both moral and artistic integrity, it nonetheless implies a belief in art's self-justification, which has often been seen as a hallmark of modernist aesthetics. As this example suggests, at the end of the twentieth century, modernist autonomy was popularly understood to be motivated by an elitist view of its own value—a position that seemed comically out of step with the economic and cultural realities of the contemporary world.

This popular view of modernist autonomy echoed scholarly positions that had been developing over the previous thirty years; by 1984, in his landmark essay on postmodernism, Fredric Jameson could confidently write aesthetic autonomy's obituary, stating that, under late capitalism, "aesthetic production today has become integrated into commodity production generally."[2] For Jameson, globalized capitalism made it virtually impossible for artists to claim independence from economic or commercial imperatives, given the hegemony of technocratic, neoliberal managerialism, and the concomitant privatization of the public sphere. Andreas Huyssen, writing about changes in museum culture in the 1990s, similarly noted that appeals to "the myths of aesthetic autonomy . . . can no longer be used by anyone with a straight face."[3] As Huyssen attests, modernist notions of autonomy no longer held sway within institutions that had become conscious of the inherently political nature of cultural intermediation. From these perspectives, modernist aesthetic autonomy seemed both impracticable and politically naïve.

But these popular and academic views of modernist autonomy tended to ignore an important fact: the concept of a "pure" autonomy had already been critiqued in many modernist works. Even George and Jerry's parodic TV show in which "nothing happens" was anticipated by André Gide's novel *The Counterfeiters* (1925), where the character Edouard strives to produce a "*pure* novel" stripped of "its concern with a certain sort of accuracy," which also eschews "dialogue . . . drawn from life" and the description of "characters," "accidents," "traumatisms," and even "outward events."[4] Gide appears to have viewed the pure novel as a sort of ideal form[5] and Eduoard's comments explicitly mirror Flaubert's own desire to write "a book about nothing, a book dependent on nothing external, which would be held together by the internal strength of its style."[6] But Eduoard's complete failure to realize this aesthetic project presents a complex and ironic undercutting of this idealization. Gide's modernist aesthetics, as *The Counterfeiters* demonstrates, do not simply argue for either art's self-justification or the creation of "pure" forms, but rather involve the self-reflexive acknowledgment of the fundamental impossibility of a "pure" autonomy. Gide's ironic and reflexive aesthetic method presents something more complex than an elitist belief in art's immanent value.

Over the last decade, there has been a renewed scholarly interest in modernist autonomy, which has increasingly sought to examine and understand this phenomenon within its own terms and contexts. This approach has been necessary because prior views on modernist autonomy frequently reflected polemical positions deriving from two of the most significant and prolonged aesthetic debates of the twentieth century. The first such debate, which mainly occurred among Marxist critics, grew out of Ernest Bloch and Georg Lukács's disagreement about German Expressionism's relationship to fascism. This dispute would develop into an ongoing exchange—taken up by such figures as Theodor Adorno, Walter Benjamin, Bertolt Brecht, and others—about whether what we now call modernist art was either elitist and reactionary or else radical and utopian.[7] Of equal importance were the postmodernism debates, in which both Jameson and Huyssen played important roles, which sought to define the mode of cultural and aesthetic production that had developed after modernism; as I will discuss in Chapter 5, proponents of postmodernism typically associated autonomy with a retrograde or conservative modernist aesthetics that had been superseded by a postmodern heteronomy. In both of these debates, positions on autonomy could not easily be separated from larger disagreements about culture and politics; while this resulted in intriguing and spirited exchanges, considerations of modernist autonomy as a specific historical and cultural phenomenon were often sidelined by what seemed to be more urgent questions—in particular the question of whether autonomy should be seen as reactionary or progressive.

While I am not seeking to dismiss the importance of these prolonged debates or account for all of the many positions articulated within them, I do want to suggest that three broad approaches to autonomy developed in their wake. The first of these approaches presupposes autonomy to be a logically coherent concept or aesthetic program, which is then situated as one pole in a binary opposition. Representative examples include Peter Bürger's influential definition of autonomy as art's separateness from life[8]; Richard Murphy's argument, itself reliant on aspects of Bürger's account, that modernist autonomy sought "to resist any kind of co-option which would limit the work's meaning"[9]; and many post-structural accounts of autonomy, such as Craig Owens's description of modernist autonomy as the "autonomy of the signifier" in its "liberation from the 'tyranny of the signified.'"[10]

The second approach, associated with such thinkers as Bloch, Adorno, and Herbert Marcuse, treats aesthetic autonomy as being, in some manner, a model for utopian social transformation. While it is important to note that many of these accounts are so conceptually rich that they cannot be simply reduced to such a formula (particularly in the case of Adorno, for whom autonomy cannot be understood, as Christoph Menke has argued, without reference to the categories of negation and sovereignty[11]), this association between aesthetic autonomy and utopia has nevertheless constituted a significant approach to the concept.

The third approach involves the claim that modernist autonomy is not integral to modernism itself. There are two variations of this argument. The first, articulated by Astradur Eysteinsson, contends that the modernist view of the work as an autonomous and "isolated aesthetic whole" cannot be reconciled with "the equally prominent view of modernism as a historically explosive paradigm"—a contradiction that leads Eysteinsson to conclude that the concept of modernism is incoherent.[12] The second, as exemplified by Fredric Jameson, views autonomy as an epiphenomenon of a deeper cultural shift, which is "the radical disjunction and separation of literature and art" from other popular and populist forms of culture.[13]

More contemporary research, however, has tried to approach autonomy in new ways by combining theory, historical research, and textual analysis to understand modernist autonomy in its own terms. Such critics as Jennifer Ashton, Charles Altieri, Nicholas Brown, Lisa Siraganian, and Andrew Goldstone have all argued that aesthetic autonomy is of key significance for any understanding of modernism, while also seeking to depict such autonomy as a complex phenomenon that is simultaneously aesthetic and political in nature. In so doing, these critics have sought to locate understandings of autonomy outside of the three traditional positions I have noted above in a manner that also transcends the traditional antipathy between aesthetic autonomy and politically committed art.

Virtually all of these more recent accounts argue that modernist claims of autonomy have typically been misunderstood. Even today, aesthetic autonomy is still commonly represented as "insisting on the retreat of art from society," disavowing any concern "with life praxis in any direct way," and seeking "to locate art in a sphere evacuated of all purposiveness."[14] In such accounts, modernist autonomy is essentially equated with the art-for-art's-sake positions articulated by *Le Parnasse* and the various decadent authors of the late nineteenth century. To be fair, even the modernists themselves—as well as many early scholars of modernism—were not always clear on how their claims of autonomy differed from these earlier ones. Nonetheless, such approaches ignore the specific historical and cultural contexts of modernism, which produce different notions of autonomy; as many scholars have noted, these differences—even if they might appear subtle—matter a great deal.

In *From Modernism to Postmodernism* (2005), Jennifer Ashton argues that autonomy is a key concept for distinguishing modernism from postmodernism, a position I will affirm, albeit in a different manner. Ashton's claim relies on a set of distinctions made by Michael Fried in his essay "Art and Objecthood" (1967). Following Fried, Ashton argues that postmodern works, as exemplified by language poetry, are art objects that invite the reader to project their own experiences onto them in a way that makes the spectator into "the author of the text."[15] Modernist autonomy, however, presumes the work of art's internal coherence, which exists prior to and regardless of any readerly interpretation.[16] Here, modernist art is characterized by the inviolability of its authorial intention, which presents a strong limitation on acceptable or possible interpretations—unlike postmodern works, which rely on a notion of authorial "attention" that invites creative, readerly interpretation. Ashton uses this distinction, among other things, to argue that Gertrude Stein's belief in the internal coherence of her own work is essentially modernist, thereby critiquing the commonly held view of Stein's work as an anticipatory postmodernism.

Ashton's claims have been taken up and extrapolated by Charles Altieri and Nicholas Brown. Brown argues that autonomy and heteronomy offer different perspectives on the same cycle of commodity exchange—a position he illustrates by contrasting Hegel and Marx's account of individual labor. Brown follows Ashton, however, in viewing authorial intention as essential for claims of autonomy: he argues that the presence of intention both limits possible interpretations and distinguishes artworks from pure commodities.[17] Altieri argues that any understanding of modernism must wrestle with the complex intentions behind autonomy, which he views as a textual reification of modernist impersonality (itself an oblique critique of political rhetoric in liberal democracies that sought to avoid or delay social reform). For Altieri, too, autonomy, as a product of authorial intent, both shapes and delimits readerly interpretations, since autonomous works "resist fixed concepts by encouraging the audience's attention to the concrete unfolding of complex and irreducible relational forces operating in several dimensions."[18] For Altieri, autonomy produces a series of complex textual effects, but these effects, at heart, are still a reification of the author's own authority and intention.

Ashton, Brown, and Altieri's claims serve as a critical response to other recent accounts of modernist autonomy. On the one hand, they refute Jameson and Eysteinsson's denial of autonomy's importance for modernism. On the other hand, this linking of autonomy and authorial intention problematizes historicist, pluralistic notions of modernism, as exemplified by Douglas Mao and Rebecca Walkowitz's notion of the "New Modernist Studies."[19] In arguing for the centrality of modernist authorial intention, Ashton, Brown, and Altieri all suggest that any concept of modernism must derive from modernists' own accounts of their practice, rather than a broader study of modernist institutions, networks, and cultural production. While I will similarly attempt to ground concepts of modernism within the parameters generated by modernist literary works, I remain more skeptical—for reasons I will enumerate later—of the adequacy of intention for conceptualizing modernist autonomy.

Lisa Siraganian's *Modernism's Other Work* (2012) extends Ashton's insights by focusing on autonomy's relationship with politics. Siraganian argues that autonomy was "always conceived simultaneously and deliberately as an aesthetic *and* political act."[20] She notes the political elements of even the most seemingly apolitical versions of modernist autonomy, as exemplified by William K. Wimsatt and Cleanth Brooks's New Critical claim that

> poetry—or art in general—might draw off by itself and be content with an emphatic assertion of autonomy—its own kind of intrinsic worth, to be understood and savoured by its own devotees. It could be set up as a legitimate pursuit apart from, and even in defiance of, the rival norms of ethics and politics.[21]

Even Wimsatt and Brooks's relatively strong claim of autonomy is not unilateral. To have an "intrinsic worth" that is "apart from" ethics and politics, for example, is not to deny ethics, politics, or purposiveness altogether, and being "in defiance of" existing ethical and political orders arguably requires a political and ethical commitment. Although Wimsatt and Brooks's conception of autonomy is not without problems, Siraganian argues that the caricature of modernist autonomy as a complete rejection of worldly, political, ethical, and social content does not hold up under scrutiny.

By acknowledging that modernist autonomy claims always already entail a relation between the aesthetic and political, it is possible, as Jacques Rancière's work has suggested,[22] to move beyond the binary in which aesthetic autonomy is viewed as either as an elitist escape from reality or as a model for enacting utopian social change. In saying this, I am not suggesting that eminent theorists like Lukács, Adorno, and Marcuse,[23] along with many others, have failed to think diachronically, but rather that most twentieth-century positions on aesthetic autonomy have covertly operated within a mimetic paradigm that posits an essential binary between the world or "reality" and the work of art. The belief that the work of art should explicitly mirror the ideal social in order to foment revolution or that art provides a utopian space that in some sense models new social orders implies a correlation between the work of art and the world, and thereby invokes the very mimetic paradigm that much of modernist literature openly sought to oppose.[24]

Peter Bürger's analysis of the avant-garde, which I will consider in detail later in this chapter, illustrates the problem: from this perspective, his entire explanatory apparatus can be read as an inflection of the very mimetic paradigm that, according to his claims, the avant-garde was trying to overcome. In starting with the assumption that art and life are essentially distinct categories (which the avant-garde seeks to merge), his analysis ignores the possibility that "life" (however such a term is constructed) and art are co-implicated and hemmed together by a complex and overlapping web of connections that renders attempts to make categorical distinctions between the two an abstract language game.[25] The point in making this claim is not to valorize all works that flaunt their disconnection from a clear social project or program, but rather to put forward the argument that autonomy might enable a set of possibilities that are actually obscured by ideology critiques of this kind. As Siraganian points out, "Modernism's core aesthetic problem—the artwork's status as an object and a subject's relation to it—poses fundamental questions of agency, freedom and politics," which are only reinforced when "the art object's immunity from the world's interpretations" is asserted.[26]

This acknowledgment of modernist autonomy's entanglement with social, political, and cultural concerns has been extended even further by Andrew Goldstone, who argues in *Fictions of Autonomy* (2013) that "modernist attempts to secure autonomy in fact confront and make use of the artist's and the artwork's embeddedness in social life."[27] Goldstone points out that modernist assertions of autonomy typically have a specific reference; rather than refusing all worldly connection, modernists sought autonomy from certain discourses, institutions, traditions, or social forces. Goldstone argues that modernism thus presents not *an* autonomy, but versions of autonomy, among which he defines four types: "elevating the cultivation of aesthetic form over mimetic realism; distinguishing the autonomous artistic work from the less independent artist who makes it; rejecting any political or communal affiliation for artist and artistic practices alike; or, finally, disavowing reference to reality altogether."[28] This nuanced account problematizes wholesale critiques of autonomy, which, in ignoring specific contexts, omit what's distinctive about individual claims of autonomy.

Modernist assertions of autonomy are not categorical, but instead present a set of provisional claims that relate to a specific set of material practices, social orders, historical contexts, and political concerns. Moreover, these claims of autonomy are often made with varying degrees of irony and seriousness. The capacity to make such claims while simultaneously ironizing or problematizing them is, of course, a central feature of the complex rhetorical strategies of works of literature, which, unlike works of philosophy, are not bound by rules of logic to be coherent, and, unlike polemical works, are not required to present a clear and unambiguous argument or set of positions. Therefore, approaching any modernist autonomy claim as a monolithic construct or a philosophical proposition ignores those very local particularities that distinguish modernist autonomy from other versions of autonomy.

However, Goldstone's considered and sensible objection to most sweeping critiques of aesthetic autonomy actually can and should be stated in much stronger terms. The very notion that all forms of autonomy possess some coherent, conceptual framework that can be extracted from these specific historical contexts and assigned an abstract, philosophical value is, at best, dubious.[29] As Pierre Bourdieu has argued, autonomous forms of art tend to result in a "reflective and critical turn by the producers upon their own production" that causes such works to self-consciously wrestle with their own conditions of possibility.[30] The irony here is clear: claims of autonomy are never completely autonomous because they can only derive their meaning from the disavowal of an external tradition, institution, or discourse. Autonomy is thus always defined by this negative relationship to a disavowed externality, and autonomy has no content aside from *not possessing* the very content that it seeks to differentiate itself from (attempts to define modernist autonomy as an emphasis on "form" over content are also misleading, since form—which by its nature is protean—does not possess an essential character for the reason that, by relational definition, it is *not* content, and thus has no content, as such). In this sense, claims of autonomy are always shadowed by the externalities they seek to escape.

Modernist autonomy therefore does not imply either a totalizing rejection of social and political content or a belief in philosophical idealism. My suggestion is that, rather than serving as a coherent philosophical position or a model for utopia, modernist autonomy be viewed as a *rhetorical strategy or gambit* that posits the work of art's separation from political or social forces from which it can never truly be free. Assertions of autonomy, rather than being universal proclamations of art's separation from reality, can be viewed, instead, as a desire or striving for an impossible objectivity that might transcend an author's given social and historical contexts, thereby enabling the creation of a work of art that extends, breaks with, or transforms received traditions and normative discourses. Modernism's insistence on autonomy, from this point of view, is inseparable from its desire for novelty and the transcendence of tradition—ends that can be achieved only by claiming autonomy from such traditions in the first place. In this sense, autonomy is less a philosophical concept than an ambit claim that creates the necessary conditions for an art that links itself to futurity and the exploration of possible forms rather than extant ones.

One benefit of this understanding of autonomy is that—while it allows for different versions of autonomy of the kind that Goldstone discusses—it nonetheless presents a distinctive and coherent account of the larger modernist approach to autonomy. Here, autonomy serves as a necessary precondition for the modernist aesthetic project of the formal exploration of new modes of aesthetic production. It also reflects the essentially provocative nature of modernism, which has typically been characterized as producing shocking and defamiliarizing aesthetic effects. Claims of autonomy both underwrite these provocations and serve as provocative incitements in their own right.

More importantly, however, acknowledging the provocative nature of modernist autonomy claims illustrates that these claims were usually logically inconsistent, and often willfully so. Rather than presenting a coherent position, modernist notions of autonomy often ironized and undercut themselves. Indeed, the notion of the "pure novel" in Gide's *The Counterfeiters* already presents one such example. Another, taken from an author who will feature prominently later in this book, can be found in the most famous passage of Wyndham Lewis's *Tarr* (1918):

> Deadness is the first condition for art: the second is absence of soul, in the human and sentimental sense. With the statue its lines and masses are its soul, no restless inflammable ego is imagined for its interior: it has *no inside*: good art must have no inside: that is capital.[31]

While these claims have often been read as a straightforward articulation of Lewis's inhuman aesthetics, this reading, as Nathan Waddell has pointed out, is problematized by "the fact that Tarr clearly is *ironized* as a character throughout the text . . . which means we ought not to treat Tarr in any simplistic sense . . . as a 'representative' of Vorticism."[32] Here, the status of Lewis's notion of aesthetic deadness, like Gide's concept of the pure novel, is rendered deeply ambiguous. But this ambiguity is further complicated by the fact that Lewis's writing, as I will argue in Chapter 3, often appears to affirm a program of aesthetic deadness very similar to what Tarr advocates—just as Gide genuinely believed in the pure novel as an aesthetic ideal, even though *The Counterfeiters* explicitly undermines such a belief. As a result, the status of these autonomy claims remains unclear because they can be read as either sincere explications of aesthetic practice or ironic provocations.

The fact that many notable modernist works present autonomy through such irresolvable contradictions problematizes the claim—made by Ashton, Brown, and Altieri—that intention is a necessary precondition for modernist autonomy. In such works as Lewis's and Gide's, the ambiguity around the status of autonomy claims makes their relationship to authorial intent virtually impossible to determine. Part of the issue involves the way that intention is defined: Ashton relies on William K. Wimsatt and Monroe Beardsley's influential claim that "intention is design or plan in the author's mind."[33] But this proposition only begs the question of how such intention might be knowable in the first place. Ashton and Brown both derive intentions from "external" evidence in the form of essays, letters, or interviews where authors appear to describe their aesthetic designs.[34] But the connection between external authorial claims and specific works is dubious because it assumes that artists always formulate an external, or theoretical, rationale prior to the act of creation.

One needn't be a Derridean or hold a relativist belief in the validity of all interpretations to argue that such a claim is not entirely accurate. Most artists only discover their intention in the process of creation, a point that Kant makes in *The Critique of Judgment* when he notes that the "rule" or plan for a work of art does not exist prior to its existence, but rather "must . . . be gathered from the execution, i.e. from the product."[35] As a result, artists' explications of their own intent are typically posterior to the execution of their work, which suggests that such external "evidence," rather than being a true description of intent, is a specialized form of literary interpretation. A second—but hardly inconsequential—problem is that artists often exaggerate, provoke, fabricate, and adopt personas in interviews, essays, and discussions; as a result, the veracity of such external claims can never be taken as a given. Stanley Cavell has responded to this state of affairs by suggesting that the work of art itself is synonymous with the author's intent[36]; while this solution may ultimately be correct, it still does not resolve the problem of how such intention can be discerned, or what the correct relation between "external" evidence and textual interpretation should be. I agree with Ashton and Brown that external evidence does appear to be a particularly significant form of evidence, but, following Cavell, I would argue that the only sensible proposition is to test such external claims against the internal structures of a text. Terry Eagleton has noted the complexities of this hermeneutic relationship, saying that "the literary intentions that matter are those built into a work itself," and thus can only be uncovered through interpretive reading of the text.[37]

In point of fact, the problematic relation between artists' plans and their actual execution of the work is foregrounded in many modernist texts, such as Ezra Pound's "Canto CXVI," which registers a key divergence between authorial intention and the realization of the autonomous work. In "Canto CXVI," the speaker, who appears to be an avatar of Pound reflecting back on the composition of *The Cantos*, emphasizes an intentional poetic desire to "achieve the possible" while nonetheless admitting that the process of composition has been marred by "errors and wrecks"; as a result the speaker states, "I cannot make it cohere," suggesting an incapacity on the part of the poet to satisfactorily enact his intention.[38] Despite these statements of authorial failure, however, the speaker nonetheless argues for the coherence of *The Cantos* themselves, saying "it coheres all right/even if my notes do not cohere."[39] The claims for the coherence of *The Cantos*, which are imbued with a singular meaning despite having a flawed or failed set of "notes" or intentions, suggest that meaning, for Pound, is not simply derived from authorial intention. Instead, the coherence of *The Cantos* appears in spite of the failure of authorial intention.

These claims of modernist autonomy—as exemplified by Gide, Lewis, and Pound—are not consistent, logical positions, but rather are enabled by an aporetic discourse, which vacillates between contradictory claims. For Gide and Lewis, autonomy is both treated with high seriousness as a legitimate aesthetic goal and ironized, appearing as little more than a necessary-but-impossible ambit claim that posits the work of art's radical freedom. For Pound, the creation of a coherent, autonomous work is the goal of authorial intention, and yet the appearance of such a work only results through the failure of this intention. My argument is that these aporias constitute a uniquely modernist version of autonomy, which appears in the work's capacity to overcome its internal contradictions in order to present a complex, polysemous aesthetic whole that is totalizing. I will demonstrate how this totalizing autonomy manifests in the three modernist works I examine: for Wyndham Lewis, totalizing autonomy presents a means of representing in full the contradictory aesthetic impulses—both radical and conservative—behind avant-gardism itself; for William Gaddis, art's ability to transcend logical contradictions (as enacted in an unusual form of the sublime) serves as a reaffirmation of art's superiority to logic itself; for Gilbert Sorrentino, the conscious deployment of logical aporias presents a means of dissociating satire from rational discourse—and this very dissociation forms the basis for a radical claim of autonomy.

This conception of an aporetic, modernist autonomy significantly diverges from Ashton's claims that modernist autonomy reifies modernist intention in order to resist or exclude readerly interpretation. In my conception, the notion of the totalizing work as the goal of modernist autonomy requires a severing of the simple connection between author and work. The inviolability of authorial intention is problematized by the aporetic and irreconcilable nature of these autonomy claims, with the result that modernist works don't reify intention, but rather, in their execution, produce a set of meanings that surpass and transcend mere intention in the process of forming a coherent aesthetic whole. While intention does remain necessary to such a process, it no longer forms a sufficient horizon for interpretation, since the meaning available to the totalizing and inexhaustible work will always exceed the intentions of the author.

To articulate this position is not to fall back into what Todd Cronan has described as "affective formalism." Cronan's critique of affective formalism is based on his account of two different kinds of aesthetic effects: intended effects, which the artist seeks to produce in the beholder, and actual effects, which are those that occur in the beholder's mind, regardless of the artist's intention. He rejects interpretations of art based purely on viewer response (or the "actual effects" that comprise affective criticism), because they are "not up for discussion in the way intention is."[40] This is because affective interpretations rely on descriptions of experience rather than logical argumentation. Instead, Cronan views intention as a precondition for meaning, and claims that debates about the meaning of the work are inevitably debates about *intended* effects, rather than reports of the beholder's experience.

Part of the issue here regards the concept of intention itself, which Cronan—much to his credit—presents as a complex process that can never fully be explicated by the artist or "recovered" by the critic.[41] He embraces a broad notion of intention, encompassing both conscious acts of "intellectual control" and unconscious impulses that the artist may only be able to see after the completion of the work.[42] While Cronan's broadening of intention reflects the complex nature of artistic creation, it also raises questions about intention's value as a category. While I am not claiming that intention is irrelevant, or that a beholder's affective response to a work is determining, two important objections to Cronan's argument need to be stated. First, intention may not be sufficient for interpreting all works of art: the highly rhetorical novels I will analyze, for example, set in play a variety of complex—and often contradictory!—intentions that cannot always be logically subordinated to each other, and, rather than being easily resolved, produce textual paradoxes, ambiguities, and uncertainties that obscure authorial intention. Secondly, the ultimate unknowability of intention (which Cronan readily admits) renders it little more than a *theoretical object* of interpretation, which can never actually be uncovered. One could just as reasonably argue that intention is, therefore, not the object of interpretation, but its product. While I am sympathetic to interpretive regimes that seek a fidelity to authorial intention, it remains important to acknowledge that the uncertainty inherent to hermeneutics means interpretation can never produce definitive conclusions. I would argue that the modernist claims of autonomy in the satires I will examine—rather than reifying authorial intention—draw attention to precisely this problematic and indefinite relationship between intention and interpretation.

I believe that self-reflexive modernist satire presents a unique locus for understanding this complex, and, indeed, aporetic form of modernist autonomy because of its relentless and reflexive examination of modernist aesthetics. In particular, I will argue that 1) these satires express an unusually forceful claim of modernist autonomy that manifests itself in the inherently contradictory desire to transform satire—traditionally seen as an ethical and instrumental genre—into an autonomous literary form; 2) despite this vigorous assertion of autonomy, these satires are inevitably shadowed by ethical and instrumental claims because autonomy is defined by its negative relationship to a disavowed externality; 3) as a result, these satires present an explicitly contradictory form: they are genuine in their attempt to negate, disrupt, and de-instrumentalize satiric critique, but their very selection of satiric targets compromises the logical coherence of these claims; 4) the contradictory nature of these satires is very much the point, since one aspect of art's autonomy—specifically its superiority over other forms of knowledge and experience—is maintained in these satires' capacity to unify and incorporate these contradictions into an aesthetic whole; and 5) these satires therefore posit a complicated form of modernist autonomy that consists of mutually exclusive propositions.

At the same time, this formal, theoretical, and literary analysis of satire will also be supported by a larger historical argument about genre. In particular, I want to suggest that this form of satire—although an important instance of modernism in its own right—also arose from a series of historical changes wrought on satire by romanticism. In so doing, I seek to acknowledge a series of often disavowed links between romanticism and modernist aesthetics which serve to problematize modernism's claims to have broken with past traditions. I argue that modernist autonomy claims require a *fictitious* assertion of independence from historical, social, and cultural forces. As I will argue, this subgenre not only highlights the peculiarity of modernist autonomy but also illuminates aesthetic trajectories that developed out of modernism, which cannot be reconciled with postmodernism aesthetics. In this sense, these satires problematize a standard view of twentieth-century literature—which sees an exhausted modernism yielding to a new postmodern dominant—by suggesting that the modernist avant-gardes have persisted in a tradition that remains very much alive. While this analysis unfolds historically and will examine a variety of contextual questions, its main aim lies in offering the history of a previously unidentified literary genre and, therefore, I will track *internal* generic shifts rather than focusing on external, material changes. Before developing these claims further, however, I must first define the three key terms that will orient my analysis—satire, romanticism, and the avant-garde—in order to establish the conditions of possibility that gave rise to this new form of satire.

2 Satire

According to most histories of Anglophone literature, the golden age of modern satire occurred during the Restoration and the eighteenth century. Although satire has continued to persist in various forms thereafter, it has typically been relegated to the status of a minor or marginal literary form, and one that, worse still, is out of step with the times: the satirist has usually been viewed as a "true conservative,"[43] who, in exercising harsh judgment according to a moral code, is—if not simply antimodern—never in danger of being called progressive. But such preconceived notions have obfuscated a vital tradition of self-reflexive satire that has been developing since the rise of British romanticism. I will argue that romanticism initiated a shift in the dominant of satire from a neoclassical conception of satire as a form of ethical instruction to a self-reflexive paradigm that sought to exploit the aesthetic potential of satiric judgment. Out of this new romantic satire, an exemplary subgenre of self-reflexive satire developed, which I have termed "avant-garde satires of the avant-garde." This subgenre is characterized by its ambivalent relationship to the avant-garde, since representative satires make the avant-garde an object of ridicule while simultaneously employing both the formal experimentation and the critical view of tradition that characterizes the avant-garde project.

But of equal importance is this subgenre's relationship to the literary tradition of satire itself. So many scholarly definitions of satire have been proposed over the last fifty years that simply listing them produces one of satire's characteristic rhetorical maneuvers—the Rabelaisian catalogue. Satire has been variously classified as a "genre," a "semigenre," a "two-toned genre," a "mode," a "*mythos*," a "tone," a "discursive practice," a "frame of mind," a set of "tactics," a literary "bent," a "species of writing," an "open" form, a "continuous tradition," and a "literary form" for generating difference.[44] Given this lack of consensus, critics, such as Brian A. Connery and Kirke Combe, have applied Wittgenstein's concept of "family-resemblance," listing qualities that are common to but not necessary for satire.[45] Other critics have claimed that it is impossible to define satire with any terminological specificity,[46] and the problems with defining satire do seem to run deeper than the lack of an adequate taxonomy.

Theorists of satire have often noted the "protean" character of satiric texts that parodically ape the form and discourse of the object they are ridiculing.[47] This suggests that satire is not so much a genre or mode, to borrow Alastair Fowler's terminology, but rather a sort of anti-genre that inhabits other genres only to destabilize them,[48] making satire a parasitic and degenerative means of literary expression, rather than a durable form whose structures can be illuminated by careful analysis. Moreover, in a manner similar to irony, satire tends toward the production of ambiguity, which further complicates any attempt to pin down its meaning. Like irony, satire tends to be inherently *double* in its various meanings; as Fredric Bogel has pointed out, the traditional description of irony as "saying one thing and meaning another" ignores its inherent, radical ambiguity, which might be better described as "saying one thing and meaning two."[49]

Satires, such as Jonathan Swift's "A Modest Proposal" (1729), possess a clear, literal meaning (the problem of poverty in Ireland could be solved by allowing the poor to sell their children as food), which is undercut by a satiric gesture that implies a radically different meaning (the systemic treatment of the poor in Ireland is so horrible that *we may as well* be eating their children). Even though contextual clues may lead us to prefer this implicit meaning, the literal one can never be entirely cancelled out, and the reader is caught in an ambiguous zone between two competing, contradictory interpretations of the same text. In theory, arguably, it is the very ambiguity of language itself that satire communicates, although in practice not all (or even most) historical examples of satire exploit this inherent instability in the form.

Although critical disagreement surrounding the definition of satire persists, most literary criticism focusing on individual works of satire tends to sidestep these issues, remaining reliant on notions of the literary form that were proposed in the 1950s and 1960s by such critics as Alvin Kernan, Robert C. Elliott, Maynard Mack, Edward Rosenheim, and others. While these critics inevitably disagreed on many matters, it is nonetheless possible to locate a common approach to satire in all of their work, which I will term the "standard view." James A. Nichols has summarized this "standard view" thusly: satire is a literary form of "indirect aggression" mediated by a satiric persona who attacks historically specific targets that are "blameworthy" due to vices or follies that are seen as anti-normative "within a given context."[50] Under the standard view, satire functions as covert moral instruction. Satiric texts target those guilty of foolishness or moral indiscretion and ridicule them; satiric ridicule serves as an object lesson for the reader, and thereby helps to correct or eliminate similar errors of judgment in others. Satire's own excesses—its negativity, invective, and intolerance—become an evil necessary for satire to function as an instrument of moral education. Under this view, satire's primary orientation is ethical, and its aims are instrumental rather than aesthetic.

But, as the proliferation of definitions of satire I noted earlier attests, the attempt to approach all satirical works through this ethical framework is highly problematic. Notwithstanding the claims of some satirists, there is no reason to presume an ethical (or any other) intention for satire, which could just as reasonably be motivated, as Jonathan Greenberg notes, by cruelty, ill temper, misanthropy, or sadism.[51] Greenberg locates a "double movement of satire" in which the satirist critiques others in the service of reforming vices, while simultaneously delighting "in his aesthetic powers" and savoring "the cruelty he inflicts."[52] Worse still, claims about satire's ethical orientation are founded on the even more dubious assumption that satire possesses clearly defined moral and ethical norms which can be uncovered within the satirical text. Theoretically, these satiric "norms" depend solely on the contextual framework generated by the satiric persona, but these presumed "positive" values balancing satire's destructive negativity are notoriously hard to locate. Their existence is rendered even more dubious in satires, such as the fourth book of Swift's *Gulliver's Travels* (1726), in which the motif of "the satirist satirized" (as Robert Elliott first described it) appears. In texts that employ this motif, satire turns back on itself, radically undermining its previous satiric critiques and covering any visible satiric norms with a veil of ambiguity. But despite these objections regarding the moral *intent* of satire, most scholarly works on satire retain the notion that its caustic criticism is marshaled for ethical or other instrumental ends.

There are two reasons why this standard view has attracted so little criticism. First, aside from the few generic and modal studies of satire produced by Fredric

Bogel, Michael Seidel, and Leon Guilhamet, the more conceptual literary theory of the last fifty years has only infrequently been applied to scholarly readings of satirical works.[53] While many of the standard view's assumptions have been rigorously critiqued in specific works, these critiques have not permeated the field of satire studies. Second, and of greater significance, the field continues to be dominated by scholarship on British satire in the seventeenth and eighteenth centuries (which I will henceforth refer to as "neoclassical satire"), whether in the form of surveys or single-author studies, as Ashley Marshall has demonstrated through a comprehensive survey of monographs on satire.[54] The specific geographical and historical orientation of this criticism has enabled much of it to sidestep the issue of defining satire, since canonical, neoclassical satires frequently possess similar cultural contexts, relatively clear generic markers, and a reasonably unified sense of the "purpose" of satire as a literary form. The dominance of neoclassical texts in satire studies thus makes them appear exemplary, and the notion of satire derived from this specific historical and cultural context is often treated as though it were universally applicable.

My suggestion is that the standard view of satire, despite its claims of universality, reflects precisely this historical bias. In viewing satire as an ethical literary form, advocates of the standard view announce their allegiance to the neoclassical tradition inaugurated by Dryden, who in his "rules" for satire argued that "the poet is bound, and that *ex officio*, to give his reader some one precept of moral virtue; and to caution him against some one particular vice or folly."[55] The standard view thus approaches the object of its study through the prism of neoclassical satire, which, in its concern with the didactic correction of vice and folly, possessed an ethical dominant.[56]

In suggesting that neoclassical satire is animated by an ethical dominant, I am not claiming that every satire from this period is captured in all of its complexity by the standard view, or even that all satires from this period necessarily had an ethical referent or association. As Ashley Marshall has noted, eighteenth-century satire exists in "vast quantities," producing "a set of multifarious phenonemona" that resist easy categorization; much satire from this period is also "crudely executed, course, and not very literary."[57] Marshall emphasizes both the heterogeneity of satiric works and key changes in satiric practices during this period in order to contest the notion that eighteenth-century satire presents an "underlying unity" marked by "organic development."[58]

While Marshall's study offers essential analysis of an enormous body of noncanonical satire and provides new contexts for understanding canonical satires, she nonetheless acknowledges that "interpretations of particular canonical texts have been of high quality" and that her work generally does not "directly challeng[e] established readings of the principal canonical works."[59] Thus, while broader satiric practices may have differed, works of canonical satire—which are the very works that have influenced later satirical practices—do more readily conform to the "standard view" of satire. My interest is not in the significant differences among eighteenth-century satires, but rather in how practitioners of a later postromantic satire both understood and responded to satirical traditions. What matters, therefore, is the subsequent perception—based on readings of canonical works—that eighteenth-century satire was unified and grounded in ethical notions, even if such perceptions do not adequately characterize all satire in this historical period.

Moreover, the notion that canonical, eighteenth-century satire possesses an ethical dominant becomes clearer when it's read against self-reflexive, postromantic satire that eschews moral concerns. In saying that eighteenth-century satire has an ethical dominant, I am arguing that most satires from this era operated *in relation to* the notion that ethics provided or should provide the grounds of satire—in a way that postromantic satires did not. For example, while the final book of *Gulliver's Travels* may not possess explicit satiric norms, Robert C. Elliott and others have argued that its orientation is still primarily ethical.[60] Acknowledging the link between the standard view and the dominant of neoclassical satire has important repercussions, since, as Brian McHale noted in another context, doing so both makes intelligible the "systems underlying [the] heterogeneous catalogues" of traits established by the standard view and enables critics "to account for historical change"[61] in satire as a literary form, rather than applying a historically contingent, neoclassical definition to all forms of satire. In this sense, the notion of the ethical dominant of satire—which is both diachronic and acknowledges diversity within forms of satiric practice—differs in kind and character from the traditional view's restrictive definition of satiric practice.

I would argue that residues of the traditional view persist even in recent theorizations, which still conceive of satire as a literary form with an *instrumental* purpose that reflects the dominant of neoclassical satire.[62] In such readings, the conception of satire as an ethical form continues as a residual notion, since they presume that satire's harsh critiques must have a purpose in order to justify their existence. If there is no purpose to satirical attack, the bitter invective of satire would seem to be mere cruelty, and, by extension, readerly enjoyment of satire would be little more than literary sadism. Other assumptions underlying the instrumental conception of satire also reflect the continuing influence of the ethical dominant of neoclassical satire, including the notion that it is possible to produce a context in which vice and folly can be clearly demarcated, that readers of satire are motivated by a desire for instruction rather than for entertainment or aesthetic contemplation, and that authors of satire intend to produce didactic works for the benefit of the reading public—which further presumes authorial intent is something that can be unproblematically excavated from a text. Unlike other literary genres, satire is almost never seen as justified by its inherent aesthetic value, but, rather, must rely on some external discourse, concept, or argument.

In this sense, both the standard view and more recent theorizations that still view satire in instrumental terms have responded to the problem of defining satire by repressing the knowledge of their limited, neoclassical frame of reference. More importantly, these assumptions about satire's ethical or instrumental orientation have often overshadowed many of satire's most important qualities, including its tendencies toward aggression, dehumanization, symbolic violence, and the inherently double-voiced and ambiguous nature of satirical critique, which necessarily produces a lacuna between the literal and implicit meaning of its mockery. Although it is common in literary criticism to examine other kinds of texts in terms of their ideological content or their presumed effect upon an audience in a reader-response model, satire seems to be an unusual literary form that is expected to have an express purpose, which is ultimately directed at either the real world or other discourses. The satires I will examine, however, go to extraordinary lengths to try to nullify the instrumentality of their critique.

Given the problems I have noted with both the standard view and other instrumental theories of satire, I have little interest in attempting to define once and for all what satire essentially *is*. Instead, I would suggest that this multiplicity of definitions cannot be avoided because satire as a textual practice is inevitably shaped by its particular historical and cultural contexts. My interest is in placing conceptions of satire back into their generic historical context in accordance with the notion of literary dominants—as articulated by McHale and Jakobson—in the hopes of tracking this historical change. In particular, I want to suggest that the ethical dominant of neoclassical satire, which has been enshrined in the standard view of satire, was challenged by the appearance of romanticism. For my purposes, I will mostly limit my arguments to British romanticism, which is natural given that all of the texts I will examine were written in English, and owe their most obvious debts to this Anglophone tradition. As I will argue, satires produced under the influence of British romanticism tend to produce two important and distinctive effects: 1) they subject satire's ethical or instrumental grounds to ironic critique in the (not entirely successful) attempt to neutralize satire's purposiveness, and 2) they accentuate satire's value as an aesthetic form in its own right. Furthermore, I want to argue that this shift culminated in the creation of a heretofore-unidentified subgenre of the satiric novel that developed later in the twentieth century, which I have termed "avant-garde satires of the avant-garde." I will trace the development of this subgenre across a series of texts, including Wyndham Lewis's *The Apes of God* (1930), William Gaddis's *The Recognitions* (1955), and Gilbert Sorrentino's *Imaginative Qualities of Actual Things* (1971), which share many substantive, thematic, and formal characteristics.

In terms of content, all of these novels possess similar satiric targets, ridiculing the avant-garde artists and bohemian communities that comprise a series of historical, urban art "scenes." While these satires are prose works that might usually be classified as novels, they all employ plotting and characterization in a manner quite different from most modern (and even modernist) novels. Specifically, these satires present "flat" characters, avoid detailed descriptions of psychological states, and have generally anticlimactic or open-ended plots that do not offer any sense of character development. Fittingly, avant-garde satires of the avant-garde have typically received poor reviews on publication for precisely these features, which reviewers have misunderstood as novelistic failings, rather than as satirical techniques.[63] Moreover, most of these works are long and "difficult" books, which signal their adherence to the tradition of the complex and sprawling modernist novel, as exemplified by such works as Joyce's *Ulysses* (1922), Stein's *The Making of Americans* (1925), and Musil's *The Man Without Qualities* (1930–43).

Avant-garde satires of the avant-garde also share many thematic and stylistic features. They all select as objects of their satire those artists who are more concerned with material success (whether in the form of wealth, power, fame, or sex) than aesthetic merit. In a related gesture, they all raise the question of whether it is possible to distinguish "real" art from the "fake." Formally, they employ similar rhetorical tropes and structures, such as the Rabelaisian catalogue, in which items are put together into a list without obvious order or logical relation, often to comic effect. They also display an obsession with banal and clichéd language, which usually manifests in the form of long passages of dialogue that in some cases (such as in the party scenes in both *The Recognitions* and *The Apes of God*) may last for hundreds of pages. The authors of these satires also often sought to separate their own works from contemporary aesthetic tendencies that might be seen as similar, including the work of other satirists. Wyndham Lewis, in his *Time and Western Man* (1928), criticizes a wide array of modernist writers, including his fellow Vorticist, Ezra Pound. William Gaddis was famous for expressing a lack of interest in other long and difficult contemporary works (such as those produced by Thomas Pynchon), and even claimed not to have read all of Joyce; at the same time, he praised such novels as Jay McInerney's *Bright Lights, Big City* (1984). Sorrentino, although more forthcoming with praise for present and past writers, frequently cited influences that were then on the fringes of established literary canons, including William Carlos Williams's prose works, Flann O'Brien's *At Swim-Two-Birds* (1939), and Wyndham Lewis's work.

By investigating this subgenre of the satiric novel, I will not only trace the shift in satire's literary dominant inaugurated by romanticism, but also uncover aspects of satire that have too often been ignored by the standard view. Avant-garde satires of the avant-garde are important to a diachronic consideration of satire *precisely because* they exhibit qualities that contravene the standard view of satire and, accordingly, undermine the ethical dominant of neoclassical satire. These satires explicitly deny any moral, ethical, or instrumental purpose, such as in the satire of Wyndham Lewis, who proclaimed that "the greatest satire is non-moral."[64] For Lewis, satire is not a mode of ethical instruction, but rather an objective method of dehumanization that can be applied indiscriminately to all subjects, including the satirist; here satire is not a method for producing fixed judgments, but a corrosive and endless series of negations. Similarly, William Gaddis's *The Recognitions* (1955) is a satire of the art world that investigates the notion of counterfeit art only to reveal the problematic nature of origins and of authorizing discourses. Gaddis's satire lifts one mask only to reveal another mask, and removes one ground only to find another ground, or, worse still, the lack of any stable ground at all. Satire's ethical force is undermined because the very universals or satirical norms that lie behind ethical claims cannot be located and may not exist at all. Gilbert Sorrentino's *Imaginative Qualities of Actual Things* (1971) denies any moral purpose to its satire ("I have certainly no moral to draw"[65]), and also makes satirical judgments that are mutually exclusive, resulting in aporias that cannot be reconciled with a logically consistent ethics.

Not only do these avant-garde satires of the avant-garde eschew any moral didacticism, but they also attempt to disavow any instrumental aims, in order to emphasize their autonomy from the purposiveness traditionally associated with satire. Gilbert Sorrentino's *Imaginative Qualities of Actual Things* explicitly makes the point that satire lacks any real-world use, noting that "everything [art] teaches is useless insofar as structuring your life."[66] *Imaginative Qualities*, if it argues for anything at all, denounces any deployment of art for instrumental purposes; as the narrator and satiric persona of the novel scornfully observes, "You try to live in America, where they either hate art or try to use it. . . . The poem as tool. Break open somebody's door with it, or unhook a brassiere. But don't just let it stand there, useless."[67] Wyndham Lewis's *Apes of God* and William Gaddis's *The Recognitions* also employ a variety of techniques to deactivate satiric intent, including subjecting their satire to self-negation that undermines the satiric norms needed to regulate satiric critique. In negating satirical norms, the goals of the satirist are revealed as being without any coherent legitimizing grounds, and—lacking any larger program—satire becomes a purely negative agent that relentlessly unveils falsity in an infinite regress.

It's worth emphasizing, however, that these satires are not completely successful in purging satire of all purposiveness. Residues of ethical and instrumental aims remain, which generates an apparent inconsistency between these novels' autocritique and their selection of specific satiric targets, as well as their unveiling of specific forms of artistic "fraudulence." This contradiction, however, is not surprising, given that, as I have argued, modernist autonomy claims are characterized by their articulation of mutually exclusive propositions. The disjuncture between these satires' self-negation and the specificity of their satiric attack is characteristic of a modernist tendency to locate the work of art's radical autonomy within its capacity to form a totalizing whole that encompasses and transcends logical contradictions. In this sense, the contradictions within these satires comprise the basis on which they will assert themselves as autonomous works of art, rather than simple attempts to satirize "bad" art, in the way that Alexander Pope does in *Peri Bathous, or the Art of Sinking in Poetry* (1727). While this assertion of autonomy could itself be viewed as a "purpose" of a sort, this purposiveness differs significantly in character from the ethical or instrumental purposiveness of traditional satire, much in the way that, as I will argue later, Kant makes a distinction between the nature of ethical and aesthetic judgments. These satires are logically contradictory, but theirs are *productive contradictions*, which have been unleashed to generate aesthetic effects quite different from those of traditional satire.

It is also perhaps worth noting at this point that the three modernist satires I am focusing on—Lewis's *Apes of God*, Gaddis's *The Recognitions*, and Sorrentino's

Imaginative Qualities of Actual Things—are not canonical texts. Indeed, they are not even commonly viewed as central texts in modernist studies, although both Lewis and Gaddis have attracted a significant (and still growing) amount of scholarly attention over the last few decades. This status matters for two reasons. First of all, as I have argued, these texts' marginality has served to obscure an important mode of modernist, self-reflexive satire. Secondly, part of the purpose in examining these texts is to suggest that—in their textual complexity and invocation of an ironic and intentionally contradictory autonomy—these are exemplary modernist works, which deserve a far more significant place in both modernist studies and literary studies generally.

While the works I have considered present the strongest examples of this new subgenre of satire, there are a large number of works with satirical elements that exhibit, at least partially, the tendencies of postromantic satire. While it would not be possible to catalogue all of them, a list would include E.T.A. Hoffmann's *The Life and Opinions of Tomcat Murr* (1819), Herman Melville's *Pierre: or the Ambiguities* (1852), Joaquim Maria Machado de Assis's *The Posthumous Memoirs of Bras Cubas* (1881), Jose-Maria Eca de Queiros's *The Illustrious House of Ramires* (1900), James Joyce's *A Portrait of the Artist as a Young Man* (1916), Wyndham Lewis's *Tarr* (1918), André Gide's *The Counterfeiters* (1925), Flann O'Brien's *At-Swim-Two-Birds* (1939), Louis-Ferdinand Celine's *Conversations with Professor Y* (1955), Vladimir Nabokov's *Pale Fire* (1962), Mikhail Bulgakov's *Master and Margarita* (1966), Joseph McElroy's *Smuggler's Bible* (1966), Michel Butor's *Portrait of the Artist as a Young Ape* (1967), Gilbert Sorrentino's *Mulligan Stew* (1979), Gerald Murnane's *The Plains* (1982), Thomas Bernhard's *The Loser* (1983), *Woodcutters* (1984), and *Old Masters* (1985), Harry Matthews's *Cigarettes* (1987), Evan Dara's *The Lost Scrapbook* (1996), and *The Easy Chain* (2008), David Markson's *Reader's Block* (1996), David Foster Wallace's *Infinite Jest* (1996), Don DeLillo's *Underworld* (1997), Roberto Bolaño's *The Savage Detectives* (1998) and *2666* (2004), and J.M. Coetzee's *Youth* (2002) and *Summertime* (2009), along with many, many others.

It is also important to acknowledge that the satires I examine have been written by white, male authors. I would argue that these works remain the most significant examples of self-reflexive satire in terms of their literary influence, and I have selected them for this reason. However, notable works in this genre—such as Fran Ross's *Oreo* (1974) and Trey Ellis's *Platitudes* (1988)—have been produced by authors of different races and genders. At the same time, authors of self-reflexive satires do seem to be overwhelmingly white men. One possible explanation for this tendency could be located in David Trotter's notion of paranoid modernism. Trotter argues that the signal feature of paranoia is the tendency to presume that "there is no event which does not already possesses a meaning and a value," and that paranoia disproportionately affects the professional classes, which have historically been male, middle-class, and white.[68] These male, professionalized paranoias, for Trotter, manifest in modernism's privileging of a masculinist "will-to-abstraction" that "pit[s] itself against" the feminine through expert displays of technique.[69] Avant-garde satires of the avant-garde both privilege technique and meditate obsessively on questions of social position, authenticity, and meaning—reflecting the paranoid tendencies of the precarious bourgeois professional class to which most (though not all: Sorrentino was raised in a working-class family) of the authors I consider belong.

It is also worth mentioning a key omission: I have not described these texts as Menippean satires—a designation typically given to long prose works of satire. I have resisted the use of this term for several reasons. For one, there are already a variety of studies, which examine twentieth-century satire in relation to Bakhtin's notion of Menippean satire, such as Steven Weisenburger's *Fables of Subversion: Satire and the American Novel 1930–1980* (1995). I would argue that the category of Menippean satire—while useful in reading some works—can give a seeming coherence to satirical works that do not readily fit into standard categories, a point reinforced by the fact that the label of Menippean satire has frequently been applied to classical, medieval, early modern, and contemporary satires. As a category, then, Menippean satire can be a universalizing one that privileges generic taxonomy over historical change. In other words, rather than presuming that these satires are Menippean works (which they may well be) and analyzing them accordingly, my interest is to examine these satires in relation to larger literary, historical, and generic changes.

This proliferation of avant-garde satires of the avant-garde indicates the shift in the literary dominant from the ethical orientation of neoclassical satire to the aesthetic orientation of postromantic satire. The rise of British romanticism at the end of the eighteenth century is thus the decisive event that enables the creation of this subgenre. Romanticism emphasized self-reflexivity, recursion, ambiguity, and so on, which produced a form of satire that explored new and different literary and rhetorical possibilities that foregrounded, among other things, the indeterminacy and ultimately groundless nature of satiric judgment. This interpenetration of satire and romanticism results in a form of satire that displays the qualities of satiric attack and ridicule, but undermines any instrumental or ethical purpose, thereby challenging the conception of satire as an ethical and didactic form. After romanticism, satire, instead of critiquing vice and folly for purposes of moral instruction, seeks to explore the potential of satire as a "useless" and aestheticized literary form. Although this potential has always been latent in satire, and some traditional satires had, at particular moments—such as in the final book of *Gulliver's Travels*—begun to gesture in this direction, after romanticism, avant-garde satires of the avant-garde become an important (and arguably *the prevalent*) form of satire. But tracking this shift in the literary dominant of satire initiated by romanticism first requires developing a fuller understanding of the particular features of romanticism itself.

3 Romanticism

As Marc Redfield has noted, romantic studies has been marked by a "history of conceptual turbulence,"[70] which can be largely attributed to the fact that, as Marilyn Butler has pointed out, the label "romantic" was retrospectively applied to a group of British writers, such as Blake, Coleridge, and Wordsworth, who, although historically contemporaneous, did not see themselves as belonging to a unified aesthetic movement.[71] Matters become even more complicated when considering such writers as Shelley, Keats, Byron, and Thomas Love Peacock, who—despite being seen as a "second wave" of British romanticism—responded critically to the work of "first wave" romantics. None of these authors applied the word "romantic" as a term of self-description. In this sense, British romanticism is not a continuous or linear tradition, but a web of influence, response, and even critique. The diversity of what is captured by the term is so great that—forty years before the rise of deconstruction—Arthur O. Lovejoy could skeptically claim romanticism's "internal incongruities" rendered "any attempt at a *general* appraisal even of a single chronologically determinate Romanticism . . . a fatuity."[72] Although there have been important subsequent attempts by such critics as Rene Wellek, Morse Peckham, and M.H. Abrams[73] to theorize a unified field of romanticism, more recent accounts of romanticism, as Frances Ferguson suggests, have typically recapitulated this foundational debate over romanticism's coherence rather than resolving it.[74]

As a result of this conceptual turbulence, even seemingly straightforward matters, such as determining the date of romanticism's inception, have proven difficult: the traditional dating of British romanticism's commencement with the publication of Wordsworth and Coleridge's *Lyrical Ballads* in 1798 is problematized by the fact that William Blake's *Songs of Innocence and of Experience* had first appeared in 1789. Similarly contested is the influence exerted on British romanticism both by German romanticism, in general, and by the various theories of romanticism developed by members of the Jena Circle, in particular. Some critics, such as Nader Saiedi, have emphasized the direct influence of German romanticism on William Wordsworth and Samuel Coleridge, both of whom travelled to Germany in the 1790s, as well as on such authors as Thomas Carlyle, Madame De Stael, and Thomas De Quincey.[75] Others, such as Marilyn Butler, have noted that most of the "major" romantic authors, such as Blake, Shelley, Byron, and Keats, had either limited or belated interactions with German romanticism, thus rendering problematic any claim that German romanticism exerted a clear influence on its British counterpart.[76] For these reasons, as I noted earlier, I will primarily focus on how British romanticism has affected the development of Anglophone satire.

And, yet, despite the conceptual turbulence that has characterized romantic studies, it nonetheless remains possible to outline many of the most salient features of Anglophone romanticism—particularly those features which will most significantly influence the satires that I will examine. Perhaps the most useful approach is to view romanticism in historical and relational terms, as a turning away from the modes of thinking—particularly empirical and logical models of cognition—that are often associated with the Enlightenment. In saying this, I do not mean to rehash the notion of romanticism as simply embracing irrationalism, but rather, following Nader Saiedi, I am suggesting that romanticism might be usefully conceived of as an epistemological shift away from notions of objective empiricism toward a focus on how the subjective, perspectival nature of perception shapes modes of knowing.[77]

Romanticism's interest in the subjective perception of phenomena resonates with aspects of Immanuel Kant's philosophy, which itself provides a useful framework for understanding the point of departure for romantic epistemology, even if most British romantics were not directly influenced by Kant's thought.[78] Romanticism shares with Kant the notion that the relationship between mind and world is linked in a complex and heavily mediated process that can only be understood in terms of this relationship itself—rather than through recourse to separate, abstract categories of reality and perception. Moreover, as Lacoue-Labarthe and Nancy have noted, Kant articulated "an entirely new and unforeseeable relation between aesthetics and philosophy"[79] that is also characteristic of romanticism. In particular, romanticism, like Kantian philosophy, takes up the notion that "epistemological antinomies" could be resolved "through art and poetry."[80] But while art held an important place in Kant's philosophy, romanticism differs in that it elevates the work of art to an even higher standing. For the romantics, the work of art is able to enact a complexity that captures the richness and interdependence of the relations between mind and world in a manner that conventional philosophy, which is subject to the demands of logic and reason, cannot. Here, romanticism moves beyond a Kantian, transcendental framework, in that it effectively repudiates traditional philosophy's reliance on logic, arguing instead for "a poetic approach to philosophical discourse."[81] The result is that the aesthetic becomes privileged because it provides the key site for exploring the relation between perception, self, world, and other, precisely because the aesthetic is able to transcend the limits of reason. In this sense, the romantic work of art cannot really be separated from either romantic modes of thought or romantic aesthetics, because all three are bound together in their rejection of Enlightenment epistemology. Viewed from this perspective, it is then possible to claim that romanticism presents as an aestheticism, but only in the sense that its philosophical concerns cannot be disentangled from its aesthetic ones.

Romantic aesthetics also share with Kant's transcendental philosophy a concern over epistemological issues, especially regarding foundational questions of how the self comes to knowledge. In this sense, romantic literature often enacts a process of self-reflexivity that serves to question assumed knowledge and depicts how knowledge itself is shaped and transformed by the self, culture, language, and experience. One of the most important tropes associated with these epistemological concerns is romantic irony, in which a character's naïve enthusiasm is undercut by a (usually comic) moment of self-realization, presenting what Paul de Man describes as a "twofold self."[82] But whereas classical forms of rhetorical irony might use this self-realization as a means for the revelation of an underlying "truth," romantic irony foregrounds the oscillation between naivety and knowledge. As Ernst Behler has noted, whereas classical irony held on to an "underlying assumption" that "truth [is] objectively discernible and recognizable by every intelligent person," in romantic irony "the sense of an objectifiable truth has vanished, and what has been substituted is the infinite self-mirroring of the individual in the mirrors of his ego and the world."[83] The ironic revelation of grounded truths is replaced in romanticism by a post-transcendental conception of "reality" as a complex series of mediations and relations between the mind and the world, with the result that absolute knowledge remains elusive.

Similarly, romantic works of art are not directed toward the beautiful, but rather toward the romantic sublime, an experience that includes a powerful self-reflexive awareness of the contingency of that which had seemed to be real. In the romantic sublime, the individual encounters an object—traditionally of a vast physical scale or temporal duration—that appears to exceed the grasp of the imagination. In this encounter, the observer—who is unable to gain purchase on the sublime object—is made aware that the experience of "reality" is in fact mediated by an anthropomorphic perception, which masks the fact that the world is not constructed in human terms. The sublime object thus provokes a vertiginous feeling within the viewer, who has now been made aware both of the relative insignificance of the human in relation to the world and of the shaky perceptual foundations of his or her own sense of self. But this first phase of the romantic sublime yields to a visionary and *imaginative* experience of what appears to be a deeper reality, which constitutes the second phase of the sublime. In this second phase, the harmony between individual ego and the wider world is restored precisely through an imaginative act, and, in this sense, the ground of the sublime is ultimately the imagination that enables the negative experience of the sublime object to be turned into a visionary one. But again, the romantic sublime does not produce a stable ground, because the imagination itself is an open-ended faculty intimately linked with perception. It is important to note that romantic presentations of both romantic irony and the sublime typically do not reach a clear resolution—and, in fact, often willfully evade such closure. It is for this reason that the romantic form par excellence is the fragment, which by its nature is incomplete.

Romantic aesthetics emphasize the importance of both the imagination and original genius in the creation of romantic art. For romanticism, art is not simply a mimetic representation of the world, but a virtual doubling of the world that produces a heterocosm. In this sense, romantic works of art present themselves as an alternate world created by the infinite faculty of the imagination that resides in the self-authorizing capacity of original genius. The romantic original genius is often conceived of in analogy to Satan (particularly in relation to Milton's portrayal of Satan in *Paradise Lost*); in this model, Satan is envisioned as a rebellious angel, who founds a heterocosm in Pandemonium that presents a rival order to God's original creation. By extension, the romantic work of art produced by the original genius also presents another order of reality.[84] Once again, in romanticism, aesthetics and ontology cannot be easily separated from each other.

If one only understands satire in the terms put forward by the "traditional view," then romanticism's self-reflexive epistemology and aesthetic disposition would appear to be incompatible with satire's ethical and instructional aims. Romanticism has typically been construed as being uninterested in satire, and it has often been argued that romanticism effectively displaced satire at the end of the eighteenth century. Romanticism and satire, according to this account, are seen as opposing and even antithetical literary manifestations. Satire is conceived of as a rationalist, ethical discourse founded in universalist, Enlightenment principles, and characterized by intellectualized, elitist procedures (such as sustained references to classical literature) as well as rigid formal structures (such as the heroic couplet). Romanticism, on the other hand, is then viewed as a nonrational, aestheticized discourse founded in personal experience, and characterized by formal experimentation and the use of everyday language (In *Lyrical Ballads*, Wordsworth adopts the language of "the middle and lower classes of society" in order to assume the position of "a man speaking to men" [85]). Although more recent studies have demonstrated the continued persistence of satire in various popular and literary forms throughout the romantic period,[86] this conventional opposition between satire and romanticism is still often repeated.

I want to argue that, rather than displacing satire, romanticism initiated a shift in the dominant of satire from an objective, ethical paradigm, to a perspectival and aesthetic one. This new dominant of satire, which was initiated by romanticism, produced satires that display a variety of postromantic tendencies, including the use of irony, self-reflexivity, aestheticism, and a nonmimetic theory of representation. Postromantic satire also approaches satiric critique and judgment in a very different manner than neoclassical satire did. Rather than seeking to use satirical judgment for didactic purposes, this new form of satire highlights the inevitably subjective and perspectival nature of judgment itself. My examination of postromantic satire is introduced by an analysis of Thomas Love Peacock's exemplary *Nightmare Abbey* (1818), a satiric attack on romanticism and many of its major figures, which is itself arguably also an important work of romanticism.

As I will argue, the postromantic tendencies that appear in *Nightmare Abbey* later coalesce into a new subgenre of postromantic satire that I have termed avant-garde satires of the avant-garde. The tendency to attack and satirize "romanticism" explicitly while also displaying exemplary postromantic traits is shared by all of the works within this subgenre that I will consider, including Wyndham Lewis's *The Apes of God*, William Gaddis's *The Recognitions*, and Gilbert Sorrentino's *Imaginative Qualities of Actual Things*. Wyndham Lewis held the same disdain for romanticism that was displayed by his early modernist contemporaries T.S. Eliot and T.E. Hulme, and he extensively criticizes what he calls "the new romanticism" in his extended essay "The Diabolic Principle" (1929), published a year before *The Apes of God*. William Gaddis's *The Recognitions* openly critiques romantic notions of originality and individual expression, exemplified by one character's disparagement of "that romantic disease, originality."[87] Gilbert Sorrentino's *Imaginative Qualities of Actual Things* provides an even more strident critique of romantic aesthetics: "Don't tell me this is romanticism, you idiot. I know all about romanticism—that's losing with a fat check in your hand. Then you tell everyone what a whore you are. Yes, I understand you, you whore."[88] In their very choice of satire as a literary form, these writers seem to signal their allegiance to a set of neoclassical principles meant to act as a corrective to a rampant romanticism.

The matter is, however, not as clear-cut as this suggests because, as Philippe Lacoue-Labarthe and Jean-Luc Nancy note in *The Literary Absolute* (1978), "'romantics' will not give themselves this name."[89] As Martin Gurewitch has stated, such antiromantic gestures are, in fact, characteristic of romantic ironists:

> It is not unusual for a romantic ironist to purge himself, quite unsuccessfully, of the stigma of romanticism. He may be tempted to describe romanticism as a linguistic orgy, a vacuous sublimity, a gratuitous maiming of classical calm, a preposterous counterfeiting of idealism, an elephantiasis of emotions, a maddening surrender to obscurantism, a narcissistic pathology of the soul, even a spiritual vampirism afflicting an entire nation.[90]

Such antiromantic romantics usually construct romanticism itself as a naïve discourse, in which enthusiasm and irrational emotions are evoked without skepticism or irony. In point of fact, the essential figure of romanticism is not its adherence to a naïve discourse, but rather, as Jos De Mul argues, its "eternal oscillation of enthusiasm and irony."[91] This characteristic oscillation of romantic irony is typically understood as an alternation between such polar opposites as naivety and sentimentality, innocence and experience, or creative and destructive impulses. Romantic irony, as both Anne K. Mellor and Lilian Furst have argued, manifests as a relentless switching between sublime enchantment and the immediate satiric undercutting of such flights of fancy.[92] Romantic texts—like William Blake's *Song of Innocence and Experience* and Lord Byron's *Don Juan*—that employ such irony do not reveal a fixed set of meanings, but rather become ambiguous.[93] Romantic irony becomes a process of oscillation without a discrete end, with the result that texts employing romantic irony possess no clear meaning or easily summarized "moral."

Avant-garde satires of the avant-garde, as a form of postromantic satire, employ a strategy very similar to romantic irony by subjecting their own satirical critiques to further critique in order to reveal that their initial satiric judgment was based on faulty or subjective criteria. Rather than unfolding a stable, ethical vision, these satires uncover the fact that judgment is perspectival and subject to revision rather than being an absolute and final determination. Here, the satiric act does not reveal the universal moral or ethical imperatives of a given situation, but rather that judgment is contextual, and the only absolute of absolute judgment remains its absolute unavailability. In this process, these satires generate a romantic indeterminacy. This romantic indeterminacy bears a passing resemblance to Marjorie Perloff's conception of avant-garde indeterminacy insofar as both produce works that are "no longer grounded in a coherent discourse."[94] Nonetheless, my understanding of indeterminacy relies on ideas developed within the field of romanticism, which view indeterminacy as a characteristically *romantic* phenomenon. Moreover, I see this indeterminacy comprising an ambiguous relationship between a text and *external* discourses, rather than viewing it as a matter of stylistic tendencies that problematize internal symbolic orders, as Perloff does.

The satires I will examine enact this specific type of romantic indeterminacy through a variety of self-reflexive and autocritical gestures. In Wyndham Lewis's *The Apes of God*, for example, although Horace Zagreus attacks artists for unreflexively "aping" the works of others, we discover later that Zagreus's own attacks (or "broadcasts") are directly copied from his mentor, Pierpoint. In *The Recognitions*, Herr Koppel attacks "that romantic disease, originality," but his desire to copy the techniques of the old masters results in his becoming an art forger, and he is subsequently arrested for his crimes.[95] In *Imaginative Qualities*, the narrator savagely attacks the sexual perversions and fetishes of other artists, only to admit that he, too, is party to such desires: "I would prefer a maid in the shortest of skirts, wearing black nylons and high heels. But I am not writing pornography, so I'll have to save the maid (Annette)."[96] These oscillations between judgment and the self-reflexive critique of judgment produce an ambiguity that is similar to romantic irony. In some respects, this notion of self-reflexive satirical critique resembles Steven Weisenburger's concept of "degenerative satire," which he associates with postmodern satirical works[97]; unlike Weisenburger, however, I argue that such unstable modes of satire are a product of a much earlier romantic self-critique that is characteristic of romantic irony.

As I have already argued, romantic irony is a self-reflexive phenomenon, and works of romantic irony tend to enact this self-reflexivity at a formal level, resulting in texts that are openly auto-referential. The recursive judgment of avant-garde satires of the avant-garde, which resembles romantic irony, results in a similar self-reflexivity that is also reflected in textual practice; specifically, avant-garde satires foreground their own fictionality through parabasis and other metafictional devices. In Lewis's *The Apes of God*, a book appears toward the end of the novel that, as Anne Quema notes, is very likely *The Apes of God* itself.[98] In Gaddis's *The Recognitions*, we are briefly introduced to a young writer named "Willie" who is writing a novel called *The Recognitions*. In Sorrentino's *Imaginative Qualities of Actual Things*, the narrator reflects on the text itself through footnotes and other marginalia that imagine readers' responses and future reviews of the novel. This self-reflexivity presents one strategy for attempting to deactivate the instrumentality of satiric critique, since, in acknowledging their own status as cultural objects, these works undermine their authority.

Furthermore, as aesthetic rather than ethical or instrumental works, these satires approach mimesis through romanticism's conception of the work of art as an imaginative heterocosm. Traditionally, it has been understood that satire must be rigorously imitative in order for its ethical critiques to function.[99] If the objects of satire did not resemble "real" people who were attacked for their vice and folly, then the satire itself could not serve as a form of moral instruction. And yet, although these satires are often viewed as roman à clefs, whose satirical objects are based on "real people," they nonetheless deny that the characters within their pages correspond to living persons. While these satires may use "real life" as the basis for their satire, these objects are "reshaped" and transformed through the faculty of the imagination and thereby become radically different from their original models. In this gesture, avant-garde satires of the avant-garde seek to move away from a rigorously mimetic paradigm toward a paradigm that reflects Coleridge's notion of the "esemplastic" power of the imagination,[100] which results in a work of art that doesn't just reflect a set of given realities, but rather forms a unified aesthetic whole from disparate and distinct materials.

In applying these romantic tropes to the formal demands of satire, avant-garde satires of the avant-garde present a radical reimagining of both satire *and* romanticism; not only does the shift from an ethical to an aesthetic dominant represent a major transformation of satire, but also these romantic tropes are completely recontextualized in their interaction with satire's critical judgment. This is not entirely surprising, since, as Jonathan Greenberg notes, "the modernist artist" often "comes to resemble his Romantic forebear" in arguing that there is a relationship between formal technique and affect.[101] In constituting a novel hybrid of romanticism and the satirical tradition, avant-garde satires of the avant-garde no longer simply present a literary form of judgment. Rather, it is the very groundlessness of judgment that these satires demonstrate in a process that self-reflexively erodes the traditional distinction between the satirist and the object of satire.

4 Avant-garde

While satire underwent a profound generic shift in its interaction with romanticism, late-nineteenth-century satire, as Aaron Matz has argued, moved away from self-referential modes of satirical critique to embrace a "satirical realism."[102] I will argue, however, that postromantic modes of self-reflexive satire reemerged within what is perhaps the most important aesthetic milieu of the last century: the avant-garde. Virtually all twentieth-century literature responds to the avant-garde, even if, as William Marx has stated, much of this response comprised a "reactionary aesthetics" that rejected avant-gardism.[103] But as I will argue, these satires' relationship to the avant-garde is particularly ambivalent and conflicted, since they employ avant-garde techniques while simultaneously making avant-garde artists and movements the objects of their satire. This overdetermined relationship with the avant-garde became so important in the twentieth century that it produced a new subgenre of self-reflexive satire, which I have termed avant-garde satires of the avant-garde. This new subgenre takes the avant-garde as its subject and object, while simultaneously critiquing and absorbing aspects of the avant-garde project in an involuted, self-reflexive process.

Of the writers I will consider, only Wyndham Lewis, as a founder of Vorticism, was a member of a historical avant-garde, and, from the 1920s onward, he eschewed any group affiliations. Yet these satirists were not complete outsiders.

William Gaddis and Gilbert Sorrentino interacted with bohemian artistic scenes (in both cases, the Greenwich Village scene of the 1950s) and more formal avant-garde movements. Gaddis was acquainted with the Beats and was the model for the character Harold Sand in Jack Kerouac's *The Subterraneans* (1958); Sorrentino corresponded with both Ezra Pound and William Carlos Williams, and published several writers associated with the Black Mountain School in his literary journals *Neon* and *Kulchur*. These social affiliations help to illustrate the unusual textual positions of these satires, which are simultaneously both inside and outside of the traditional framework of the avant-gardes and their associated bohemias.

Tyrus Miller discusses how "the avant-garde and bohemia occupy overlapping cultural spaces," which has produced a complex, reciprocal relationship between the two, since the historical avant-gardes emerge "within the milieu of bohemia" but bohemian cultures were simultaneously reinvigorated by the avant-gardes.[104] Miller argues that the avant-gardes have sought both to identify with and to dissociate themselves from cultural bohemia "in the name of an authentic, serious, innovative and truly revolutionary artistry."[105] He lists multiples examples of avant-garde works that seek to differentiate themselves from bohemia, including both Lewis's *The Apes of God* and Sorrentino's *Imaginative Qualities of Actual Things*. He also argues that many (if not most) prominent modernists participated in contemporary bohemian cultures, while also critiquing the foppish image of the nineteenth-century bohemian, which had hardened into a cultural cliché by the early twentieth century: Wyndham Lewis and other English modernists, for example, began dressing "in dark business suits" so as not to be confused with earlier aesthetes and dandies.[106] But as Mary Gluck has pointed out, the critical gestures of such artists could be construed as an internal critique that constitutes an "ironic bohemia," rather than a genuine anti-bohemianism.[107]

While all of the novels I examine satirize historical bohemian communities, these works break down stable distinctions between an "authentic" avant-garde and a "false" bohemia through their self-reflexive satire. In this claim, I elaborate on Peter Brooker's argument that there is no such thing as "the modernist bohemian" but rather "the strategic adoption of different bohemian personae."[108] Following this logic, the modernist avant-gardes—rather than creating stable bohemian identities—inhabited some aspects of the traditional bohemian persona, while rejecting others in ways were often contradictory or at least not logically consistent. In this sense, bohemia does not form a traditional object of satire, but rather presents a series of surfaces that can be productively critiqued and played off each other for aesthetic ends. I would argue that what might appear as satires of bohemia are, in reality, self-reflexive critiques of the avant-garde.

Untangling these satires' complicated textual interactions with avant-gardism first requires establishing a conception of the avant-garde itself. Like satire and romanticism, definitions of the term "avant-garde" have been so vigorously contested that even some of its most famous theorists have argued for dispensing with them altogether.[109] Some of the problems with defining the avant-garde are internal to scholarly discourse: avant-garde movements produced works across media—incorporating literature, the visual arts, and, in many cases, aspects of theatre and dance—but the scholarly fields corresponding to these various art forms have often employed key terms related to the avant-garde in very distinct ways. Modernism—a term often used in contradistinction to the avant-garde—for example, means one thing when applied to literature but means something very different when applied to the visual arts.

Moreover, as Hans Enzensberger pointed out in "The Aporias of the Avant-Garde" (1962), the concept of the avant-garde is internally contradictory. Enzensberger notes that the avant-gardes' orientation toward the future, which is present in their claim to be "en avant," is problematized by the fact that all "that can be affirmed is what *was* 'out front,' not what is there."[110] From this perspective, the avant-garde always operates in the future-perfect tense, determining what will have been in advance of current trends. This unusual temporal condition, as Enzensberger argues, means that many who claim to be avant-garde will turn out to be nothing of the sort: "Whoever becomes rigid about objective necessity, the demands of the medium, and compulsory evolution is already in the wrong. Every such doctrine relies on the method of extrapolation: it projects lines into the unknown."[111] The aporetic nature of the avant-garde, however, should perhaps not be surprising, given that modernist autonomy, as I already argued, is similarly characterized by such contradictions. In this sense, the avant-garde's incoherence actually suggests an affinity with modernism's contradictory modes of autonomy, although it does also problematize attempts to define the avant-garde as a concept.

The idea of the avant-garde is also rendered problematic by the twofold manner in which the term is employed. In its everyday or generic use, "avant-garde" simply describes artworks and artists that employ experimental aesthetic techniques that run contrary to (or more technically, "ahead of") dominant forms of cultural production.[112] Such a definition of avant-gardism can even be applied in a "transtemporal sense" to describe "whatever is the most current (most progressive) movement" of a given period, with the result that "painters of the early Renaissance can, in this sense, be readily discussed as avant-garde."[113] More often than not, however, being avant-garde in this generic sense implies the notion not only of being aesthetically innovative or ahead of one's time, but also of being opposed to culturally normative, traditional forms of representation. Under this notion of avant-gardism, one could speak, for example, of Mallarmé, Virginia Woolf, and Donald Barthelme as "avant-garde" writers.

But many scholars have drawn a sharp distinction between this generic use of the term and its more specialized reference to a series of early twentieth-century movements, such as Dadaism, Surrealism, Futurism, and Vorticism, which are typically known as the "historical avant-gardes." The most famous and influential example of this argument remains Peter Bürger's *Theory of the Avant-Garde* (1974), which, inspired by Marxist ideology critique, argues that the essential characteristic of the historical avant-gardes lay in their desire to achieve a sublation (Bürger employs the Hegelian term "*Aufhebung*"[114]) of art with the praxis of life:

> The intention of the avant-gardiste may be defined as the attempt to direct towards the practical the aesthetic experience (which rebels against the praxis of life) that Aestheticism developed. What most strongly conflicts with the means-end rationality of bourgeois society is to become life's organizing principle.[115]

For Bürger, the avant-gardes' characteristic works, in merging art with the practice of life, present a form of anti-art that seeks nothing less than a totalizing critique of the bourgeois institution of art. Decisively for Bürger's account, however, this attempt to sublate art and life fails, although this very failure is paradoxically accompanied by the avant-gardes' "success" within the institution of art. Instead of demolishing the bourgeois institution of art, the avant-gardes' critique of art is recuperated and "recognized by the institution as art," with the result that "avant-garde categories such as rupture and shock gain admittance to the discourse of art."[116] Hereafter, avant-garde gestures lose both their force and their significance, becoming little more than an exhausted set of fashions and trends circulating within the bourgeois institution of art.

One of the prime effects of Bürger's theory, as Benjamin Buchloh and Hal Foster have noted,[117] has been to privilege the historical avant-gardes as a locus of genuine rupture at the expense of virtually all other contemporary and subsequent forms of art that would appear to share many formal, aesthetic, and even political similarities with the historical avant-gardes. Several authors have responded to Bürger by arguing for the inclusion of other groups and artists within the concept of the avant-garde.[118] Perhaps the most prominent among those excluded are the various artists now classed as modernists, many of whom both interacted with and were influenced by members of the historical avant-gardes. In Bürger's account, modernism is little more than a late instantiation of a tradition of bourgeois, autonomous aestheticism that began sometime in the nineteenth century.[119] As I have already noted, this claim problematically elides nineteenth-century aestheticists like the Symbolists and the decadents with early-twentieth-century modernists, who typically saw their work in opposition to these earlier traditions. Moreover, as Astradur Eysteinsson has pointed out, there are many artists whose work blurs the boundaries between modernism and the avant-garde in such a manner that a simple division of these categories cannot be maintained.[120] Over the last decade in particular, a great deal of scholarship on early-twentieth-century art and literature has sought to emphasize the continuities between modernism and the avant-garde rather than making sharp distinctions between the two.[121]

Later avant-garde movements, typically known as the "neo-avant-gardes" are also rendered problematic by Bürger's theory. As Tyrus Miller has described it, "At the heart of the existence of a neo-avant-garde is an intolerable contradiction: an avant-garde whose newness is defined by its seeming repetition, at a later date, of an earlier historical formation."[122] For Bürger, the neo-avant-gardes become nothing more than empty repetitions of avant-gardism, since the revolutionary, avant-garde gesture has been consecrated and reabsorbed into the institution of art as yet another aesthetic maneuver. This particular critique of neo-avant-gardism reaches its apotheosis in Paul Mann's *The Theory-Death of the Avant-Garde* (1991). Following a Baudrillardian logic, Mann argues that the neo-avant-gardes reconstruct themselves in an endless series of repetitions and manufactured crises that mimic consumer trends, and this repetition of trends places the contemporary avant-gardes in a discursive space where they are neither fully "alive" nor completely "dead."[123] More recently, however, critics such as Anna Katharina Schaffner have openly questioned the validity of such dismissals of neo-avant-gardism.[124]

From my perspective, Bürger's thesis suffers from more fundamental problems. Not only does it unconsciously reintroduce a mimetic separation of art and life, as I argued earlier, but it also uncritically accepts the avant-garde's own claim to possess a radical novelty that marks a rupture with all prior traditions. By positioning the appearance of the avant-garde as an exceptional historical event, Bürger effectively recapitulates the "myth" of the "originality of the avant-garde" (to borrow Rosalind Krauss's phrase). Bürger's argument that the avant-garde presents a unique system-wide critique of the bourgeois institution of art absolutely depends on the claim that the historical avant-gardes constitute an aesthetic development that is genuinely unprecedented. In this sense, the problem with Bürger's argument is not only that it too emphatically separates the historical avant-gardes from the contemporary and subsequent movements—such as modernism and the neo-avant-gardes—that shared many of the historical avant-gardes' concerns and cultural networks,[125] but also that it takes at face value the historical avant-gardes' claim to present a novel critique of the traditional institution of art. But, despite the rhetorical assertions of revolutionary intent within the manifestoes of the various historical avant-gardes (a rhetorical gesture also favored by many among the modernists and neo-avant-gardes), the historical avant-gardes' critiques of art were both anticipated and heavily influenced by prior movements—the most significant of which, by far, was romanticism.

The influence of romanticism on the twentieth-century avant-gardes was already well established prior to the appearance of Bürger's *Theory of the Avant-Garde*; Renato Poggioli, in his book also titled *The Theory of the Avant-Garde* (1962), devoted an entire chapter to the correspondences between the avant-garde and romanticism.[126] Moreover, Poggioli also points out that even the avant-garde's own belief that it had severed all ties with romanticism is itself unoriginal, since this "belief was shared by followers of art-for-art's-sake and of the Parnasse, by the decadents and symbolists, finally by the realists and naturalists," all of whom thought "they had transcended romanticism solely because they had overcome psychological sentimentality or aesthetic idealism."[127] Scholars as diverse as Pierre Bourdieu, Paul Hamilton, Herbert Read, Peter Gay, Michael Lowy and Robert Sayre[128] have documented the influence of romanticism on a number of the historical avant-gardes. Philippe Lacoue-Labarthe and Jean-Luc Nancy have perhaps been the most emphatic about this connection, stating baldly that "without any exaggeration" the Jena Circle is "the first 'avant-garde' group in history. At no point, in any case, does one discern the least departure from this nearly two-hundred-year-old form on the part of what calls itself the 'avant-garde' today."[129]

Some of these claims may, however, overstate the case. My contention is *not* that the avant-garde is identical to romanticism, but rather that romanticism both creates the conditions of possibility required for the emergence of the avant-garde and anticipates many of its key features. While attempting to offer a systematic delineation of the avant-garde's historical debts to romanticism lies beyond the scope of my argument, I will briefly consider some of the more explicit correspondences between the two by examining one paradigmatic, romantic text: Wordsworth's preface to the *Lyrical Ballads*. Written in 1800, two years after the first publication of *Lyrical Ballads*, this preface demonstrates a variety of tendencies that, without being expressly avant-garde, appear as something like a proto-avant-gardism. The preface foregrounds its own novelty, even explaining that its contents "are to be considered as experiments" that will cause readers to "struggle with feelings of strangeness and awkwardness,"[130] while simultaneously serving to provide an interpretive frame that makes this new poetry legible, by explaining the ways in which it differentiates itself from prior traditions. Seen in this light, the preface to the *Lyrical Ballads* serves as a precursor to the avant-garde manifesto. Even the dual authorship of the poetry within *Lyrical Ballads* anticipates the avant-garde practice of producing work through the prism of group affiliations, rather than as individuals.

But, more importantly, the preface to the *Lyrical Ballads* anticipates the avant-garde in exactly Bürger's sense, since it, too, displays a nascent desire to sublate the categories of life and art through the medium of the work of art. This inchoate attempt to merge life and art appears when Wordsworth addresses the linguistic register of his poetry, which has attempted to adapt "the language of conversation in the middle and lower classes of society" to "the purposes of poetic pleasure."[131] My argument is that the historical avant-gardes' attempts to merge art and life present a hypertrophic development of this romantic tendency to reenvision the everyday through an aesthetic lens, and in this sense the avant-garde does not so much represent a break with its romantic precursors as a radicalized reenvisioning of certain aesthetic concepts already imminent to the discourse of romanticism itself. Bürger's claim that the historical avant-gardes' attempt (and fail) to sublate art and life is not necessarily incorrect, but the assumption that this attempt itself is novel and constitutes a ground for establishing the distinctiveness of the historical avant-gardes is deeply problematic.

My argument is that avant-garde satires of the avant-garde actually anticipate many aspects of Bürger's critique, although without replicating the problematic claim of the historical avant-gardes' exceptionality. They also depict the failure of the avant-gardes' attempts to merge art and life, and they frequently satirize the manner in which avant-gardism has become imbricated with bohemian "lifestyle" choices—one of many instrumental traces that remains in these aestheticized works of satire. A character in Wyndham Lewis's *The Apes of God* describes this process as the "societification of art,"[132] itself an extrapolation of a concept that Lewis had already articulated when he coined the term "bourgeois bohemian" in his 1918 novel *Tarr*. This critique of art that is "used" as a means of lifestyle enhancement prefigures the situation that Bürger has described as the "false actualization" of the avant-garde's project, resulting in an "aestheticization of every day life."[133] (It's also worth underscoring the contradictory nature of Lewis's critique, which is an instrumental critique of instrumentalism!).

But while their critiques prefigure Bürger's, avant-garde satires of the avant-garde also retain an essential difference: they locate the exhaustion of the avant-garde in its inaugurating gesture. The avant-garde is always already hopelessly indebted and repetitive, and—even more critically—*completely unaware* of its own indebtedness. These satires suggest that what *appears* to be avant-garde is, in fact, only the exhausted, dead repetition of previous sources, inheritances, and antecedents. By denying the exceptional nature of the avant-garde, they suggest that the avant-garde's claim to have broken with tradition is baseless. Instead, this subgenre of satire seeks to reveal that the avant-garde's claims of radical novelty are a form of repression that results in the unconscious repetition of prior traditions.

Although avant-garde satires of the avant-garde remain hostile to the avant-garde's project by rejecting its claims to represent a genuine rupture with tradition, they nonetheless do not constitute an absolute rejection of avant-gardism as such, nor can they be dismissed as simply being conservative or "*arrière-garde*" works. In this sense, the satires I examine differ in character from the many contemporaneous parodies and satires of modernism collected by Leonard Diepeveen in *Mock Modernism: An Anthology of Parodies, Travesties, Frauds, 1910–1935* (2014), which often attack modernism through more stable satiric norms, by accusing it of being obscure, pretentious, or absurd. The works I examine undertake a more complex project; as Lisa Siraganian has noted in relation to the work of William Gaddis, what appears to be a "'neo' rear-guard satire of the contemporary art world" actually "reinvents the avant-garde by imagining criticism incorporated into art."[134] This rejection of the avant-garde's claim to radical novelty does not constitute a return to a prior aesthetic mode, but rather a search for more adequate grounds upon which to found a legitimately original avant-garde. But these satires are not able to articulate this project in explicit terms. Having rejected any ethical or utilitarian grounds for their satire, it remains impossible for them to posit any kind of explicit program that could be attached to their critique. Nonetheless, their critique cannot be reduced to a simple negativity, since the figure of critique they produce is hypertrophic—critiques are themselves critiqued and negations themselves negated in a theoretically endless process.

This endless process of critique presents an attempt to avoid the exhaustion of the avant-gardes—in which art becomes nothing more than dead repetition—by relentlessly revealing and negating the conditions of possibility that make this form of satire possible in the first place. In so doing, these works become self-reflexive and aware of their own indebtedness, rather than unconsciously re-presenting what has come before. For this reason, avant-garde satires of the avant-garde often disapprovingly depict unconscious repetition, whether satirizing the banal and clichéd conversations of people on the street or the way New York poets in the 1950s cribbed from William Carlos Williams's *Paterson* (1946–58). These unconscious repetitions serve as a counterpoint to the radical self-reflexivity of postromantic satire, which consistently negates and critiques the norms that underlie its own satiric judgments. Paradoxically, it is only through this process of relentless negation that avant-garde satires of the avant-garde can escape exhaustion. In employing this figure, however, these satires also mark their own difference from the objects of their satire—another residue of satiric instrumentality.

This relentless self-criticism recalls Giorgio Agamben's discussion of Hegel's description of romantic irony as a "self-annihilating nothing," in which he notes precisely this capacity of art to survive only through its infinite self-negation:

> Art does not die but, having become a self-annihilating nothing, eternally survives itself. Limitless, lacking content, double in its principle, it wanders in the nothingness of the *terra aesthetica*, in a desert of forms and contents that continually point it beyond its own image and which it evokes and immediately abolishes in the impossible attempt to found its own certainty.[135]

In this gesture of infinite negation, whereby the work of art must contain its own critique, its own transcendence of itself, the strange hyperromanticism of these texts appears. But it is through these inexhaustible negations that these works attempt to overcome exhaustion and open themselves to new aesthetic possibilities, rather than instrumental aims. This complicated form of self-negation seems to be precisely what William Gaddis had in mind when he choose, as the cover illustration for his novel *The Recognitions*, a drawing of a dragon swallowing its own tail—the ouroboros, which, in an anticipation of romanticism's aesthetics, was the symbol employed by medieval alchemists to signify both unity and infinity.

Paradoxically, these avant-garde satires strive to negate or destroy themselves in the attempt to transcend their own limits. By admitting and negating the principles on which they are based, they seek to avoid the failure and exhaustion of the avant-garde. But it is worth emphasizing that even this paradoxical form of transcendence has a romantic precedent, since it recalls the romantic notion of the fragment. The fragment, too, is intentionally incomplete, destroyed, or partial. But it is precisely the incomplete nature of the fragment that allows it to suggest something larger than the complete work of art; effectively, the fragment is able to transcend the limits of the completed work, by admitting its own incompleteness. As Jan Luc Nancy and Philippe Lacoue-Labarthe have noted, "The fragment combines completion and incompletion within itself" in ways that allow it "to designate its own incompletion, to master it."[136] Put another way, this constant attempt at self-transcendence also constitutes these works' claim of autonomy. They seek to generate a totalizing, organic whole which surpasses (rather than merely reflecting) artistic intent; the generation of such a totalized autonomous work, however, both requires a keen sense of aesthetic history and the intentional deployment of internal contradictions, which will be resolved within the individual work.

On one hand, then, this subgenre of postromantic satire is a late re-presentation of many aspects of the romantic project, such as the fragment. On the other hand, however, it also constitutes an attempt to respond to and surmount the internal contradictions of the historical avant-gardes. In this dual movement, avant-garde satires of the avant-garde illustrate the historical relation between romanticism and the twentieth-century avant-gardes, which has often been ignored and repressed amid claims for the radical novelty of modern art. Ultimately, this odd subgenre that eschews any ethical grounding and instead presents an unyielding, self-reflexive negativity can only be understood as *Nachträglichkeit*—a belatedness that results in an obsessive desire to continue wrestling with both the traumas and the contradictions that have arisen from the various avant-gardes' attempts to overcome tradition. But this obsessiveness also presents a challenge to most histories of twentieth-century art, which see the concerns of the avant-garde as having been relegated to the dustbin of history. In re-interrogating avant-gardism, this subgenre generates a complex and self-reflexive concept of autonomy while also suggesting that the aesthetic developments of the early twentieth century (and, indeed, of romanticism before it) continue to exert an influence on contemporary cultural production.

5 Chapter summaries

Having outlined the four key terms of my investigation—autonomy, satire, romanticism, and the avant-garde—it's worth briefly sketching out the shape of my argument in relation to the specific texts I will consider. Chapter 2, "The Romantic Satire of Romanticism," tracks the shift in the literary dominant of satire from ethics to aesthetics through a close reading of Thomas Love Peacock's *Nightmare Abbey* (1818), an exemplary satire that has been reshaped by romanticism. Although *Nightmare Abbey* appears to be a straightforward attack on romantic tropes and authors, the novel self-reflexively critiques its own satire in a recursive process that resembles romantic irony. In so doing it undermines its satiric norms and problematizes the authority of the satiric persona, who traditionally embodies satire's ethical intent. By employing a romantic self-reflexivity, the novel severs its connection to a transcendent, ethical ground, which, in turn, enables the novel to explore the aesthetic possibilities of satire as a literary form.

Nightmare Abbey undermines its apparent ethical grounding through a variety of formal and rhetorical strategies. First, it deploys allusion and paratextual metacommentary to contradict the judgments of its satiric persona. Secondly, it surreptitiously engages in a dialogue with Peacock's own long poem, *The Philosophy of Melancholy* (1812), which was published six years earlier and effusively praised the same literary melancholia that *Nightmare Abbey* satirizes; I will argue that, in so doing, the novel makes satiric critique a matter of subjective perspective instead of objective judgment. Finally, the novel employs the comedy of humors to enact a dialogism that diminishes the authority of the satiric persona. In these ways, *Nightmare Abbey* utilizes self-reflexivity to reveal the partial, subjective, and incomplete nature of satiric judgment.

The chapter concludes by arguing that *Nightmare Abbey*'s self-reflexivity extends and revises romantic aesthetic principles in general and the oscillating function of romantic irony in particular. Like romantic irony, self-reflexive satire becomes an unfolding, inconclusive, and theoretically inexhaustible process. Such satiric judgments, which lack transcendent, ethical grounds, now function like Kantian aesthetic judgments in relying on subjective rather than objectively universalizable criteria. But self-reflexive satire also differs from romantic irony: instead of oscillating between positive and negative poles, satiric judgment employs only the negative pole in a recursive fashion to generate romantic indeterminacy. This reliance on negativity means that romantic satire never produces an explicitly positive or affirmative moment. In this way, romantic satire also revises romanticism within the generic logic of satire. The result is nothing less than a new, romantic form of satire oriented toward aesthetics rather than ethics.

Chapter 3, "Modernism against Itself," examines the formation of the subgenre of avant-garde satires of the avant-garde. Although its self-reflexivity and focus on aesthetics is prefigured by romantic satires like *Nightmare Abbey*, this distinct subgenre develops in the wake of the modernist avant-gardes, which provide both the subject and context of its satire. This subgenre is characterized by its simultaneous critique and affirmation of the modernist avant-gardes. On the one hand, this satiric subgenre ridicules the avant-gardes' claim to have broken entirely with tradition, which is instead revealed as an unconscious suppression of prior influences, including that of romanticism itself. On the other hand, this subgenre takes up elements of the avant-gardes' utopian project, albeit in an apophatic form, with the result that it becomes a key textual site both for wrestling with the contradictions of the avant-gardes and for understanding their lasting influence.

I will explore the contours of this new subgenre through an analysis of Wyndham Lewis's *The Apes of God* (1930), a self-proclaimed work of autonomous, "non-moral" satire that mocks avant-garde artists in 1920s London. The novel establishes clear satiric norms that condemn these artists as unoriginal apes, whose "avant-garde" works are hopelessly indebted. But these norms are undermined in a series of "staged reversals," which reveal the satiric persona to be unoriginal much like his satiric targets. *The Apes of God* extends this self-reflexive critique through a series of allusions to other works that prefigure its satire, culminating in a reference to a key intertext, E.T.A. Hoffmann's "Report of an Educated Young Man," whose entire premise is intentionally appropriated in *The Apes of God*. In this gesture, the novel attempts (not entirely successfully) to remove any traces of satiric instrumentalism.

Nonetheless, *The Apes of God*'s playful foregrounding of its own indebtedness presents a genuine attempt to respond to the avant-gardes' (false) claims to have broken with tradition. Lewis views these fictitious claims of novelty as a problem, because they enable prior traditions to reassert themselves unexpectedly in a return of the repressed. As I will argue, Lewis saw his "non moral" satire as nothing less than an alternate vision for a more authentic avant-garde that would be founded on a paradigm of self-reflexivity, rather than radical novelty. In satire, Lewis sought a literary form that could explore new aesthetic avenues by engaging in an open and sustained critique of tradition, rather than simply attempting to transcend it, as the avant-gardes had done. Lewis's aesthetic project thus presents a fundamental revision of the purpose of satire, which is no longer a literary form of ethical didacticism, but rather the exemplary form for wrestling with the contradictions of an overdetermined modernity upon which a genuine avant-garde might be founded. As I will argue, while Lewis's satire thus does articulate a purpose, the nature of this purposiveness differs from the means-end rationalism of traditional satire.

Chapter 4, "Exhausting Modernism," examines how William Gaddis's *The Recognitions* (1955) extends and intensifies self-reflexive satire's mode of recursive critique, which, as I will argue, constitutes a late modernist revision of this subgenre of avant-garde satires of the avant-garde. Pervaded by a sense of cultural exhaustion caused by the collapse of the modernist avant-gardes, late modernist works remain deeply skeptical of modernist notions like originality and authenticity. Instead of advancing explicit, utopian programs, they employ modernist prose techniques to produce a sustained textual ambiguity that seeks to avoid any clear resolution in order to prolong a state of ambiguity. Fittingly, *The Recognitions* shrouds its satiric judgment behind a veil by providing contradictory information about the targets of its satire. This technique constitutes an intensification of the methods used to undermine satiric authority, since the reader faces an unresolvable textual indeterminacy and therefore cannot assess the validity of the novel's satiric judgment.

But this late modernist ambiguity is counterpoised with a paradoxical imperative to revive the exhausted avant-garde project even though such a task is acknowledged to be fundamentally impossible. *The Recognitions'* satire reflects this conflicted imperative in its desire to reaffirm a modernist notion of aesthetic autonomy despite the fact that the negative recursion of postromantic satire makes explicit, positive affirmation impossible. The novel resorts to apophatic means, re-marshaling the force of satiric critique to an indirectly "positive" end: it launches an attack on aesthetic autonomy in order to cleanse this concept of its exhausted connotations, so that autonomy can be obliquely reasserted in a purified form.

The novel's oscillation between critique and apophatic affirmation ultimately results in the production of an "ambivalent sublime," in which the "negative" moment of the sublime (blockage) and its restorative "conclusion" (uplift) occur simultaneously. This suspension of the plot of the sublime constitutes the goal of *The Recognitions'* satire: while the ambivalent sublime is a natural extension of the late modernist preference for unresolvable ambiguity, it also implicitly affirms the unique capacity of the work of art to contain and even unify binary opposites into an aesthetic whole. The ambivalent sublime thus constitutes an apophatic reaffirmation of the autonomy of art. This represents an intensification of the aesthetic turn in Lewis's satire, since satire orients itself wholly toward the creation of an aesthetic experience of the sublime. At the same time, however, it is also an attenuation of the project of the modernist avant-gardes, since *The Recognitions* presents a purely aesthetic utopianism that can be achieved only by transcending— rather than confronting—its contexts and its conditions of possibility.

In Chapter 5, "Aporia and the Satiric Imagination," I focus on Gilbert Sorrentino's *Imaginative Qualities of Actual Things* (1971), a text that appears to be a postmodern reworking of the avant-garde satires of the avant-garde. Unlike the other texts in this subgenre, which first establish a clear set of norms that are later subverted, *Imaginative Qualities* openly proclaims its lack of any norms, both flaunting and reveling in the groundlessness of its satire. Satiric tendencies are exploited for aesthetic ends and performatively amplified, as satiric outrage becomes indistinguishable from harsh invective. Elsewhere, the satiric persona frequently notes his similarity to many of the characters in the novel, rather than seeking to differentiate himself from his satiric targets, as is the case in traditional satire. These tendencies reflect a variety of traits associated with literary postmodernism. The novel's antifoundationalist denial of ethical grounds and satiric norms recalls Lyotard's postmodern rejection of grand narratives, and its playful exploration of satiric tropes recalls the Derridean notion of the free play of signifiers, both of which have been proposed as key features of postmodern texts.

But *Imaginative Qualities'* relationship to postmodernism is more complicated than it seems, since the novel both emphasizes the influence exerted upon it by modernist works and articulates a modernist notion of autonomy. As I will argue, *Imaginative Qualities* revises a modernist aesthetic in postmodern terms to produce a complicated hybrid of the two that still belongs in the modernist tradition, but reimagines key elements of this legacy. The novel's postmodern antifoundationalism ironically provides the means to reassert apophatically a modernist autonomy through the rhetorical figure of the aporia. By introducing a willfully illogical and contradictory set of propositions into the text, *Imaginative Qualities* halts the formation of any coherent norms—a gesture that comprises yet another intensification of these satires' self-reflexive methods. But the text also posits its own isolation from grounded discourses as a form of autonomy in the modernist sense.

As I will argue, however, the notion of autonomy advanced in *Imaginative Qualities* nonetheless radically differs from most accounts of modernist aesthetics. Rather than reestablishing the self-sufficiency of the work of art, *Imaginative Qualities'* claim of autonomy invokes the romantic conception of the imagination in an attempt to reconfigure the relation between the fictional and the actual in a manner that evades both the utilization of art and the aestheticization of life. In its reimagining of this relation, the novel echoes the avant-gardes' utopianism, albeit in an oblique form. This unusual mode of autonomy reconstitutes satire as an apophatic utopianism forged in the groundless ground of the imagination.

In my concluding chapter, "Satire and Radical Apophasis in Evan Dara's *The Easy Chain*," I consider how the notion of autonomy in avant-garde satires of the avant-garde is intimately linked to a set of political and social contexts that cannot be separated from the generic history of satire as a form. In particular, their deactivation of ethical grounds can be read as a democratizing gesture that disaggregates the relation between authority, norms, ridicule, and control that animated traditional forms of satire. Autonomy is commonly understood either as a form of philosophical idealism or as an absolute rejection of the social. In contrast, I will propose that these satires' autonomy claims—which, as I have argued are a rhetorical provocation linked to the uncovering aesthetic possibilities—do not represent a willful dismissal of reality, but rather a utopian desire closely related to their exploration of possible rather than extant forms.

Finally, I argue that this form of satire continues to exert a force on contemporary literature, through a reading of Evan Dara's *The Easy Chain*, a novel that amplifies the apophatic tendencies of this satiric subgenre by making the avant-garde itself a palpable absence within the text. The negative presence of an autonomous avant-garde sharpens the book's social critique, which has as one of its chief concerns the impossibility of asserting a modernist conception of autonomy under the material conditions of late capitalism. Through this apophatic gesture, *The Easy Chain* views autonomy not as a disinterested aestheticism, but as a provocation to think through a series of questions about how economic structures affect culture and society under global capitalism. *The Easy Chain* exemplifies the particular power of this unusual form of satire, which has endured precisely because of its capacity to track the complicated relation between art and its social and political contexts without resorting to reductionist positions.

Notes

1   Larry David and Jerry Seinfeld, "The Pitch," *Seinfeld,* season 4, episode 3, directed
    by Tom Cherones, aired September 16, 1992 (Culver City, CA: Sony Pictures
    Home Entertainment, 2005), DVD.

2   Fredric Jameson, "Postmodernism, or the Cultural Logic of Late Capitalism,"
    New Left Review 146 (July–August 1984): 53.

3   Andreas Huyssen, *Twilight Memories: Marking Time in a Culture of Amnesia*
    (New York: Routledge, 1995), 22.

4   André Gide, *The Counterfeiters,* Trans. Dorothy Bussy and Justin O'Brien
    (New York: Vintage, 1973), 73–4.

5   Kurt Weinberg, *On Gide's* Prométhée: *Private Myth and Public Mystification*
    (Princeton, NJ: Princeton University Press, 1972), 17.

6   Gustave Flaubert, *The Letters of Gustave Flaubert: 1830–1857,* Ed. and Trans.
    Francis Steegmuller (Cambridge, MA: Harvard University Press, 1980), 154.

7   For an excellent overview of the key elements of this debate, see Theodor Adorno,
    Walter Benjamin, Ernst Bloch, Bertolt Brecht and Georg Lukács, *Aesthetics and
    Politics* (London: Verso Books, 1977).

8   Peter Bürger, *Theory of the Avant-Garde,* Trans. Michael Shaw (Manchester:
    Manchester University Press, 1984), 51.

9   Richard Murphy, *Theorizing the Avant-Garde: Modernism, Expressionism, and the
    Problem of Postmodernity* (Cambridge: Cambridge University Press, 1998), 30.

10 Craig Owens, "The Discourse of Others: Feminists and Postmodernism," *The
    Anti-Aesthetic,* Ed. Hal Foster (New York: The New Press, 1983), 59.

11 Christoph Menke, *The Sovereignty of Art: Aesthetic Negativity in Adorno and
    Derrida,* Trans. Neil Solomon (Cambridge, MA: MIT Press, 1999), xi.

12 Astradur Eysteinsson, *The Concept of Modernism* (Ithaca, NY: Cornell University
    Press, 1990), 16.

13 Fredric Jameson, *A Singular Modernity: Essay on the Ontology of the Present*
    (London: Verso, 2002), 176. Although it may seem odd, Georg Lukács's rejection
    of aesthetic autonomy also falls within this category; as Bela Kiralyfalvi has
    argued in *The Aesthetics of Gyorgy Lukacs* (Princeton, NJ: Princeton University
    Press, 1975), Lukács viewed aesthetic autonomy as an illusion, since capitalist
    societies did not free artists, but rather turned them into the producers of
    commodities (144). Jameson's dismissal of autonomy thus rearticulates Lukács's
    view that autonomy claims simply mask the commodification of art.

14 Mark M. Freed, *Robert Musil and the NonModern* (New York:
    Continuum, 2011), 117.

15 Jennifer Ashton, *From Modernism to Postmodernism: American Poetry and Theory in the Twentieth Century* (Cambridge: Cambridge University Press, 2006), 6.

16 Ashton, *Modernism to Postmodernism*, 2.

17 Nicholas Brown, "The Work of Art in the Age of Its Real Subsumption under Capital," *Nonsite*, March 13, 2012. Retrieved at http://nonsite.org/editorial/the-work-of-art-in-the-age-of-its-real-subsumption-under-capital.

18 Charles Altieri, "Why Modernist Claims for Autonomy Matter," *Journal of Modern Literature* 32.3 (Spring 2009): 12.

19 Douglas Mao and Rebecca L. Walkowitz, "The New Modernist Studies," *PMLA* 123.3 (May 2008): 737–48.

20 Lisa Siraganian, *Modernism's Other Work: The Art Object's Political Life* (Oxford: Oxford University Press, 2012), 3. My emphasis.

21 Cited in Siraganian, *Modernism's Other Work*, 16.

22 Jacques Rancière, *The Politics of Literature* (Cambridge: Polity, 2011), 5. Rancière has explored the inherently political nature of autonomy at length in such works as *The Politics of Aesthetics* (2000), *The Politics of Literature* (2006), *Dissensus* (2010), and *Aisthesis* (2011), among others.

23 Siraganian, in *Modernism's Other Work*, notes that Adorno's thought can actually be read as supporting the notion that autonomy is always already co-implicated with politics (49). Christoph Menke, in *The Sovereignty of Art*, reads Adorno's theory as an attempt to navigate between two different reductionist views of aesthetics (3–6), a point that resonates with my claims. Herbert Marcuse, in *The Aesthetic Dimension: Towards a Critique of Marxist Aesthetics*, trans. Herbert Marcuse and Erica Sherover (Boston: Beacon Press, 1978), articulates a position very similar to mine, noting that, "literature can be called revolutionary in a meaningful sense only with reference to itself, as content having become form. The political potential of art lies only in its own aesthetic dimension" (xii). The key distinction is that Marcuse sees such autonomous art as a model for social change—a position of which I am more skeptical.

24 Adorno was very critical of avant-garde works that, in his estimation, had inadvertently retained a mimetic orientation; as Martin Scherzinger notes in "In Memory of a Receding Dialectic: The Political Relevance of Autonomy and Formalism in Modernist Music," *The Pleasure of Modernist Music: Listening, Meaning, Intention, Ideology* (Rochester, NY: University of Rochester Press, 2004), Adorno's infamous critique of twelve-tone music is based on the claim that it "had reproduced the fate it attempted to elude and thus degenerated into its opposite" (82).

25 For one extended examination of the material history of the book as both artefact and commodity, see Roger Chartier, *The Order of Books: Readers, Authors, and*

Libraries in Europe between the Fourteenth and Eighteenth Centuries, Trans. Lydia G. Cochrane (Stanford: Stanford University Press, 1994).

26 Siraganian, *Modernism's Other Work,* 3.

27 Andrew Goldstone, *Fictions of Autonomy: Modernism from Wilde to de Man* (Oxford: Oxford University Press, 2013), 4.

28 Goldstone, *Fictions of Autonomy,* 4.

29 Tobin Siebers points out, in "Allegory and the Aesthetic Ideology," *Interpretation and the Allegory: Antiquity to the Modern Period,* Ed. John Whitman (Leiden; Boston: Brill, 2000), that "Kant chose to represent human autonomy aesthetically" because to define freedom "on the basis of predetermined concepts" would effectively "define it out of existence"; as a result, Kant realized freedom could "be defined only on its own terms, and since 'its own terms' are not even comprehensible . . . he proposed an analogy" to the "beautiful object" which, "like freedom, is its own definition" (479).

30 Pierre Bourdieu, "The Historical Genesis of a Pure Aesthetic," *Analytic Aesthetics,* Ed. Richard Shusterman (Oxford: Basil Blackwell, 1989), 157.

31 Wyndham Lewis, *Tarr* (Oxford: Oxford University Press, 2010), 265.

32 Nathan Waddell, *Modernist Nowheres: Politics and Utopia in Early Modernist Writing, 1900–1920* (London: Palgrave Macmillan, 2012), 179.

33 William K. Wimsatt and Monroe Beardsley, "The Intentional Fallacy," *The Sewanee Review* 54.3 (July–September 1946): 469. See also Ashton, *From Modernism to Postmodernism,* 22.

34 Ashton, for example, grounds her analysis of Stein in a wide array of essays and lectures that theoretically reflect her artistic intent. Brown, similarly, compares statements by James Cameron (in relation to his film *Avatar* [2009]) and David Simon (in relation to this TV series, *The Wire* [2002–08]) to clarify his concept of intent.

35 Immanuel Kant, *Critique of Judgment,* Trans. James Creed Meredith. Ed. Nicolas Walker (Oxford: Oxford University Press, 2007), 138–9.

36 For an excellent overview of Cavell's position on intention, see David Rudrum, *Stanley Cavell and the Claim of Literature* (Baltimore: Johns Hopkins University Press, 2013), 78.

37 Terry Eagleton, "Unhoused," *The London Review of Books* 30.10 (May 22, 2008): 19–20.

38 Ezra Pound, *The Cantos* (New York: New Directions, 1998), 815–16.

39 Ibid., 817.

40 Todd Cronan, *Against Affective Formalism: Matisse, Bergson, Modernism* (Minneapolis, MN: University of Minnesota Press, 2013), 26.

41 Ibid., 11, 14.

42   Cronan, *Against Affective Formalism,* 13.

43   Robert C. Elliott, in "The Satirist and Society," *Satire: Modern Essays in Criticism,*
      Ed. Ronald Paulson (Englewood Cliffs, NJ: Prentice-Hall, 1971), argues that the
      "satirist claims with much justification to be a true conservative" who is operating
      "within the established framework of society, accepting its norms, appealing to
      reason . . . as the standard against which to judge the folly that he sees" and thus
      acts as a "preserver of tradition" (213).

44   Alvin Kernan, in *The Cankered Muse: Satire of the English Renaissance*
      (New Haven; London: Yale University Press, 1959), argues that "satire is a distinct
      artistic genre with a number of marked characteristics" (vii). John Snyder, in
      Prospects of Power: Tragedy, Satire, the Essay, and the Theory of Genre (Lexington,
      KY: University Press of Kentucky, 1991), claims "satire is a semigenre only, a
      genre that stops itself from becoming a fully distinct alternative to other genres"
      (101). David Noakes, in *Raillery and Rage: A Study of Eighteenth Century Satire*
      (Brighton: The Harvester Press Ltd., 1987), views satire as "a two-toned genre,
      being both sweet and sour, a weapon and a toy" (17). Michael Seidel, in *The
      Satiric Inheritance: Rabelais to Stern* (Princeton: Princeton University Press,
      1979), denies that satire constitutes a genre, arguing instead that it is a mode,
      albeit "a subverting and subversive" one (14). Northrop Frye, in *The Anatomy of
      Criticism* (Princeton: Princeton University Press, 1957), sees satire as a "mythos"
      whose central theme is "the disappearance of the heroic" (228). Ronald Paulson,
      in *The Fictions of Satire* (Baltimore: Johns Hopkins University Press, 1967), argues
      that there is an important distinction between considering a specific work of
      satire and considering satire as a larger category, since "without an article 'satire'
      refers more to a tone than a form" (v). Paul Simpson, in *On the Discourse of
      Satire: Towards a Stylistic Model of Satirical Humour* (Amsterdam; Philadelphia:
      John Benjamins Publishing Co., 2003), contends that "satire manifests a level
      of organisation which is of a sufficiently higher-order status to constitute a
      discursive practice" (8). Charles A. Knight, in *The Literature of Satire* (Cambridge:
      Cambridge University Press, 2004), argues that viewing "satire as a pre-generic
      form, as a frame of mind" is productive because it halts the formation of satire
      "as an exclusive category allowing some works to be included and more left
      out" (14). James W. Nichols, in *Insinuation: The Tactics of English Satire* (The
      Hague; Paris: Mouton & Co. N.V., 1971), describes satire as a set of tactics, but
      tentatively notes that these "tactics" also "suggest, I think, that satire may be a
      genre in some useful sense of the term" (12). George A. Test, in *Satire: Spirit and
      Art* (Tampa: University of South Florida Press, 1991), suggests that "satire may
      more easily be explained and understood as a bent possessed by many human
      beings but more highly developed in some individuals and expressing itself in

an almost endless variety of ways" (12). Edward W. Rosenheim, in *Swift and the Satirist's Art* (Chicago; London: University of Chicago Press, 1963), claims that, while satire constitutes a "species of writing," it is not "what is ordinarily regarded as a ... literary 'form'" (11). Dustin Griffin, in *Satire: A Critical Reintroduction* (Lexington, KY: University Press of Kentucky, 1994), states that satire is an open form because of its "formal ... reluctance to conclude" and "its more general rhetorical and moral features" that demonstrate a "preference for inquiry, provocation, or playfulness rather than assertion and conclusiveness" (186). Gilbert Highet, in *The Anatomy of Satire* (Princeton: Princeton University Press, 1926), notes that "satire as a distinct type of literature with a generic name and continuous tradition of its own, is usually believed to have started in Rome" (24.) Fredric V. Bogel, in *The Difference Satire Makes: Rhetoric and Reading from Jonson to Byron* (Ithaca; London: Cornell University Press, 2001), argues that satire's most important feature lies in "the impulse to convert an initially ambiguous relation of identification and division ... into one of pure division" (48).

45   Brian A. Connery and Kirke Combe, "Theorizing Satire: A Retrospective and Introduction," *Theorizing Satire: Essays in Literary Criticism* (New York: St. Martin's Press, 1995), 4–5.

46   Robert C. Elliott, in "The Definition of Satire: A Note on Method," *Yearbook on Comparative and General Literature,* 11 (1962), suggests that "there are no properties common to *all* of the uses" of satire, and that any delineation of a central principle for satire would be "so general, as to be useless for purposes of definition" (22). Christopher Yu, in *Nothing to Admire: The Politics of Poetic Satire from Dryden to Merrill* (Oxford: Oxford University Press, 2003), also contends that any attempt to create "a definition of satire that is valid for all historical moments and cultural situations" would be "doomed to resort to partial truths and pointless generalizations" (4). Test, in *Satire: Spirit and Art,* similarly argues that "what is commonly referred to as satire is merely the aesthetic manifestation of a universal urge so varied as to elude definition" (1).

47   Charles A. Knight, "Satire, Speech, and Genre," *Comparative Literature,* 44.1 (1992): 22.

48   There has been a considerable debate as to whether satire constitutes a genre or a mode, to use the terminology deployed by Alastair Fowler in *Kinds of Literature: An Introduction to the Theory of Genres and Modes* (Cambridge: Harvard University Press, 1982). For two representative examples of the opposing sides of this debate, see Leon Guilhamet, *Satire and the Transformation of Genre* (Philadelphia: University of Pennsylvania Press, 1987) and Michael Seidel, *The Satiric Inheritance: Rabelais to Stern.* Surprisingly, both Seidel and Guilhamet come to similar conclusions about how satire inhabits and deforms other genres.

49 Bogel, *The Difference Satire Makes,* 68.

50 My citations for this standard view of satire come from Nichols summary of them in *Insinuation* (35).

51 Jonathan Greenberg, *Modernism, Satire, and the Novel* (Cambridge: Cambridge University Press, 2011), 5.

52 Ibid., 7.

53 There are, however, several important works that have applied literary theory to satire: Mikhail Bahktin's account of the carnivalesque in Menippean satire informs, for example, Steven Weisenburger's *Fables of Subversion: Satire and the American Novel, 1930–1980* (Athens, GA: University of Georgia Press, 1995); a wide range of recent literary and cultural theories are deployed in *Cutting Edges: Postmodern Perspectives on Eighteenth-Century Satire* (Knoxville, TN: University of Tennessee Press, 1995), edited by James E. Gill; and aspects of Foucault's thought are deployed by Rose A. Zimbardo, in *Zero Point: Discourse, Culture, and Satire in Restoration England* (Lexingtion, KY: The University Press of Kentucky, 1998).

54 Ashley Marshall, *The Practice of Satire in England: 1658–1770* (Baltimore, MD: Johns Hopkins University Press, 2013), 10.

55 John Dryden, *The Essays of John Dryden* Vol. 2., Ed. William Patton Ker (Oxford: Clarendon Press, 1900), 104. Zimbardo, in *At Zero Point,* argues that the ethical orientation of neoclassical satire is asserted in Dryden's preference for Horace over Juvenal "as the favoured model," which had the effect of both "reconstruct[ing] the generic profile of satire in line with new modern thinking," and "project[ing] upon that new generic model a *conceptual* design for satire that has shaped our understanding of the genre for three hundred years" (141).

56 Roman Jakobson, "The Dominant," *Selected Writings, Vol. 3: Poetry of Grammar and Grammar of Poetry* (The Netherlands: Walter de Gruyter, 1981), 751–56. My interpretation of Jakobson's concept has been guided by Brian McHale's account in *Postmodernist Fiction* (New York; London: Metheun, 1987), 6–11.

57 Marshall, *The Practice of Satire in England,* xi.

58 Ibid., xiii.

59 Ibid., xi–xii.

60 Elliott, *The Power of Satire,* 219. See also Griffin, *Satire,* 27.

61 McHale, *Postmodernist Fiction,* 7.

62 Seidel, in *The Satiric Inheritance,* suggests that satirists "elaborate a fable . . . they attempt to displace themselves from," but he also returns to a form of moral universalism by arguing that "the real satiric subject is the degenerative spirit in human nature," which "is so universally formed" (11). Bogel, in *The Difference Satire Makes,* argues that "satirists identify in the world something or someone

that is both unattractive and curiously or dangerously like them . . . something, then, that is *not alien enough*" and then create their satire "as a textual machine or mechanism for producing difference" (41–42). For Bogel, satire still has an instrumental purpose, at least from the perspective of the satirist. Snyder, in *Prospects of Power,* locates a purpose behind satire through "the selection of necessarily rational means for attaining symbolic superiority over its targets" (97). Knight, in *The Literature of Satire,* affirms satire's instrumentality, saying that satire "attacks real offenders; it reveals disorders of the discourse that it imitates or disorders in the world to which that discourse refers" (47). Guilhamet, in *Satire and the Transformation of Genre,* also retains an instrumental notion of satire, arguing that it "points out what is in contrast to the good" (8).

63   Wyndham Lewis's first attempts at theorizing satire in *Satire and Fiction* (1930) were prompted by (what he felt were) incompetent reviews of *The Apes of God.* The negative reviews of William Gaddis's *The Recognitions* prompted a book-length response by Jack Green called *Fire the Bastards!* (1962). Gilbert Sorrentino produces imaginary negative reviews of his novel within the text of *Imaginative Qualities of Actual Things.*

64   Wyndham Lewis, *Men Without Art,* Ed. Seamus Cooney (Santa Rosa, CA: Black Sparrow Press, 1987), 85.

65   Gilbert Sorrentino, *The Imaginative Qualities of Actual Things* (Normal, Il: Dalkey Archive Press, 1991), 70.

66   Ibid., 215.

67   Ibid., 137.

68   David Trotter, *Paranoid Modernism: Literary Experiment, Psychosis, and the Professionalization of English Society* (Oxford: Oxford University Press, 2001), 5–6.

69   Ibid., 10.

70   Marc Redfield, "Aesthetics, Theory, and the Profession of Literature: Derrida and Romanticism," *Studies in Romanticism,* 46 (Summer/Fall 2007): 240.

71   Marilyn Butler, *Romantics, Rebels and Reactionaries: English Literature and Its Background, 1760–1830* (New York; Oxford: Oxford University Press, 1982), 7–9.

72   Arthur O. Lovejoy, "On the Discrimination of Romanticisms," *PMLA* 39.2 (June, 1924): 252.

73   Rene Wellek, in "The Concept of 'Romanticism,'" *Comparative Literature* 1.2 (Spring, 1949), summarizes romanticism's aesthetic program as "imagination for the view of poetry, nature for the view of the world, and symbol and myth for poetic style" (147). Morse Peckham, in "Towards a Theory of Romanticism," *PMLA* 66.2 (March, 1951): 5–23, argues that Wellek's position is actually very close to Lovejoy's view in *The Great Chain of Being* (1936) that romanticism is a form of organicism. M.H. Abrams, in "English Romanticism: The Spirit

of the Age," *Romanticism Reconsidered: Selected Papers from the English Institute,* Ed. Northrop Frye (New York; London: Columbia University Press, 1963), pays particular attention to the influence of the French Revolution on romanticism (29).

74 Frances Ferguson, "On the Numbers of Romanticisms," *ELH* 58.2 (Summer, 1991): 471–98. Ferguson presents an excellent overview of how the Lovejoy/ Wellek debate has continued to inform the work of subsequent prominent critics of romanticism, such as Geoffrey Hartman, Harold Bloom, Jerome McGann, and Paul de Man.

75 Nader Saiedi, *The Birth of Social Theory: Social Thought in the Enlightenment and Romanticism* (Lanham, MD: University Press of America, Inc., 1993), 65.

76 Marilyn Butler, "Romanticisms in England," *Romanticism in National Context,* Eds. Roy Porter and Mikulas Teich (Cambridge: Cambridge University Press, 1988), 37–8.

77 Saiedi, *Birth of Social Theory,* 78.

78 Ernst Behler, in *Irony and the Discourse of Modernity* (Seattle; London: University of Washington Press, 1990), sees Kant's "Copernican turn in philosophy" as symptomatic of Romanticism in its "switch of perspective from the objects of perception to the perceiving subject" (40).

79 Philippe Lacoue-Labarthe and Jean-Luc Nancy, *The Literary Absolute: The Theory of Literature in German Romanticism,* Trans. Phillip Barnard and Cheryl Lester (Albany, NY: SUNY University Press, 1988), 29–30.

80 Saiedi, *Birth of Social Theory,* 78.

81 Ibid., 79.

82 Paul de Man, "The Rhetoric of Temporality," *Interpretation: Theory and Practice,* Ed. Charles S. Singleton (Baltimore: The Johns Hopkins Press, 1969), 197.

83 Ernst Behler, "The Theory of Irony in German Romanticism," *Romantic Irony,* Ed. Frederick Garber (Amsterdam; Philadelphia: John Benjamins Publishing Company, 2008), 80.

84 Peter Schock, "*The Marriage of Heaven and Hell*: Blake's Myth of Satan and Its Cultural Matrix," *ELH* 60.2 (Summer, 1993): 451–2.

85 Williams Wordsworth and Samuel Taylor Coleridge, *Lyrical Ballads* (London: J. & A. Arch, 1798), i.

86 Two prominent scholarly investigations into romantic satire include Steven E. Jones, *Satire and Romanticism* (New York: St. Martin's Press, 2000) and Steven E. Jones, Ed., *The Satiric Eye: Forms of Satire in the Romantic Period* (New York: Palgrave Macmillan, 2003).

87 William Gaddis, *The Recognitions* (New York: Penguin, 1993), 89.

88 Sorrentino, *Imaginative Qualities,* 127.

89   Lacoue-Labarthe and Nancy, *The Literary Absolute,* 6.

90   Morton Gurewitch, *The Comedy of Romantic Irony* (Lanham, MD: University Press of America, Inc., 2002), 6.

91   Jos De Mul, *Romantic Desire in (Post)Modern Art and Philosophy* (Albany, NY: SUNY University Press, 1999), 10. See also Behler, "The Theory of Irony in German Romanticism," 43.

92   Anne K. Mellor, *English Romantic Irony* (Cambridge, MA: Harvard University Press, 1980), 24. Lilian Furst, *Fictions of Romantic Irony* (Cambridge, MA: Harvard University Press, 1984), 229.

93   David Simpson, *Irony and Authority in Romantic Poetry* (London: Macmillan, 1979), 190.

94   Marjorie Perloff, *The Poetics of Indeterminacy: Rimbaud to Cage* (Princeton, NJ: Princeton University Press, 1981), 18.

95   Gaddis, *Recognitions,* 89.

96   Sorrentino, *Imaginative Qualities,* 107.

97   Weisenburger, *Fables of Subversion,* 26–29.

98   Anne Quema, *The Agon of Modernism: Wyndham Lewis's Allegories, Aesthetics, and Politics* (London: Associated University Presses, 1999), 70.

99   Snyder, *Prospects of Power,* 145–46. See also Knight, *The Literature of Satire,* 38–39.

100 Samuel Taylor Coleridge, *Biographia Literaria* Vol. 1, Part 2 (London: William Pickering, 1847), 173.

101 Greenberg, *Modernism, Satire, and the Novel,* 19.

102 Aaron Matz, *Satire in an Age of Realism* (Cambridge: Cambridge University Press, 2010), 35.

103 William Marx, "The Twentieth Century: The Century of the Arrière-Gardes?" *Europa! Europa?: The Avant-Garde, Modernism and the Fate of a Continent,* Eds. Sascha Bru et al. (Berlin: Walter de Gruyter GmbH & Co., 2009), 65.

104 Tyrus Miller, "The Avant-Garde, Bohemia, and Mainstream Culture," *The Cambridge History of Twentieth-Century English Literature,* Eds. Laura Marcus and Peter Nicholls (Cambridge: Cambridge University Press, 2005): 100.

105 Ibid., 101.

106 Ibid., 108.

107 Mary Gluck, *Popular Bohemia: Modernism and Urban Culture in Nineteenth-Century Paris* (Cambridge, MA: Harvard University Press, 2005), 15.

108 Peter Brooker, *Bohemia in London: The Social Scene of Early Modernism* (London: Palgrave Macmillan, 2007), 8.

109 Peter Bürger, in "Avant-Garde and Neo-Avant-Garde: An Attempt to Answer Certain Critics of *Theory of the Avant-Garde,*" *New Literary History* 41.4 (2010),

argues that definition "runs the risk of depriving the concept [of the avant-garde] of what keeps it alive: the contradictions that it unites within itself" (695).

110 Hans Magus Enzensberger, "The Aporias of the Avant-Garde," *The Consciousness Industry: On Literature, Politics, and the Media* (New York: Seabury Press, 1974), 25–7.

111 Ibid., 27.

112 Richard Kostelanetz, in "Introduction: What is Avant-Garde?" *The Avant-Garde Tradition in Literature* (Buffalo, NY: Prometheus Books, 1982), argues for this more generalized notion of the avant-garde (3–6). Renato Poggioli, in *The Theory of the Avant-Garde,* Trans. Gerald Fitzgerald (Cambridge, MA: Harvard University Press, 1968), views the avant-garde as a "sociological" rather than "aesthetic" phenomenon (46).

113 Bürger, "Avant-Garde and Neo-Avant-Garde," 696.

114 Ibid., 699.

115 Bürger, *Theory of the Avant-Garde*, 34.

116 Bürger, "Avant-Garde and Neo-Avant-Garde," 705.

117 Benjamin Buchloh, *Neo-Avantgarde and Culture Industry: Essays on European and American Art from 1955 to 1975* (Cambridge, MA: MIT Press, 2000), xxiv. Hal Foster, *The Return of the Real: The Avant-Garde at the End of the Century* (Cambridge, MA: MIT Press, 1996), 14.

118 Richard Murphy, in *Theorizing the Avant-Garde: Modernism, Expressionism, and the Problem of Postmodernity* (Cambridge: Cambridge University Press, 1999), proposes that the German expressionists should be considered an avant-garde under the terms that Bürger established. Josephine M. Guy, in *The British Avant-Garde: The Theory and Politics of Tradition* (New York: Harvester Wheatsheaf, 1991), argues for including Walter Pater, William Morris, and Oscar Wilde in the avant-garde.

119 Bürger, "Avant-Garde and Neo-Avant-Garde," 708.

120 Astradur Eysteinsson, "'What's the Difference?' Revisiting Concepts of Modernism and the Avant-Garde," *Europa! Europa?: The Avant-Garde, Modernism and the Fate of a Continent,* Eds. Sascha Bru et al. (Berlin: Walter de Gruyter GmbH & Co., 2009), 34.

121 Two examples of more recent studies that acknowledge the frequent overlapping of these categories include Sascha Bru, *Democracy, Law, and the Modernist Avant-Gardes: Writing in the State of Exception* (Edinburg: Edinburgh University Press, 2009) and Lawrence Rainey, *Institutions of Modernism: Literary Elites and Public Culture* (New Haven; London: Yale University Press, 1998). I will return to this issue in Chapter 3, which focuses on the work of Wyndham Lewis.

122 Tyrus Miller, *Singular Examples: Artistic Politics and the Neo-Avant-Garde* (Evanston, IL: Northwestern University Press, 2009), 4.

123 Paul Mann, *The Theory-Death of the Avant-Garde* (Bloomington, IN: Indiana University Press, 1991), 39.

124 Anna Katharina Schaffner, "Inheriting the Avant-Garde: On the Reconciliation of Tradition and Invention in Concrete Poetry," *Neo-Avant-Garde*, Ed. David Hopkins (Amsterdam; New York: Rodopi, 2006), 109–12.

125 Members of the "historical avant-gardes" frequently interacted and shared networks of cultural transmission with those artists who would subsequently be deemed "modernists." These correspondences are so numerous that claims of the "radical" difference between these groups seem hard to support from a historical perspective. That being said, offering anything like a comprehensive account of these shared networks lies beyond the ambit of this study. Lawrence Rainey, in *Institutions of Modernism*, presents one detailed example of the way in which modernists and the avant-garde developed within the same cultural and social milieu by considering the relationship between F.T. Marinetti and Ezra Pound (10–41).

126 Poggioli, *The Theory of the Avant-Garde*, 55. Jochen Schulte-Sasse, in his foreword to Bürger's *Theory of the Avant-Garde*, argues that Poggioli's position threatens to reduce the concept of the avant-garde to "an empty slogan" that would "no longer [be] able to help us distinguish romanticism, symbolism, aestheticism, the avant-garde, and postmodernism from each other" (viii). From my perspective, I do not see how acknowledging a line of historical influence necessarily dissolves the distinctions between such movements.

127 Poggioli, *Theory of the Avant-Garde*, 48.

128 Pierre Bourdieu, *The Rules of Art: Genesis and Structure of the Literary Field*, Trans. Susan Emanuel (Cambridge, UK: Polity Press, 1996), 67–68; Paul Hamilton, "'A Shadow of Magnitude': The Dialectic of Romantic Aesthetics," *Beyond Romanticism: New Approaches to Texts and Contexts 1780–1832*, Ed. Stephen Copley (London; New York: Routledge, 1992), 25; Herbert Read, "Surrealism and the Romantic Principle," *Surrealism*, Ed. Herbert Read (London: Praeger, 1971), 19–91; Peter Gay, *Modernism: The Lure of Heresy, from Baudelaire to Beckett and Beyond* (New York: W.W. Norton & Co., Inc., 2008), 45; and Michael Lowy and Robert Sayre, *Romanticism Against the Tide of Modernity* (Durham, NC: Duke University Press, 2001), 214.

129 Lacoue-Labarthe and Nancy, *The Literary Absolute*, 8.

130 Wordsworth and Coleridge, *Lyrical Ballads*, i–ii.

131 Ibid., i.

132 Wyndham Lewis, *Apes of God* (Santa Barbara, CA: Black Sparrow Press, 1981), 123.

133 Bürger, "Avant-Garde and Neo-Avant-Garde," 705.

134 Siraganian, *Modernism's Other Work*, 125.

135 Giorgio Agamben, *The Man Without Content,* Trans. Georgia Albert (Stanford: Stanford University Press, 1999), 56.

136 Lacoue-Labarthe and Nancy, *The Literary Absolute*, 50.

2

The Romantic Satire of Romanticism: Thomas Love Peacock's *Nightmare Abbey*

1 Antiromantic romanticism

In most historical surveys of British literature, the hegemony of neoclassical aesthetics (and, by extension, the exemplarity of satire) is overturned in the late eighteenth century by the aesthetic movement of romanticism, which privileges emotion and personal aesthetic experience and rejects the use of heightened literary rhetoric in favor of "everyday" language. Romanticism's exemplary forms become the lyric poem and the novel. After the rise of romanticism (and notwithstanding the significance of major satirical works, such as Byron's *Don Juan*), it is claimed that satire ceases to be a culturally dominant literary form. But this historical opposition between satire and romanticism is problematized by the appearance of forms of satire in which satiric judgment becomes subjected to romantic self-reflexivity. This self-reflexivity is characterized not only by the presentation of effusive emotion and enthusiastic belief, but also by the inherent self-critical investigation and satirical undercutting of such moments, as naïve, idealistic visions of the world are undermined by actual experience.[1]

Understanding self-reflexivity as an essential characteristic of romanticism also implies that romanticism is not a naïve discourse, but a self-interrogating one that attempts to contain its own transcendence and its own critique. Incorporating romantic self-reflexivity into satire results in a profound shift within the genre: instead of offering objective judgments based on ethical principles, satire becomes a recursive, self-questioning form that interrogates satirical judgment's capacity for objectivity. In this sense, romanticism results not so much in the eradication of satire (an assertion, which, as more recent studies have shown, is historically inaccurate[2]), as in a shifting of its literary dominant. Rather than simply eclipsing neoclassical satire, romanticism reshapes satire, which ceases to be a purely instrumental mode of ethical instruction, and instead becomes—like romantic cultural products in general—increasingly focused on the aesthetic. After romanticism, satire privileges self-reflexivity over objective judgment, and aesthetic exploration over ethical instruction (although residues of satiric instrumentality remain). This shift in the literary dominant of satire can be observed in one of romanticism's exemplary satiric texts, Thomas Love Peacock's *Nightmare Abbey* (1818).

Nightmare Abbey—like all of Peacock's satires—primarily consists of dialogue between its characters, and its plot is easily summarized. Christopher Glowry and his son, Scythrop Glowry, occupy an enormous dilapidated estate, called Nightmare Abbey, which is constantly visited by eminent romantic literary figures. Scythrop—a recent university graduate and aspiring man of letters—becomes romantically entangled with two women, Marionetta (his penniless cousin) and Stella, a woman with an enigmatic past who takes asylum in Scythrop's tower, "seeking refuge from an atrocious persecution."[3] Scythrop duplicitously woos both women, but his father uncovers Scythrop's deception, and both women leave in anger. In utter torment, Scythrop begs the women to come back and marry him even though he cannot choose between them. He threatens to commit suicide with a pistol, in emulation of Goethe's *Sorrows of Young Werther* (1774), if they do not return. Ultimately, Scythrop receives two missives, which tell him that the women have become engaged to two other men who had been visiting the abbey. Noting that the time of his proposed suicide has already passed, Scythrop decides to forego the act, remarking that his recent experiences "qualify me to take a very advanced degree in misanthropy" and, as a result, "there is a very good hope that I may make a figure in the world."[4]

Nightmare Abbey might seem an odd choice for examining the romantic transformation of satire, since it could be read as a straightforward satirical critique of one of romanticism's most important literary genres: the gothic. *Nightmare Abbey* explicitly parodies many of the gothic's most familiar tropes, including gloomy towers, mysterious damsels in distress, and paranormal phenomena, all in the apparent service of belittling both the excesses of gothic literature and its reliance on a series of seemingly formulaic genre devices. Indeed, *Nightmare Abbey*'s parody of romanticism extends beyond the gothic to include satirical attacks on the writers of the "Satanic School," such as Byron—represented in the novel by a character named Mr. Cypress, who does nothing but recite lines from *Childe Harold's Pilgrimage* (1812–18).

In caricaturing these authors' obsessions with the supernatural and tendency toward brooding fits of melancholy, *Nightmare Abbey*'s satire appears to be a fictionalized variation on Robert Southey's attack on those romantic writers who are "characterized by a Satanic spirit of pride and audacious impiety":

> Men of diseased hearts and depraved imaginations, who, forming a system of opinions to suit their own unhappy course of conduct, have rebelled against the holiest ordinances of human society, and hating that revealed religion which, with all their efforts and bravadoes, they are unable entirely to disbelieve, labour to make others as miserable as themselves, by infecting them with a virus that eats into the soul![5]

On an initial reading, *Nightmare Abbey* appears to come to similar—if less virulent—conclusions about the value of romantic literature in general. Although *Nightmare Abbey*'s satire focuses on the gothic preoccupations and melancholic disposition of "Satanic" romanticism, its inclusion of roman à clef portraits of other romantics, such as Coleridge, and explicit echoing of works of German literature, including Goethe's *Sorrows of Young Werther*, suggest a critique of romanticism in all of its forms. *Nightmare Abbey* thus might seem to be a neoclassical attack on the romantic—an anachronistic and ultimately reactionary response to an upstart tradition that has displaced satire as the central mode of high-cultural literary production. From this perspective, Peacock appears as little more than a cultural conservative, objecting to the new aesthetic "avant-garde" of romanticism (and, as I argued in the introduction, romanticism does comprise a "potential avant-gardism"[6] in that it made possible the conditions of the avant-garde).

The coterie of writers satirized in *Nightmare Abbey* also appears to comprise a proto-bohemian cultural formation. Indeed, it is common to associate romanticism with the historical appearance of bohemian cultures. Orlo Williams, for example, locates the origins of bohemia in Paris in 1830.[7] Mary Gluck similarly associates the origins of bohemianism with romantic artists in France in the 1830s, who "performed their identities through outrageous gestures, eccentric clothes, subversive lifestyles" and thus "were identified for the first time not by what they did, but by how they lived and what they looked like."[8] Gluck argues that this new association between artists and a certain lifestyle presents a "contrast with the older generation of Romanticists,"[9] but *Nightmare Abbey* critiques earlier romantics precisely for their privileging of gothic fashions and gloominess (in dress, architecture, and personal bearing), which presage the eccentric and subversive lifestyle choices displayed by later bohemians. Whether or not the romantics satirized by Peacock constitute a bohemia in the full sense,

I would argue that *Nightmare Abbey* foregrounds and satirizes the connection between artistic production and artistic lifestyle, which became so prevalent in bohemian cultures.

Regardless, any view of *Nightmare Abbey* as a conservative critique of romanticism is undermined by several of the novel's unusual textual features, including a superabundance of intertextual references that complicate the straightforward identification of the targets of *Nightmare Abbey*'s satire. In most satirical works, the objects of satire are human beings whose ineptitude or questionable morals have led them into vice and folly; Robert Kiernan has argued that *Nightmare Abbey* is a roman à clef that satirizes major contemporary figures in Anglophone romanticism, including Samuel Taylor Coleridge, Lord Byron, and Percy Bysshe Shelley.[10] But in *Nightmare Abbey* the objects of the satire seem to be literary texts rather than people; Klaus Schwank notes that, in the novel, "reality exists only as a frame for the representation of literary objects."[11] And the characters in the novel do not so much speak for themselves as refer to other *texts*. Flosky, for example, constantly references Kant and many of his other assertions are glosses on Coleridge's published literary criticism. Mr. Cypress speaks in verse cribbed from Byron's *Childe Harold's Pilgrimage*, and *Nightmare Abbey* encourages intertextual identification by attaching footnotes to each of Cyprus's speeches, which name the chapter and line of the original from which they are drawn. Whereas Jonathan Swift's *The Battle of the Books* (1704) employed books to stand in for the people who were debating the relative merits of ancient and modern texts, *Nightmare Abbey* employs characters that seem to stand in for *books*.

But the fact that the satiric target of *Nightmare Abbey* is literature should be no surprise given that one of the most striking textual features of the novel is its sustained, heavy use of allusion. This relatively brief, 30,000-word novel refers to an enormous number of other fictional, philosophical, and political works, including Dante's *Purgatorio* (1308–21), Rabelais's *Gargantua and Pantagruel* (1532–64), Shakespeare's *A Midsummer Night's Dream* (1594–96), *Hamlet* (1599–601), *Henry IV* (1596–99), *Henry V* (1599), and *Macbeth* (1603–07), Ben Jonson's *Every Man in His Humour* (1598), Thomas Rogers's "Leicester's Ghost" (1605), Cervantes's *Don Quixote* (1605–15), Robert Burton's *Anatomy of Melancholy* (1621), Milton's *Comus* (1634), Samuel Butler's *Hudibras* (1663–78), Jean-Francois Regnard's *Le Destrait* (1697), George Berkeley's *A Treatise Concerning the Principles of Human Knowledge* (1710), Jonathon Swift's "The Lady's Dressing Room" (1732), Henry Carey's satirical play *Chrononhotonthologos*

(1734), Alexander Pope's *Dunciad* (1743), Samuel Johnson's *Dictionary* (1755), Edmund Burke's *A Philosophical Enquiry into the Origin of Our Ideas of the Sublime and Beautiful* (1757), Goethe's *The Sorrows of Young Werther* (1774) and *Stella* (1782), Johann Adam Weishaupt's various writings on the Illuminati (1786–95), Pierre Denys de Montfort's *Histoire Naturelle des Mollusques* (1802), Robert Forsyth's *Principles of Moral Science* (1805), Cesare Sterbini's libretto for *The Barber of Seville* (1816), William Godwin's *Mandeville* (1817), Lord Byron's *Manfred* (1817) and *Childe Harold's Pilgrimage* (1818), and Samuel Coleridge's "Kubla Khan" (1797), "Christabel" (1800), and the *Biographia Literaria* (1817). In addition to these references to specific texts, *Nightmare Abbey* also makes more generic references to various thinkers and authors—including Thomas Reid (1710–96), Immanuel Kant (1724–804), Friedrich Schiller (1759–805), and Robert Southey (1774–843)—and mentions a variety of ancient and classical authors, such as Homer, Virgil, Pliny, Cicero, Socrates, Aesop, and Pausanias, as well as multiple books of the Bible, including Ecclesiastes, Job, and Revelations.

Nightmare Abbey is a book that is quite literally composed of other books. Although allusion is hardly a novel trope, the extent and form of the allusion within *Nightmare Abbey* suggests that it is being deployed for purposes beyond its traditional uses; *Nightmare Abbey* functions like other romantic texts, which, as M.H. Abrams famously argued,[12] do not mimetically reflect the world, but rather ground themselves in other works of literature. But Peacock's use of allusion is more complicated still, since it frequently involves a restructuring and reappropriation of the source material itself. Giorgio Agamben has noted (using, appropriately, a quotation) that the "particular power of quotations arises, according to Benjamin, not from their ability to transmit that past and allow the reader to relive it but, on the contrary, from their capacity to 'make a clean sweep, to expel from the context, to destroy.'"[13] The decontextualizing function of quotation becomes explicit in Peacock's use of allusion in which he often builds new quotations from fragmented sections of the work of other writers. An epigraph to *Nightmare Abbey* from Butler's *Hudibras*, for example, is in fact a rhyming quatrain composed of two couplets taken from completely different sections in the original, a decontextualization pushed further by the altering of certain words from the original text as well.[14] For Peacock, allusion functions not just as an appeal to an extant tradition, but a literal reshaping of that tradition for the purposes of the text. In *Nightmare Abbey,* allusion enables the creative reappropriation and re-presentation of tradition for the aesthetic purposes of the text itself. The result is that allusion becomes a dialogic figure, since the quoted material does not just refer to an outside text but actively reshapes and, thus, reimagines the source text itself.

But intertextual reference does not provide the only dialogic figure in *Nightmare Abbey*, since Peacock's novel is in dialogue not only with other texts but also with *itself*. In particular, the text explicitly comments on itself through the means of paratexts—typically footnotes—that respond to assertions made within the main body of the text. At one point, for example, the narrator partially recounts a conversation between two characters, stating that "Mrs. Hilary hinted to Marionetta that propriety, and delicacy, and decorum, and dignity, &c. &c. &c."[15] In a footnote accompanying this line, the narrator explains the deployment of ampersands instead of words: "We are not masters of the whole vocabulary. See any Novel by any literary lady."[16] The result of such moments is that satire presented within the main body of text is opened up to yet another layer of possible critique and commentary, rather than being portrayed as absolute or unequivocal.

Taken in concert, the textual oddities within *Nightmare Abbey* introduce a slippage between satirical language and the authority of the satiric persona: not only are linguistic utterances revealed as complex assemblages of sources and intertexts, but also the absolute authority of any statement remains in doubt, because all statements may either be creatively reappropriated or be subjected to further metacommentary. Both the appearance of such metacommentary and the refashioning of "original" texts thus suggest gaps in the sovereign authority of the satiric persona, which is unquestionable in traditional satires. Moreover, *Nightmare Abbey*'s unusual intertextual reference, quotation, and metatextual commentary complicate readers' relationship both to the satire and the satiric persona, since, in including and interacting with extensive extratextual material, the satiric persona is diffused in the chorus of other voices and other texts within the novel. Robert Kiernan has also examined the elaborate nature of the novel's jokes, which often employ complex puns and repetitive conceits, producing a humor that often seems more open-ended and suggestive than traditional satirical critique.[17]

While these devices do not completely undermine the satiric persona, they do challenge its authority. The relationship between the text and the satiric persona's authority becomes compromised further still when one considers what is perhaps *Nightmare Abbey*'s most important intertext—albeit one never explicitly named in the novel: Peacock's own earlier, long poem *The Philosophy of Melancholy* (1812). I will argue that this work exerts an important, but heretofore unidentified, influence on *Nightmare Abbey*'s own satire.

2 The Philosophy of Melancholy

While *Nightmare Abbey* satirizes various aspects of romanticism, Peacock's own letters indicate he had one primary concern about romantic literature: its excessive focus on melancholia. In a letter written to Shelley during *Nightmare Abbey*'s composition (May 30, 1818), Peacock states, "I think it necessary to 'make a stand' against the 'encroachments' of black bile,"[18] a position which he would reaffirm in a subsequent letter, dated September 15, 1818, which states that the "object of *Nightmare Abbey*" is to "bring to a sort of philosophical focus a few of the morbidities of modern literature, and to let in a little daylight on its atrabilarious complexion."[19] The paratexts of the novel reflect this emphasis, with the novel's epigraph taken from Ben Jonson's *Every Man in His Humour* (at the suggestion of Shelley), which specifically satirizes a melancholic disposition: "Your true melancholy breeds your perfect fine wit, sir. I am melancholy myself, divers times, sir; and then do I no more but take pen and paper presently, and overflow you half a score or a dozen of sonnets at a sitting."[20] Through this epigraph, the text seeks to affirm the link between melancholy and romantic literature.

But this attack on melancholy in literature seems particularly odd, given that, six years prior to composing *Nightmare Abbey*, Peacock himself published a book-length poem entitled *The Philosophy of Melancholy* (1812), which earnestly invokes a variety of characteristic gothic tropes ("ivied abbeys," "mouldering towers," and communication with ghosts), and praises specific gothic works, including Anne Radcliffe's *Mysteries of Udolpho* (1794), which *Nightmare Abbey* echoes at points, and Joshua Pickersgill's *The Three Brothers* (1803), whose narrative recounts a Faustian bargain that would go on to influence Byron's own Satanism. More importantly, however, the central concern of this poem—which is written in heroic couplets and prefaced by extensive explanatory remarks so that the "philosophical" meaning of each section would not be lost on the reader—is to investigate the close connection between melancholy and artistic creativity:

> Why joys the bard, in autumn's closing day,
> To watch the yellow leaves, that round him sail,
> And hear a spirit moan in every gale?
> To seek beneath the moon, at midnight hour,
> The ivied abbey, and the mouldering tower,
> And, while the wakening echoes hail his tread,
> In fancy hold communion with the dead?[21]

These questions are more or less rhetorical, since the poem unequivocally views melancholy—and the "contemplation of vicissitudes" that melancholy encourages—as nothing less than a fundamental principle that gives order to perception, by encouraging the "mind" to ascend "from the observation of apparently discordant particulars, to the knowledge of that all-perfect wisdom, which arranges the whole in harmony."[22] Here, Peacock views melancholy not as an affliction of the humors (as he will in *Nightmare Abbey*), but as a means to a deeper understanding of reality that also results in more profound artistic achievement: "In art, as in nature, those pleasures, in which melancholy mingles, are more powerful, and more permanent, than those which have their origin in lighter sensations."[23] Melancholy, for the speaker of this long poem, appears as an aesthetic and philosophical concept that orders both the work of art, and, indeed, life itself.

Elsewhere in the poem, the speaker extolls the visionary powers enabled by melancholy, which appear to be inextricably tied up with a very romantic notion of creative genius: "From the deepest night creative genius brings/ The brightest flow of [melancholy's] exhaustless springs."[24] The overtones are unmistakably romantic: the darkness of night separates the phenomena of conscious perception from their referents in the real world, thereby serving to emphasize the *transformative powers* of the imaginative genius, who can turn the "deepest night" into the "brightest flow" of artistic production. For the younger Peacock, melancholy's role in the production of great art reflects a romantic belief in the power of original artistic production. In his arguments for the visionary capacities of the melancholic genius, the speaker of *The Philosophy of Melancholy* sounds a great deal like the characters who will later populate *Nightmare Abbey*.

Indeed, in *Nightmare Abbey* such visionary tendencies are ridiculed, as in the satirical portrait of Mr. Flosky, who "lived in the midst of that visionary world in which nothing is but what is not. He dreamed with his eyes open, and saw ghosts dancing round him at noontide."[25] The visionary genius of *The Philosophy of Melancholy* reappears as a witless dreamer in *Nightmare Abbey*. Melancholy itself—which *The Philosophy of Melancholy* describes as being the sole source of "virtue, of courage, and of genius," "the finest efforts of art, in painting, music, poetry and romance," and "all-perfect wisdom"[26]—is depicted in *Nightmare Abbey* as being little more than a pose evoked by a particular group of fashionable authors and their literary coterie. This satiric critique again appears explicitly in descriptions of Mr. Flosky, who possesses both a "very fine sense of the grim and tearful" and is notable for his ability to "relate a dismal story with so many minutiae of supererogatory wretchedness."[27] The gothic receives similar treatment in *Nightmare Abbey*, and is ridiculed as being little more than a formulaic and fashionable trend in contemporary letters, that readily lends itself to parody.[28]

Even though it has not been previously noted, it is difficult, given the two texts' diametrically opposed views on melancholy and the gothic, not to read *Nightmare Abbey* as a response to *The Philosophy of Melancholy*. Although it is more common to regard *Nightmare Abbey*'s satire as an attack on contemporary romantic writers like Coleridge, Shelley, and Byron, it covers almost exactly the same literary territory as *The Philosophy of Melancholy*, while contradicting it at every turn: what *The Philosophy of Melancholy* praises, *Nightmare Abbey* satirizes. Seen in this light, rather than being a satire of romanticism, *Nightmare Abbey* equally can be considered a refutation of *The Philosophy of Melancholy* that critiques and ironizes Peacock's own prior work. But such a connection can only be inferred, since—despite the many allusions within the pages of *Nightmare Abbey*—*The Philosophy of Melancholy* is never mentioned by name.

And yet the omission of any reference to *The Philosophy of Melancholy* in *Nightmare Abbey* may simply have reflected the fact that virtually no one had read it. After an initial print run in 1812, which yielded exactly two reviews, *The Philosophy of Melancholy* remained out of print until the publication of Peacock's complete works in 1927.[29] Although not specifically mentioned, the poem's underwhelming reception and its youthful enthusiasm recall a treatise written by Scythrop in *Nightmare Abbey*, entitled "Philosophical Gas; or, a Project for a General Illumination of the Human Mind." Although the title suggests that the work is little more than hot air, Scythrop assumes that this tract, which is inspired by "the distempered ideas of metaphysical romance and romantic metaphysics," will "set the whole nation in a ferment," resulting in revolution.[30] But Scythrop's idealism is absurdly undercut; "a letter from his bookseller" informs "him that only seven copies had been sold . . . concluding with a polite request for the balance."[31] Scythrop remains unperturbed, stating, "Seven copies . . . have been sold. Seven is a mystical number, and the omen is good. Let me find the seven purchasers of my seven copies, and they shall be the seven golden candlesticks with which I illuminate the world."[32] Scythrop's naïve enthusiasm resembles that of the speaker in *The Philosophy of Melancholy*, who boldly exclaims, "Oh melancholy! blue-eyed maid divine!/Thy fading woods, thy twilight walks, be mine!"[33]

The differences that divide *The Philosophy of Melancholy* from *Nightmare Abbey* can best be understood as illustrating the opposing poles of naïve enthusiasm and a world-weary cynicism, with the latter providing the satirical critique of the former. *The Philosophy of Melancholy* and *Nightmare Abbey*, one might say, comprise a diptych not dissimilar to William Blake's *Songs of Innocence and of Experience* (1798–94). Such an understanding is further strengthened by the fact that *Nightmare Abbey* explicitly foregrounds the movement from innocence to experience—particularly in relation to the experience of love. Mr. Glowry's cynical state within the novel is attributed to the fact that "he had been deceived in an early friendship: he had been crossed in love; and had offered his hand, from pique, to a lady, who accepted it from interest, and who tore asunder the bonds of a tried and youthful attachment."[34] These early disappointments cause Glowry to look "upon human learning as vanity" and believe "that there was but one good thing in the world, *videlicet*, a good dinner."[35] Glowry's son, Scythrop, finds his own naivety in love tempered by experience: after being restrained from marrying Emily Girouette as a result of a dowry dispute, Scythrop is disillusioned when "three weeks after the tragical event, the lady was led a smiling bride to the alter, by the Honourable Mr. Lackwit; which is neither strange nor new."[36] The narrator of *Nightmare Abbey* emphasizes the importance of this event for Scythrop: "It was his first disappointment, and it preyed deeply on his sensitive spirit."[37] Although much of *Nightmare Abbey* is composed of long scenes of dialogue without much action, the novel revolves around Scythrop's continuing experiences and disappointments in love.

Nightmare Abbey's satire thus presents a literary enactment of the relationship between innocence and experience. The thematization of this relationship problematizes any attempt to account for the novel in traditional terms as the condemnation of vice and folly for the purposes of edification. The relationship between the satire and the object of satire is complicated in *Nightmare Abbey* by its manifestation as a form of authorial *self-critique*, rather than a straightforward neoclassical attack on a romantic other. If *Nightmare Abbey* is a response to *The Philosophy of Melancholy*, then the satire does not assert an unequivocal or universal morality but rather critiques innocence from the perspective of experience. Satiric critique in *Nightmare Abbey* constitutes a moment of self-understanding by coming to grips with the limitations and failures of the claims written in an earlier text. In this mode of satire, folly becomes an unavoidable condition of the human being who lacks experience, rather than a moral failing to be addressed by literary inculcation.

That being said, the autocritique in *Nightmare Abbey* does not necessarily mean that it must be viewed as a romantic work. *Nightmare Abbey* could simply be a satirical repudiation of a previous, youthful interest in romantic literature that Peacock, over time, came to reject in favor of neoclassical principles. Since it is the satiric persona (which is, of course, separate from the actual person of the author) who forms the absolute ground of judgment, it would seem that Peacock's personal relationship to romanticism and romantic writing is ultimately irrelevant to the satire of *Nightmare Abbey*. But such responses are insufficient, because they ignore the character of the relationship between innocence and experience that is presented in *Nightmare Abbey*, which does not simply proceed from ignorance to authoritative knowledge.

Nightmare Abbey repeatedly suggests that while experience (and the self-ironizing insight that accompanies such experience) may reveal the folly of past innocence, it in no way insulates the self from future folly. Mr. Glowry's disappointments in love and friendship result in his concluding (in an echo of the book of Ecclesiastes) that "all is vanity"; his misanthropy appears to be a disproportionate response to the experience of disloyalty that is ultimately even more absurd than his previous innocence. In the case of Scythrop, his initial disappointment in love in no way stops him from making bad decisions regarding romantic relationships over the course of *Nightmare Abbey* (and, in fact, quite the opposite is the case). At the end of the book, it remains unclear if Scythrop has actually been able to draw any larger understanding or "moral" out of his experiences, since he says "these repeated crosses in love qualify me to take a very advanced degree in misanthropy; and there is, therefore, good hope that I may make a figure in the world."[38] Has Scythrop really accepted a misanthropic view of the world, or has he instead understood that adopting a fashionable "pose" of romantic misanthropy might be useful in matters of worldly advancement? In *Nightmare Abbey*, experience does not clearly lead to a position of greater enlightenment.

In the conclusion of *Nightmare Abbey*, then, there appears to be a disjuncture between the specific satirical critique advanced and any normative beliefs underlying the satirical critique. According to traditional conceptions, satire must possess a set of norms, which are the ethical values that form the basis of the satirist's critique, but a critical self-satire based on experience will never produce a set of norms, because, although it may illuminate prior follies, experience does not produce a set of normative rules for living. *Nightmare Abbey*'s exploration of the relationship between innocence and experience undermines its satiric norms, which are notoriously opaque. As James Nichols has noted, Peacock's novels are "so idiosyncratic that they can hardly be said to correspond with any generally accepted system of values—or even to be a 'system' at all," and even though "Peacock's novels are unquestionably satires," the "norms Peacock uses are exceedingly difficult to state in general terms, and all but defy rational analysis."[39] That the novel encompasses opposing claims in this way is not entirely surprising, given that, as Robert Kiernan has noted, Peacock was fond of inhabiting positions that appeared mutually contradictory.[40] In *Peacock Displayed* (1979), Marilyn Butler puts it even more succinctly: "If Peacock believes in anything he has not shown what." [41]

Both *Nightmare Abbey*'s implicit dialogue with *The Philosophy of Melancholy* and its explicit representation of the relationship between innocence and experience therefore undermines the authority of the satiric persona on two fronts: 1) the satirical persona's satire appears to be as much a matter of *perspective* (i.e., the perspective of "experience" rather than of "innocence") as it is a matter of reasoned, objective judgment, and 2) the resulting opacity of any satiric norms within *Nightmare Abbey* destabilizes its critiques, which no longer appear as objective, universalizable judgments, because there is no underlying logic to their application. As a result, the satire in *Nightmare Abbey* is unmoored from reason and universal judgment, which have traditionally been invoked to present a solid basis for satire's ethical didacticism.

My claim that the satire within *Nightmare Abbey* is more a matter of perspective than universal judgment is further reinforced by the novel's deployment of the comedy of humors, which enacts a dialogic indeterminacy in which no single character can claim complete understanding or authority. Moreover, the characters within *Nightmare Abbey* are motivated by their natural dispositions or humors, with the result that their judgments are inherently subjective and partial.[42] Most importantly, the text suggests the satiric persona is not exempt from dispositional bias, and, as a result, *Nightmare Abbey*'s satire doesn't produce grounded, ethical judgments. In undermining the fixed and determinate nature of satiric judgment, *Nightmare Abbey's* satire instead begins to resemble romantic irony, which, as David Simpson has argued, "consists in the studied avoidance on the artist's part of determinate meanings."[43] In *Nightmare Abbey,* the authority of the satirist—whose judgment, in traditional satires, is typically beyond any reproach—is opened up to criticism in a similarly self-reflexive process. *Nightmare Abbey,* then, for all of its attacks on romantic writers and ideas, exemplifies how satire was historically altered by contemporary romantic conceptions.

3 Indeterminacy and the comedy of humors

Nightmare Abbey's employment of the comedy of humors produces a dialogic text in which no single voice—not even the satiric persona—can claim absolute authority, thereby creating an indeterminacy that unmoors its satire from any objective grounds. While this might superficially resemble Marjorie Perloff's concept of avant-garde indeterminacy in *The Poetics of Indeterminacy* (1981), I am applying a notion of romantic indeterminacy, which significantly differs from Perloff's account and has a long and distinct history within the field of romanticism studies. Geoffrey Hartman's account of romantic indeterminacy predates Perloff's by a year,[44] and views indeterminacy as a foundational aspect of romanticism itself. This indeterminacy does not result from a breakdown in an internal symbolic order (as it does for Perloff), but rather is a textual effect that seeks either to disavow or render uncertain any referent to a grounding external discourse. In arguing for the romantic indeterminacy of *Nightmare Abbey*, I am not, therefore, suggesting that the novel stylistically resembles avant-garde writings, but rather arguing that it problematizes any coherent discourse or concept that might legitimize it or otherwise provide an extratextual "rule" for its interpretation.

There are many moments in *Nightmare Abbey* that exemplify this tendency by suggesting that satirical attacks are based on subjective and perspectival criteria, rather than logical, objective grounds. When Mr. Flosky says "novelty is the bane of literature," for example, any profundity attached to this statement is immediately undermined by his addendum "except for my works, and those of my particular friends."[45] Many characters within *Nightmare Abbey* take a position very similar to that of the satiric persona in the novel, in which they bemoan the fallen state of contemporary letters as being subject to fads or fashion. But rather than serving to further the satiric persona's critique of romanticism, these critical perspectives on "fashionable literature" are themselves satirized. Mr. Asturias, for example, offers a jeremiad attacking "our fashionable belles lettres" that extensively catalogues its failures:

> I have known many evils, but I have never known the worst of all, which, as it seems to me, are those which are comprehended in the inexhaustible varieties of *ennui*: spleen, chagrin, vapours, blue devils, time-killing, discontent, misanthropy, and all their interminable train of fretfulness, querulousness, suspicions, jealousies, and fears: which have alike infected society and the literature of society; and which would make an Arctic ocean of the human mind, if the more humane pursuits of philosophy and science did not keep alive the better feelings and more valuable energies of our nature.[46]

It would be an understatement to say he protests too much. Mr. Asturias's diatribe against the "literature of society"—which, in many ways, resembles the attack on the "Satanic School" that Robert Southey would articulate in 1821 in *A Vision of Judgment* (a text to which Byron would satirically respond with his own *A Vision of Judgment* in 1822)—possesses a hyperbolic intensity that marks it as a target of satire. His harangue spills over into the Rabelaisian catalogue (one of many moments in which *Nightmare Abbey* reveals its own intertextual debts to the history of satire) with the result that Mr. Asturias's vehemence is dramatically undermined by his overly intricate restatement and categorization of the "varieties of *ennui*" and his extreme notion that a vogue for melancholy could actually succeed in making "an Arctic ocean of the human mind." Both his meticulous, critical typology of black bile and his estimate of its effects comically exceed any reasonable measure of judgment.

Here we have the motif of the satirist-satirized in miniature; the excessiveness of Mr. Asturias's tirade makes not only Mr. Asturias, but also such negative critical vehemence automatically suspect. If Mr. Asturias has avoided that "worst kind of evil" in melancholy, such scrupulous avoidance has not made him immune to folly. While Mr. Asturias's argument begins by attacking melancholy, it turns out, in the final analysis, to be simply antiliterary, finding room only for the useful and the instrumental. What begins as a critique of fashionable trends in literature ends in an unmitigated condemnation of a literary culture that should cede its dominion to science. But even the validity of Mr. Asturias's science must be called into question; although he is allegedly an ichthyologist (he is named after a starfish), Asturias's great scientific exploration lies in the search for a literal chimera: he seeks mermaids, of course. What could be more natural? Even the scientists in Peacock's world are hobbled by hobbyhorses and an ungrounded Laputan logic that leads them into error.

Moreover, the swerving authority of satirical attacks like Mr. Asturias's serves to reemphasize the problem generated by the lack of satiric norms in *Nightmare Abbey,* since its characters cannot be neatly divided into the categories of the wise and the foolish. The authority of the satiric persona is undermined by the ambiguity regarding the validity of the speaking positions of other characters in the book. While the melancholy disposition of Scythrop, Flosky, and Stella/Celinda clearly mark them as targets of satire, even those immune to melancholy find themselves satirized. What *Nightmare Abbey* demonstrates is the capacity for all of its characters to engage in folly. Even Mr. Hilary, the most seemingly reasonable of all the abbey's inhabitants—whom many critics have identified with Peacock himself—is not without flaws. His relentless good humor becomes yet another form of excess; after Marionetta (Mr. Hilary's penniless niece) and Scythrop have called off their marriage, he makes light of the situation, but Christopher Glowry angrily points out his poor taste:

> "Ah!" said Mr. Glowry, "you are a happy man, and in all your afflictions you can console yourself with a joke, let it be ever so bad, provided you crack it yourself. I should be very happy to laugh with you, if it would give you any satisfaction; but really, at present, my heart is so sad, that I find it impossible to levy a contribution on my muscles."[47]

Hilary's sanguine disposition undermines his authority just as the Glowries' melancholy undermines theirs. Their humors are indicated by their names: Glowry, recalling the word "glower," suggests sullenness, whereas Hilary suggests the Greek "hilaros" or "cheerful." Scythrop Glowry is doubly dour, since Scythrop is Greek for "sad-faced."[48] While the Glowries' melancholy seems absurd in many everyday situations, Mr. Hilary's cheerfulness is similarly out of place in such a serious moment as the ending of Marionetta and Scythrop's engagement.

Hilary is every bit as motivated by his sanguine humors as the Glowries are by their black bile, and thus when Hilary says things like "the highest wisdom and the highest genius have been invariably accompanied with cheerfulness,"[49] he is *only* expressing his own humors in the literal, classical, and medical sense. Hilary's statement is no more definitive than *The Philosophy of Melancholy's* claims that "philosophical melancholy . . . is the most copious source of virtue, of courage, and of genius."[50] Neither point of view is authoritative; rather *Nightmare Abbey* enacts a dialogic indeterminacy in which a multiplicity of viewpoints are advanced and given equal weight even though the positions taken by its many speakers are frequently at odds with one another.

It is humors—whether melancholy or sanguine—that motivate the characters in *Nightmare Abbey*. The connection is made explicit through *Nightmare Abbey's* epigraph, which comes from Ben Jonson's *Every Man in his Humour* (1601): "Oh! It's only your fine humour, sir. Your true melancholy breeds your perfect wit, sir."[51] While most characters suffer from an atrabilarious excess resulting in melancholy, Mr. Hilary and Mr. Asterias have an excess of blood that produces an overly sanguine dispositions, while Mr. Listless's phlegmatic disposition is expressed in his name. Therefore, none of the characters in *Nightmare Abbey* appears to be reliable or authoritative, because each is dominated by a humor that reveals the limitations of their point of view.

The deployment of the comedy of humors in the novel suggests that the satiric persona's critique may also be motivated by an inherent disposition rather than reasoned critique. Of the four medical humors, only three explicitly appear within *Nightmare Abbey*: black bile (melancholy), phlegm (laziness), and blood (cheerfulness). The remaining humor—yellow bile, or choler—is the one related most closely to anger and invective, and the only voice in the narrative which consistently displays a choleric temperament is the satiric persona[52]:

> Mr. Burke was a very sublime person, particularly after he had prostituted his own soul, and betrayed his country and mankind, for £1,200 a year. . . . Our immaculate laureate [Robert Southey] . . . is another sublime gentleman of the same genus: he very much astonished some persons when he sold his birthright for a pot of sack; but not even his *Sosia* [i.e. former self] has a grain of respect for him. . . . At best, he is a mere political scarecrow, a man of straw, ridiculous to all who know of what materials he is made; and to none more so, than to those who have stuffed him, and set him up, as the Priapus of the garden of the golden apples of corruption.[53]

Here satiric critique elides into a ranting, acerbic vitriol. From the bitter reference to Burke as "sublime" (which presents a pun on the more archaic meaning of sublime as being "of lofty appearance or bearing") to the description of Southey as a hapless puppet of a corrupt government (presumably a reference to Southey's tenure as poet laureate under a Tory government, which—given his youthful allegiance to progressive politics—appeared hypocritical, especially after the surreptitious republication of his early, radical play *Wat Tyler* [1794] in 1817, the year before *Nightmare Abbey*'s composition), this satiric tirade seems primarily driven by outrage. But this choleric outburst, along with others in the novel, indicates that the satiric persona may also be subject to an excess of humors. The choleric nature of satirical vehemence levels the apparent distinction between the satiric persona and the other characters in the novel. *Nightmare Abbey* thus problematizes the satiric persona's authority (even though authoritative judgment is precisely what the satiric voice strives for), because satiric invective, in this context, suggests a choleric disposition, rather than a rational project of universal enlightenment through objective satirical critique. This gesture implicitly reduces the satiric persona to one voice among many in the polyphonic chorus of the text.

The deauthorization of the satiric persona produces another strange effect. Despite striving for an absolute judgment of the world, the satiric persona's desire to critique actually reveals the subjective and perspectival nature of that desire. This is a key effect of romanticism on satire as a literary form. Whereas neoclassical satire reflected the rationality of Enlightenment thinking in demanding that satire's critiques be founded upon clear ethical norms, satirical judgment in romantic satire instead ends up revealing the disconnect between aesthetic works and such norms. In this gesture, the dominant of satire shifts from the ethical orientation of neoclassical satire toward a self-reflexive, romantic satire whose dominant is aesthetic. After romanticism, satire increasingly seeks to reveal that satirical judgment is not grounded in logical or objective discourses. In this circular formation, wherein the exercise of satiric authority through satiric judgment reveals the fictitious foundations of its authority, Peacock's satirical method resembles romantic irony.

4 Satire after romantic irony

Romantic irony—a concept that such critics as Jos De Mul, Azade Seyhan, and Andrew Roberts argue is closely affiliated with the self-reflexivity at the heart of romanticism's aesthetic project[54]—provides a key frame of reference for understanding how romantic modes of thinking instigated a shift in satire's literary dominant. This shift can be detected in *Nightmare Abbey,* which, as I have argued, registers the profound changes that romanticism effects on the dominant of satire by means of the novel's extensive intertextual reference, its autocritical dialogue with Peacock's earlier poem *The Philosophy of Melancholy,* and the dialogic indeterminacy regarding the authority (or lack thereof) of speaking positions in the text. Not only does the novel use these means to foreground the perspectival and experiential nature of satiric judgment in a manner that problematizes the authority of the satiric persona, but also, as I will argue, it approximates the oscillating function of romantic irony by means of a self-negating satiric recursion. This recursive function constitutes a rejection of the ethical dominant of neoclassical satire as embodied in the "standard view" of satire, because it undermines both the satiric norms and the objective grounds that are meant to be the foundations of satiric critique. Instead, *Nightmare Abbey* presents a subjective judgment that suggests an orientation with aesthetics rather than ethics—a shift that its alignment with romantic irony makes clearer.

While this new form of satiric judgment *resembles* romantic irony, it also retains some essential differences, which I will delineate. Understanding these differences is important for coming to terms with both *Nightmare Abbey* and the other satires I will examine, which have been written in the wake of romanticism.[55] The differences between the recursion of self-reflexive satire and romantic irony demonstrate that satire did not passively absorb romantic modes of thinking, but rather that both satire's form and its intent were reconstituted within a matrix of romanticism, and the end result of this process constitutes a reenvisioning of both satire and romanticism.

But assessing these similarities and differences first requires establishing the concept of romantic irony. Romantic irony, however, has tended to resist definition because of an inherent categorical ambiguity: whereas irony is traditionally identified as a rhetorical trope, the conception of romantic irony, as articulated by Schlegel and other romantic writers, elevates the rhetorical gesture of irony to the level of a philosophical doctrine or a mode of existence.[56] To complicate matters further, it is common to understand notions of romantic self-reflexivity—and even the concept of romanticism in toto—through the lens of romantic irony, with the result that romantic irony appears as not just *a form,* but rather *the exemplary form* of romantic self-reflexivity.[57] Romantic irony thus functions as something like the paradigm of romantic self-reflexivity; as Giorgio Agamben has argued, the paradigm is a figure that both exemplifies and makes intelligible its own concept,[58] much in the way that romantic irony both provides an instance of and simultaneously defines conceptions of romantic self-reflexivity. In this sense, then, romantic irony resists definition because it transgresses the categories of exemplarity and abstract principle.

Resistance to definition is also one of romantic irony's defining characteristics, because what romantic irony signifies is not a static concept, but rather an unfolding process. Romantic irony comprises a restless oscillation between seemingly opposing poles of thought, and this continual shifting of opposites is romantic irony's chief attribute; as many scholars have argued, the goal of romantic irony is to resist reification and stasis through this continual play of opposites, in which a character's idealism is revealed as naivety in a moment of skeptical enlightenment.[59] But this moment of skepticism isn't the "end" of romantic irony, which is, in fact, a theoretically limitless process since, as Paul de Man has argued, "to know inauthenticity is not the same as to be authentic."[60] Enlightened skepticism becomes only one moment in an unfolding process rather than a telos. It is precisely this oscillation between naivety and partial enlightenment that constitutes the romantic mode of existence, since as Jos De Mul has pointed out, "Schlegel once defined the romantic as a life-feeling that oscillates between enthusiasm and irony."[61]

Romantic irony—much like romanticism in general—has often been defined in opposition to satire. Lilian Furst, for example, opposes the romantic ironist to the satirist, noting that, although both use irony, the satirist has "a firm allegiance to a set of convictions" that are "grounded in ethical standards" and the "authoritative pre-eminence of the judge," while the romantic ironist "does not have the absolute certainty to do that" and possesses "an enquiring mode" that "does not presume to hold out answers."[62] My claim, however, is that this seemingly sharp distinction is eroded by the recursion of self-reflexive satire, which problematizes the grounds of the satiric persona's convictions. *Nightmare Abbey*, by highlighting the subjective nature of satiric judgment, similarly reveals satirical critique to be contingent, rather than authorized by a grounded ethical discourse.

Instead of producing objective judgments based on ethically indexed certainties, recursive satiric judgment, like romantic irony, initiates an unfolding process that is theoretically endless. Satiric recursion opens up an infinite regress, because satiric judgment subjects itself to critique that may always be subjected to further critique. Under such recursion, no judgment can be deemed absolute. But rather than rendering satiric critique invalid, the contingency of satiric judgment is then—much like romantic irony—elevated to a philosophical principle or a mode of existence: rather than calling attention to vice and folly, *Nightmare Abbey*'s satiric judgment suggests that humans are fundamentally incapable of making absolute or objective judgments because rational thought processes cannot be separated from the embodied person making such judgments.

Although no absolute ground appears from which objective judgment could be formed, the desire for such transcendent or absolute judgment continues. This desire is a manifestation of romantic desire (itself a concept closely linked to romantic irony), which Jos De Mul has argued is always characterized by a "tragic consciousness of the final achievability of this desire"; romantic desire stems from a wish to reconcile "the infinite with *here and now*," a principle that is already implicit in romanticism's view of nature as "an organic, living totality" that constitutes a unity of all opposites.[63] In this sense, while romantic desire *appears* impossible to sate, it is also a representation of a belief that this impossible distance can nonetheless be overcome. Like romantic irony, then, romantic desire involves the play of opposites (in this case the desire, on one hand, and the knowledge that the desire cannot be fulfilled, on the other hand) *as a means of* expressing a relation that cannot be captured by either logic or traditional means of representation. *Nightmare Abbey* approximates such romantic desire: although it portrays human judgment as based on partial truths resulting in an unfolding process that has no discrete ending, the desire for an objective form of judgment remains, as evidenced by various characters, including the satiric persona, who attempt to locate grounds to support their critiques. Romanticism thus reshapes satire, which now reveals a romantic indeterminacy behind its caustic judgments and demonstrates an unfulfilled and unfulfillable desire for absolute judgment. After romantic irony, it is not simply that satire's *telos* ceases to be ethical, but that it ceases to have a *telos* at all, because its judgment has become subjective and always open to further critique.

Where neoclassical satire modeled satiric judgment on *ethical* judgment, romantic satire's subjective judgment reflects the paradigm of aesthetic judgment, which is both "groundless"[64] and increasingly reliant on individual "taste" rather than any transcendental criteria.[65] Once again, Kant's philosophy provides a useful frame of reference for conceptualizing the relationship between aesthetic judgment and the ungrounded judgment produced by romantic satires, even if most British romantics were not aware of his work (although Kant is explicitly named in *Nightmare Abbey*). Aesthetic judgments, following Kant, are typically understood as intensely held subjective positions that are essentially different in kind from either objective or ethical assessments.[66] More specifically, aesthetic judgments lack objective grounds, even though the desire for such universal grounding is often implicit within the act of judgment itself.[67] Romantic satires can be said to possess an aesthetic dominant, not only because they inhabit satiric tropes for aesthetics ends, but also because they produce judgments of the same subjective and ungrounded order. The aesthetic orientation of romantic satire is already explicit in *Nightmare Abbey's* rumination on aesthetic matters, which is so extensive that, as I have argued, the subject matter of the novel appears to be nothing less than literature itself.

While *Nightmare Abbey's* approximation of romantic irony is essential for grasping the new aesthetic dominant of its satire, it remains essential to note the key differences between romantic irony and the recursive judgment of romantic satire. The shift in satire's dominant is not simply a matter of the passive absorption of romantic tropes and concerns, since satire's formal traits and thematic concerns affect how *Nightmare Abbey* (along with the other satires that I will examine) have adopted aspects of romanticism, with unsuspected resonances often resulting in quite surprising—and, in many cases, counterintuitive—permutations of satirical forms. While *Nightmare Abbey's* recursive satire resembles romantic irony in a variety of respects, this does not mean that it ceases to be satire, because the shift of satire's literary dominant prompted by romanticism always unfolds within satire's specific logic. For example, satire's reliance on logic and reason problematizes any attempt to present the positive or "naïve" moment of romantic irony, because this moment would be in danger of being recuperated as a ground or norm forming the basis for the satire's unfolding critique. If romantic satire presented such positive moments, it would undermine romanticism's larger critique of reason by re-instilling a grounded, normative basis for satiric critique.

In order to avoid this consequence, romantic satire operates by using only the negative "pole" of romantic irony in a recursive fashion. If romantic irony can be roughly characterized as the oscillation between an affirmative experience and the satirical critique of that experience, then postromantic satire necessarily differs in that no positive or affirmative moment need be presented. Instead of reaching for a privileged *idealistic* vision of the world as romantic irony does, satires that have been generically transformed by romanticism search for a negative, satiric vision, only to discover that such judgments lack absolute grounds, and are therefore always themselves susceptible to further critique. Like romantic irony, this relentless negativity instigates an endless process, albeit one marked not by endless oscillation but by ceaseless recursion: when satiric judgment is revealed to be grounded on faulty premises, the negativity of satiric critique is itself negated as the logic of satire turns back in on itself. Whereas the oscillation of romantic irony—despite the critiques that have been offered of it by Hegel, Kierkegaard and many others—is a process without end that is meant to result in the revelation of a romantic "infinite" or "absolute," the infinite regress of postromantic satire always appears as a diminishment of something with no larger ambit than to prove again and again the general "falsity" of all things. In this way, satire engages with the romantic through a process of creative reinterpretation that also complicates and extends the concept of romanticism itself by reimagining romantic irony from within the "rival" tradition of satire.

Nightmare Abbey constitutes a romantic satire in that it uses the literary characteristics of satire to present a romantic indeterminacy, and provides an example of how romanticism alters the literary dominant of satire while still operating within the specific logic of satire itself. Over the next several chapters, I will examine how the shift in satire's literary dominant eventually produced a new subgenre of postromantic satire, which I have termed avant-garde satires of the avant-garde. I will examine the evolution of this new satiric subgenre as it elaborates on and reacts to the dynamic between satire and romanticism that can be seen in its earliest form in *Nightmare Abbey*. While all of the texts that I will consider present a fundamentally romantic aesthetic orientation, each deploys satiric tropes in a manner that both extends and responds to this romantic inheritance in novel ways that, as I will argue, are also inextricably bound to the trajectory of avant-garde art in the twentieth century—itself another phenomenon significantly influenced by romanticism. In their complicated engagement with the traditions of satire, romanticism, and the avant-garde—an engagement that receives its first rehearsal in *Nightmare Abbey*—these satires present an important development of the romantic tradition, and, even more significantly, constitute a genuinely new reconception of the purpose and form of satire, making this subgenre perhaps the most vital form of satire to appear after the rise of romanticism.

Notes

1   There is an extensive literature that supports the notion of romanticism as a
    discourse that, rather than being naïve, attempts to transcend itself by containing
    its own critique. I have already cited two prominent examples of this reading of
    romanticism in Mul's *Romantic Desire* and Saedi's *The Birth of Social Theory*. Some
    other important accounts of romanticism's self-reflexivity include Niklas Luhmann,
    "A Redescription of 'Romantic Art,'" *MLN* 113:3 (1996): 506–22; Andrew Michael
    Roberts, "Romantic Irony and the Postmodern Sublime," *Romanticism and
    Postmodernism*, Ed. Edward Larrissy (Cambridge: Cambridge University Press,
    1999), 141–56; and David Simpson, *The Academic Postmodern: A Report on
    Half-Knowledge* (Chicago; London: University of Chicago Press, 1995).

2   Steven E. Jones, *British Satire, 1785–840*, 5 Vols. (London: Pickering and
    Chatto, 2003).

3   Thomas Love Peacock, *Nightmare Abbey* (Oxford: Woodstock Books, 1992), 137.

4   Ibid., 218. These final lines were absent from the first printing of *Nightmare Abbey*,
    which ended with Scythrop calling for another glass of madeira. The new ending
    was added to later editions by Peacock.

5   Robert Southey, "Preface," *A Vision of Judgment* (London: Longman, Hurst, Rees,
    Orme, and Brown, 1821), xx. See also Mario Praz, *The Romantic Agony*, 2nd Ed.
    (Oxford: Oxford University Press, 1970), 53–94. Praz offers an important account
    of the "satanic school" of Romanticism.

6   Lacoue-Labarthe and Nancy, in *The Literary Absolute*, argue that the Jena Circle
    "is the first 'avant-garde' group in history. At no point, in any case, does one

discern the least departure from this nearly two-hundred-year-old form on the part of what calls itself the 'avant-garde' today" (8). Poggioli, in *The Theory of the Avant-Garde,* does not hold to the "categorical, literal, or absolute definition of romanticism as the first avant-garde," but nonetheless views romanticism as a "potential avant-gardism" and contends that "the hypothesis of historical continuity between romanticism and avant-gardism now seems irrefutable" (52). Bourdieu, in *The Rules of Art,* notes that several avant-garde tendencies were already present in romanticism, including their similar "distaste for high society" and the "bourgeois" (357) and their preference for organizing "artists and writers in an ideal community, grouped in the same circles around a magazine like *L'Artiste* . . . which incited many writers to take up art criticism" (67).

7   Orlo Williams, "The Parisian Prototype," *On Bohemia: The Code of the Self-Exiled,* Eds. Cesar Grana and Marigay Grana (London: Transaction Publishers, 1990), 62.

8   Gluck, *Popular Bohemia,* 27.

9   Ibid.

10   Robert Kiernan, *Frivolity Unbound: Six Masters of the Camp Novel* (New York: Continuum, 1990), 31. Kiernan identifies Mr. Flosky as Coleridge, Mr. Cypress as Byron, and Scythrop Glowry as Shelley. Shelley was both one of Peacock's closest friends, and an occasional antagonist. Andrew Bennett, in *Romantic Poets and the Culture of Posterity* (Cambridge: Cambridge University Press, 1999), presents essential context regarding the two authors' friendship (163–66). Marilyn Butler, in *Peacock Displayed: A Satirist in His Context* (London/Boston: Routledge, 1979), offers a brief but detailed account of Shelley's influence on the composition of *Nightmare Abbey* (103–05).

11   Klaus Schwank, "From Satire to Indeterminacy: Thomas Love Peacock's *Nightmare Abbey,*" *Beyond the Suburbs of the Mind: Exploring English Romanticism,* Eds. Michael Gassenmeier and Norbert H. Platz (Essen: Verlag Die Blaue Eule, 1987), 158.

12   M.H. Abrams, *The Mirror and the Lamp: Romantic Theory and the Critical Tradition* (Oxford: Oxford University Press, 1971), 47–69.

13   Agamben, *The Man Without Content,* 104.

14   Thomas Love Peacock, *The Letters of Thomas Love Peacock* Vol. 1, Ed. Nicholas A. Joukovsky (Oxford: Clarendon Press, 2001), 123.

15   Peacock, *Nightmare Abbey,* 45.

16   Ibid.

17   Kiernan, *Frivolity Unbound,* 32–7.

18   Peacock, *Letters,* 123.

19   Ibid., 152.

20   Peacock, *Nightmare Abbey,* xi.

21　Peacock, "The Philosophy of Melancholy," 190.

22　Ibid., 186.

23　Ibid., 198.

24　Ibid., 220.

25　Peacock, *Nightmare Abbey,* 14–15.

26　Peacock, "The Philosophy of Melancholy," 186.

27　Peacock, *Nightmare Abbey,* 14.

28　Peacock presents the most explicit such parody in *Nightmare Abbey* when Mr. Flosky is leafing through a stack of recently published gothic works: "'Devilman, a novel.' Hm. Hatred—revenge—misanthropy—and quotations from the Bible. Hm. This is the morbid anatomy of black bile—'Paul Jones, a poem.' Hm. I see how it is. Paul Jones, an amiable enthusiast—disappointed in his affections—turns pirate from ennui and magnanimity" (58).

29　Peacock, *Works* Vol. 6, 342–43. *The Philosophy of Melancholy* was reviewed in *The Anti-Jacobin Review* in April 1812. Although it has not been previously noted, *The Philosophy of Melancholy* also received one other contemporary review in *The New Review, or Monthly Analysis of General Literature,* Vol. 1 No. 2 (February 1813): 148. This anonymous review critiques the poem's exaltation of melancholy in a manner that anticipates the very critiques that Peacock will employ in *Nightmare Abbey* six years later—including a passing allusion to Ben Jonson's *Every Man in His Humor*: "The author of this poem, like Ben Jonson's Master Stephen, is 'mightily given to melancholy' . . . and has sung its praises in the volume before us. We fear, upon the whole, that the bulk of society . . . will find more gratification in [']The laugh that charms the grosser sons of earth['] than in those sensations which it is the object of this work to excite" (148).

30　Peacock, *Nightmare Abbey,* 21–22, 26.

31　Ibid., 25.

32　Ibid., 25–26. Peacock had his own share of analogous publishing disappointments, as he notes in a letter to E. T. Hookam from August 18, 1810, where he discusses the reprinting of his collection *Palmyra* (1805):

> Richardson's bill—the expense of printing—the little probability of encouragement from the *trade* to a work of which the first edition was *strangled in its birth*—and many other considerations—induce me to think it will be better to defer the publication till some other work of mine shall have obtained a degree of popularity, which I do not expect will be the case in the course of the ensuing winter—The temple of Fame must be gained by slow approaches, not taken by storm. What do you think? (*Letters* 58).

33　Peacock, "The Philosophy of Melancholy," 191.

34　Peacock, *Nightmare Abbey,* 2.

35 Ibid., 4.

36 Ibid., 7.

37 Ibid.

38 Ibid., 218.

39 Nichols, *Insinuation*, 26.

40 Kiernan, *Frivolity Unbound*, 19.

41 Butler, *Peacock Displayed*, 8. No consensus exists on whether or not *Nightmare Abbey* is even a satire. Gurewitch, in *The Comedy of Romantic Irony*, argues that *Nightmare Abbey* is not "romantic irony" but rather "the ironic mockery of romanticism" constituting a "virtually unhedged" satiric critique of romanticism (25). Thomas Schmid, in *Humor and Transgression in Peacock, Shelley, and Byron: A Cold Carnival* (Lewiston, NY: The Edwin Mellen Press, 1992), claims that, because it lacks definable norms and self-consciously reflects on its own production, *Nightmare Abbey* is not a satire at all (115, 131). Kiernan, in *Frovolity Unbound*, considers the novel to be an example of "camp humor" (37).

42 While *Nightmare Abbey* is not usually considered a comedy of humors, various critics have noted the indeterminate and perspectival nature of *Nightmare Abbey*. Butler, in *Peacock Displayed*, states that "Peacock proceeds as an artist" rather than a "controversialist," and in this turn he reveals his satire to be "carried along in some degree with the new aestheticism" of the nineteenth century with its emphasis on the "irrational and the subjective" (123). Schmid, in *Humor and Transgression*, notes that the lack of a clear authorial presence "leaves the reader strangely bereft of any confidence in his own position as judge of these targets and follies" suggesting both the reader's own "complicit[y] in the follies he would judge" and "analogous follies of his own" (114). Schwank, in "From Satire to Indeterminacy," contends that the "narrator as satirist no longer commands that Archimedean point outside the world he satirizes which would enable him to posit a value system by which to judge the world he is creating" (157).

43 Simpson, *Irony and Authority in Romantic Poetry*, 190.

44 Geoffrey Hartman, *Criticism in the Wilderness: The Study of Literature Today* (New Haven: Yale University Press, 1980), 265–69.

45 Peacock, *Nightmare Abbey*, 61.

46 Ibid., 97–98.

47 Ibid., 131.

48 Claude A. Prance, *The Characters in the Novels of Thomas Love Peacock 1785–1866 with Bibliographical Lists* (Lewiston, NY: The Edwin Mellen Press, 1992), 37.

49 Peacock, *Nightmare Abbey*, 164.

50 Peacock, "The Philosophy of Melancholy," 186.

51 Peacock, *Nightmare Abbey*, xi.

52 The notion of the "satiric persona" as a performative narratorial mask separate from the person of the author was first developed in the late 1950s by Alvin Kiernan in *The Cankered Muse* (New Haven, CT: Yale University Press, 1959); he argues that the "satirist must be regarded as but one poetic device used by the author to express his satiric vision, a device which can be dispensed with or varied to suit his purpose" (15).

53 Peacock, *Nightmare Abbey*, 134.

54 Mul, *Romantic Desire*, 23–24; Saiedi, *The Birth of Social Theory*, 68; and Roberts, "Romantic Irony and the Postmodern Sublime," 141–56.

55 D.C. Muecke, in *The Compass of Irony* (London: Methuen, 1969), argues that "To study Romantic Irony is to discover how modern Romanticism could be, or, if you like, how Romantic Modernism is" (182).

56 For more on romantic irony's resistance to definition, see Claire Colebrook, *Irony* (London; New York: Routledge, 2004), 46–49. On romantic irony as a philosophical concept rather than a rhetorical trope, see William Egginton, *A Wrinkle in History: Essays on Literature and Philosophy* (Aurora, CO: The Davies Group, 2007), 115. The difficulty of defining romantic irony is further compounded within the Anglophone tradition, since there was no contemporary theorist of romantic irony in English—and Schlegel's concept of romantic irony was largely unknown to British romantics.

57 Colebrook, in *Irony*, notes that "'Romantic irony' has since been identified with romanticism in general, with Friedrich Schlegel's fragments often providing the theory through which English Romantic irony can be read" (46). Theodor Adorno, in *Kierkegaard: Construction of the Aesthetic*, Trans. Robert Hullot-Kentor (Minneapolis: University of Minnesota Press, 1989), registers the entanglement of romantic irony with romanticism, noting that it is "the electrifying clash of perceived reality and reflexive subjectivity" of romantic irony which "constitutes the formal principle of German romantic prose" (6).

58 Giorgio Agamben, "What Is a Paradigm?" *The Signature of All Things: On Method*, Trans. Luca D'Isanto and Kevin Attell (Brooklyn, NY: Zone Books, 2009), 17.

59 Simpson, *Irony and Authority in Romantic Poetry*, 190; Mellor, *English Romantic Irony*, 24; Furst, *Fictions of Romantic Irony*, 229; Gurewitch, *The Comedy of Romantic Irony*, viii; and De Man, "The Rhetoric of Temporality," 197.

60 De Man, "The Rhetoric of Temporality," 198.

61 Mul, *Romantic Desire*, 64.

62 Furst, *Fictions of Romantic Irony*, 8–9.

63 Mul, *Romantic Desire*, xvii, 7–8.

64 Paul Hamilton, "From Sublimity to Indeterminacy: New World Order or Aftermath of Romantic Ideology," *Romanticism and Postmodernism*, Ed. Edward

Larrissy (Cambridge: Cambridge University Press, 1999), 19. See also Christopher
J. Knight, *Hints and Guesses: William Gaddis's Fiction of Longing* (Madison:
University of Wisconsin Press, 1997), 38.

65   Agamben, *The Man Without Content,* 13–27. Agamben offers a brief critical history
of the notion of individual "taste."

66   Kant, in *Critique of Judgment,* argues that aesthetics judgments are inherently
subjective rather than objective, but goes on to note that, while aesthetic judgments
do not "rest on any concept" and cannot be grounded in logic, they are also "of a
special kind" that "does not join the predicate of beauty to the concept of the object
taken in its logical sphere, and yet does extend this predicate over the whole sphere
of *judging subjects*" (46).

67   Again, the inherent desire for a universal ground for aesthetic judgment already
appears, up to a point, in Kant's *Critique of Judgment* under the concept of a
"universal voice" (47). For Kant, while aesthetic judgments are not universal, they
nonetheless are referred back to the *idea* of a "universal voice," which is to say that
such judgments strive for some form of universality, even if they are not able to
attain it. In this sense, the relation between the judgments of self-reflexive satire
and aesthetic judgment correspond. Thierry De Duve, in *Kant After Duchamp*
(Cambridge, MA: The MIT Press, 1996), offers a very clear explication of the
grounds of aesthetic judgment in relation to other forms of judgment in Kant's
thought (301–12).

3

Modernism Against Itself: Wyndham Lewis's *The Apes of God*

1 Self-reflexive satire and the modernist avant-gardes

I have already argued that the historical interaction between satire and romanticism produced a shift in the literary dominant of satire from an ethical to an aesthetic orientation. I now want to examine a new subgenre of self-reflexive satire that coalesced in the aftermath of the modernist avant-gardes.[1] Aaron Matz has persuasively argued that, in the late nineteenth century, satiric impulses became intertwined with the dominant mode of literary writing: realism. This "satirical realism" is characterized by its austerity, which results in a "comedy that does not make us laugh"; not only were such modes of Victorian satire "not inherently funny," but also they eschewed "self-referential tendencies" and suppressed the "playful self-awareness" that—as I have argued—are characteristic of postromantic satires like Peacock's *Nightmare Abbey*.[2] But if self-reflexive satire was briefly displaced by this mode of "satirical realism" in the Victorian era, I want to suggest that self-reflexive satire reemerges as a key mode of satire after the appearance of the modernist avant-gardes.

The rise of these avant-gardes arguably constitutes the most significant aesthetic event of the twentieth century; as William Marx has argued, avant-gardism so influenced twentieth-century aesthetics that all art produced in its wake has had to respond to the questions raised by it, either directly or indirectly—and even those works that might be described as comprising the *arrière-gardes* (a designation that, for Marx, includes both works that belatedly imitate the gestures of earlier avant-garde experiments and works that are openly hostile to avant-gardism) have inevitably been shaped by their *negative or conservative* response to the avant-gardes.[3] In this broad context, I want to suggest that the modernist avant-gardes exerted a unique influence on postromantic, self-reflexive satires because of the complicated manner in which they reframed the aesthetic issues that, after romanticism, had become part of the fabric of satire—and the result was the creation of this new satiric subgenre of avant-garde satires of the avant-garde.

Thierry de Duve has offered a very useful—if not unproblematic—approach for conceptualizing how the modernist avant-gardes reframed aesthetics. Duve contrasts the modernist avant-gardes' new aesthetics with Kantian philosophy (once again) to argue that the point of reference for avant-garde aesthetics was no longer the beautiful, as it was for Kant, but rather the institution of art itself:

> With the readymade . . . the shift from the classical to the modern aesthetic judgment is brought into the open, as the substitution of the sentence "this is art" for the sentence "this is beautiful." To say of a snow shovel that it is beautiful (or ugly) doesn't turn it into art. That judgment remains a classical judgment of taste pertaining to the design of the snow shovel. The paradigmatic formula for the modern aesthetic judgment is the sentence by way of which the snow shovel has been baptized as a work of art.[4]

In Duve's account, the avant-garde work of art exercises the taste of the viewer by first raising the question of whether the object is worthy of aesthetic contemplation. For Duve, the modernist avant-gardes reframed aesthetics by making this question the content of the work. Modulating Duve's claim into a slightly different key, the avant-garde work of art contains a new imperative to question the relationship between itself, the institution of art, and the traditions upon which that institution is founded. The uniqueness of the avant-gardes, following this logic, lies precisely in this critical questioning.

Although I will offer objections to Duve's account, it *does* present a good description of how many of the modernist avant-gardes regarded their own project as a rupture with tradition. Under this view, the modernist avant-gardes question both the traditional institutions of art that became entrenched in the nineteenth century and contemporaneous bourgeois social mores.[5] In this account, the modernist avant-gardes also respond to a variety of the social, political, and technological conditions of modernity that manifested around the turn of the twentieth century: the transformations of everyday life wrought by new forms of technology like automobiles, telephony, and air travel; the increased access to education and literacy that opened up official cultures to critique from new and different perspectives; and the turmoil caused by a series of drastic political upheavals and international conflicts in the West—the most significant of which was the First World War. The modernist avant-gardes were in many cases also either influenced by or in dialogue with nineteenth-century and fin de siècle thinkers—like Bergson, Darwin, Durkheim, Freud, Marx, Nietzsche, Schopenhauer, Weber, and others—whose work sought to isolate or wrestle with these material conditions that were seen to constitute a novel modernity. The writers and artists working in the wake of these systematic social, cultural, and political developments in the Western world—which were often experienced as crises, shocks, or traumas—increasingly felt that this new modernity required an art that was radically different from and even hostile to traditional conceptions of the work of art.

Duve's account implicitly allies itself with this rupture thesis, since the avant-garde work of art (as exemplified by the readymade) cannot be separated from its self-reflexive interrogation of its relation to tradition (in raising the question of whether or not it constitutes a work of art). For Duve, this self-reflexivity produces the avant-garde rupture, since the question of what art is replaces the Kantian aesthetic paradigm. It is the avant-garde's self-reflexivity about its own relationship to tradition that also enables its transcendence of tradition with the somewhat paradoxical result that tradition, although overturned, remains important as a negative concept—an aporia that Hans Magus Enzensberger viewed as endemic to all conceptions of the avant-garde.[6]

Although the modernist avant-gardes' approaches to shaping a "new" art differed wildly, they were linked, as Jo Anna Issak has argued, by their *critical* stance toward tradition, their shared rejection of humanistic aesthetics, their increased emphasis on style and form, and their suspicion of mimetic representation.[7] Some movements, such as Imagisme, which argued for "direct treatment of the 'thing,'" conceived the artist's task as producing a language commensurate with this new "reality"[8]; other movements, such as Dadaism, as represented in Tristan Tzara's manifesto, attacked the notion of artistic representation head-on by proposing a set of practices that would produce an "anti-art." But despite these differences, the modernist avant-gardes all suggested that any authentic—and authenticity itself, whether viewed as desirable or undesirable, is a key concern of the modernist avant-gardes—form of modern art would present a radical critique of traditional representation. Unsurprisingly then, the modernist avant-gardes produced artworks that self-reflexively analyzed their own complicated relationship to tradition, resulting in what Jeff Wallace has described as an "interweaving of critical and creative activities" that "typifies the self-consciousness we have come to find in modernism across all the arts."[9] The prevalence of the *Kunstlerroman* in the modernist novel—as in Joyce's *Portrait of the Artist as a Young Man* (1914), Proust's *In Search of Lost*

Time (1913–27), Virginia Woolf's *To The Lighthouse* (1927), and Wyndham Lewis's own *Tarr* (1918)—suggests the extent to which the modernist avant-gardes believed that their radical aesthetics required a self-reflexive examination of the roles of both the artist and the work of art.

The problem, however, with this portrayal of the modernist avant-gardes' "rupture" with tradition is that—as I have already noted in the introduction—it ignores the modernist avant-gardes' many antecedents and precursors, chief among which was romanticism, a movement that is also typically presented both as a response to and a critique of the material conditions of early modernity. Duve's claim, for example, that the modernist avant-gardes overturned a Kantian paradigm of beauty, largely ignores the fact that romanticism—in its privileging of the sublime over the beautiful, employment of romantic irony, and use of formal devices like the fragment—had already moved beyond a Kantian aesthetic framework. Even those precursors that the modernist avant-gardes were willing to acknowledge—such as Baudelaire and the French Symbolist poets—illustrate the problem with the "rupture" thesis, since the nascent avant-gardism of the Symbolists actually precedes the various upheavals to which the modernist avant-gardes were meant to respond. In an influential article on the concept of modernism, Susan Stanford Friedman has suggested that modernism's claims to radical novelty often cannot be supported, and instead constitute an "(illusory) break with the past" and "a willed forgetting of tradition."[10]

In contrast to the "rupture" thesis, it can be argued that many of the characteristic features of the modernist avant-gardes derive from their paradoxical claim to a novelty that they do not possess. As Jonathan Greenberg argues, modernism's often-critical response to those nineteenth-century movements that presage the modernist avant-gardes, such as Symbolism, betray "an anxiety born by proximity."[11] Friedman makes an even more emphatic claim, noting that "the more modernity protests its absolute newness, the more it suppresses its rootedness in history. And the more that history is repressed, the more it returns in symbolic forms to haunt and disrupt the illusionary and ideological mythology of the new."[12] In Friedman's account, the modernist avant-gardes thus present not a genuinely novel reframing of the aesthetic, as Duve claims, but rather a reframing that is shadowed by the repressed knowledge of its own fictitious originality. As I will argue, this paradoxical formation exerted a profound influence on postromantic satire, which, with its orientation toward the aesthetic, attempted to confront this aporia head-on by revealing the *indebtedness* of the avant-garde—itself something of an obsession in these satires (although this critique, as I will argue, is itself undermined in a not entirely successful attempt to avoid creating a new external ground for satire). Thus, the paradoxical aesthetics of the modernist avant-gardes now provide the context, object, and subject matter of these satires.

But I also want to suggest that the modernist avant-gardes influenced the form of this new subgenre of satire by enabling an aphophaticism, which, although immanent to the new aesthetic orientation of romantic satire, had not yet been explored. While these self-reflexive satires critique the modernist avant-gardes' claims of novelty, they also participate in the avant-garde project by attempting to produce an art that is adequate for representing the contradictions of modernity—a task they undertake with an urgency that is characteristic of the modernist avant-gardes. The problem for the satires in this subgenre, however, is that they can never explicitly articulate *any* aesthetic program, since such an articulation would create a new legitimating ground for satire. As I will argue over the course of the next several chapters, all of the satires within this subgenre attempt to surmount this contradiction by indirectly or apophatically suggesting a means for overcoming the problem of the avant-garde's indebtedness. In this sense, avant-garde satires of the avant-garde not only interrogate the most important developments in twentieth-century aesthetics but also seek to locate in themselves the archetype for an art yet to come—a major development for a literary form often seen to present little more than a conservative nostalgia for tradition.

2 Wyndham Lewis's "satire for its own sake"

Wyndham Lewis was uniquely placed to understand the paradox of avant-garde aesthetics: only he and Ezra Pound—as cofounders of Vorticism—could claim beyond any doubt to be both members of the historical avant-gardes and eminent practitioners of Anglophone modernism. As I will seek to demonstrate, Lewis's *The Apes of God* presents the strongest example of this new subgenre of postromantic satire that wrestles with the contradictions of the modernist avant-gardes' aesthetics. The explicit subject of *The Apes of God* is art and it appears to be a straightforward satire of "avant-garde" artists in 1920s London—particularly those painters and writers associated with the Bloomsbury Group. In so doing, Lewis's novel also constitutes, at least in part, an attack on the contemporary mode of British bohemianism that Bloomsbury represents. As I will note later, much of the novel's satiric norms seem driven by a critique of bohemianism as a "lifestyle" adopted by the wealthy classes. Indeed, Bloomsbury has frequently been singled out as a "'lifestyle modernism' of high bohemia" whose "relative wealth" and connections to important institutions enabled it to criticize certain social norms, and, with relative safety, embrace "pacifism, unconventional manners, and liberal sexual attitudes."[13]

As Peter Brooker has noted, Lewis's attack on Bloomsbury had already begun in his first published novel, *Tarr* (1918), which transports Bloomsbury to a "Parisian stage" in order to reveal it as "a flaccid imitation of a feeble French original."[14] Brooker also points out that Lewis's engagements with bohemian communities were complex and included periods of both extensive engagement (from 1909 to the early 1920s) and withdrawal (when Lewis went "underground" in the early 1920s).[15] As Brooker suggests, these positions were not a rejection of bohemianism, but rather exemplify the modernists "strategic adoption of different bohemian personae."[16] Brooker argues that even this later withdrawal produced Lewis's "last bohemian persona as the crowned 'Enemy'" in the short-lived journal of the same name.[17] These complicated allegiances are reflected in the ambiguity of the satire in *The Apes of God,* which seems to attack contemporary artists and bohemians, only to undermine the basis of this satiric critique.

The action of the novel is initiated by a hanger-on in London's art scene, the infamous prankster and socialite Horace Zagreus, who becomes the mentor of the youthful "genius," Daniel Boleyn (who in reality is both simple-minded and naïve). Zagreus gives Dan a letter (called "The Encyclical") from Zagreus's own mentor, Pierpoint (a figure who seems to resemble Lewis). Even though Pierpoint himself never appears in the novel, his letter orchestrates the main action of the plot, informing Dan that the majority of artists in London's art scene are not in fact real artists at all, but rather "apes of God"—figures who have chosen to live a bourgeois-bohemian lifestyle making "art," but whose own creative output merely copies the work of other, superior artists. Under Zagreus's orders, Dan observes and catalogues the behavior of various "apes." Pierpoint's "Encyclical"—which appears to outline the contours of the novel's satiric critique of the larger novel—therefore seems to establish something like the satiric norms of *The Apes of God* itself.

Although the book mocks the artist-apes described within its pages, the seemingly stable, satirical norms presented in Pierpoint's "Encyclical" are undermined through a series of what I will describe as "staged reversals" of satiric critique, as well as a complicated web of allusions to representations of the artist as ape that undermine the novel's critique of the avant-garde's lack of originality. In these gestures, the novel's employment of self-reflexive judgment takes the recursive form of romantic satire that, as I have argued, can be found in *Nightmare Abbey*. However, *The Apes of God* differs from *Nightmare Abbey* both in its choice of satiric objects (the modernist avant-gardes instead of romanticism) and its avant-garde desire to locate a form of art adequate to modernity. The novel attempts to meet this second task, as I will argue at the end of this chapter, by enacting a hyper-mimetic mode of representation that indirectly undermines mimesis itself. This contradictory desire both to critique and to advance elements of the avant-garde program comprises the distinctiveness of the subgenre of avant-garde satires of the avant-garde. Nonetheless, *The Apes of God* still operates within the new paradigm of romantic satire, which, with its aesthetic dominant, removes satire's ethical grounding.

The clearest example of the novel's staged reversals occurs in the chapter "Chez Lionel Kein, Esq.", which initially appears to be a satire of Kein as a "pseudo-Proust,"[18] whose allegedly "avant-garde" novels are shameless imitations of the French novelist. Zagreus baits Kein by asking him a seemingly innocent question: "I've always regarded you, Li, as—can you guess?—*a perfect Proust-Character!* How does that accommodate you?" Here and elsewhere in the chapter, Kein does not even *know* that he is being satirized, just as he remains unaware that his own work's indebtedness to Proust borders on plagiarism. Kein seems to serve as a synecdoche for a larger problem, namely that the modernist avant-gardes (as embodied by the apes in the novel) claim to have created a novel art that breaks with tradition, even though their aesthetics comprise an unconscious or repressed continuation of tradition. The avant-garde's claim to an originality that breaks with tradition can be maintained only by repressing the knowledge of its precursors, such as romanticism.

In various polemical writings, Lewis supports such a position, arguing that the modernist avant-gardes' claims of novelty are not credible: "In its popular sense, 'modern' is used to convey a liberal outlook in all things—not much more than that. As applied to pictures, music, and books, a rupture of tradition is indicated; a tendency to do something *new* is expressed. New? Well, surprising, and, in England, 'shocking.'"[19] In reality, the avant-gardes recycle older practices and claim them as new: "We see every month or so things announced as 'new' that we have all seen before, many times over: which is merely silly."[20] In representing the old as if it were new, the modernist avant-gardes reveal a necessary amnesia at the heart of their radical project: "Modernism, which is merely the nervous jingo exaggeration of the more futile novelties of the Zeitgeist, has enunciated it: we see it possessed of a meretricious colour more reminiscent of the revivalist or salvationist army-technique."[21] Lewis suggests that the modernist avant-gardes, rather than presenting something genuinely new, have recycled older techniques producing an unoriginal pastiche.

Zagreus's argument seems to advance a very similar point, reflecting what appears to be Lewis's satirical intent. Zagreus's discussion of Proust (who, as Aaron Matz has argued, was a key influence on Lewis's own conception of satire[22]) serves as a pretext to ruminate on the notion of the roman à clef novel and the relation between satire and the "real" world. He dismisses as inauthentic a Proustian fiction that "pretends to approach its material with the detachment of the chemist or the surgeon" even as it deploys a conservative, nineteenth-century aesthetics identified with "the work usually of a writer for the salon and the tea party."[23] Having satirized the ultimately indebted and inauthentic form of avant-gardism that Kein represents, Zagreus articulates a rival aesthetics virtually identical to those propounded by Lewis in his expository texts, calling for a radical form of satire that would apply its brutal critique without any regard to the morality or virtue of the subjects it portrays. Such a satire would seek to dehumanize all of its subjects: "Were we mercilessly transposed into Fiction, by the eye of a Swift, for instance, the picture would be intolerable. . . . *Every* individual without exception is in that sense objectively unbearable."[24]

Lewis describes satire as radically objective observation (rather than as a form of ethical judgment) in a pamphlet entitled "Satire and Fiction" (1930, reprinted as part of *Men without Art* [1934]). Like Zagreus, Lewis claims that "the greatest satire is non-moral," and argues for separating satire from any ethical ground.[25] Outlining a vision of "'satire' *for its own sake*,"[26] Lewis retains the method of satirical critique while denying its ethical grounds; instead of an ethical critique, Lewis's satire presents a dehumanizing vision that can be applied indiscriminately to all of humanity. Satire now becomes first and foremost an aesthetic experience (which manifests through laughter), but it also spills over into metaphysical territory, since satiric mockery provokes laughter at the absurdity of humanity. Lewis's satire thus resembles earlier forms of aestheticized satire, but, as Jonathan Greenberg has argued, it also differs in emphasizing "technique, form, and control" in ways that resonate with modernism's broader investments in artistic expertise.[27]

Lewis termed his new form of nonmoral satire the "external approach,"[28] emphasizing the idea of satire as an artistic method opposed to the common modernist use of stream-of-consciousness techniques. Rather than representing the internal human consciousness in action, Lewis's satire is the literature of "the Great Without," which focuses on the external, material elements of humanity.[29] For this reason, characters within Lewis's satire must be portrayed as mechanical and flat, as if they were the living "dead."[30] Lewis's new theory of satire requires seeing the human from an inherently inhuman perspective, and, for this reason, human beings must be depicted not as living persons but as dead things. In a reversal of Henri Bergson's dictum that laughter is predicated on the notion of a person behaving like a thing, Lewis argues that laughter is caused by "a thing behaving as if it were a person."[31] As Jonathan Greenberg notes, however, Lewis's dehumanizing strategy still retains the essential relation in Bergson's formation, even if it inverts it.[32]

The apparent similarity between Lewis's and Zagreus's positions creates a significant problem for the entire theory of nonmoral satire. If Zagreus were little more than a textual mechanism for broadcasting Lewis's theory of satire, then it would undermine the claim that *The Apes of God* presents a new form of satire, because the theory of nonmoral satire would constitute precisely the kind of norms that enabled the ethical critique of neoclassical satire. This is problematic, since Lewis argues in *Men without Art* that satire should not only excise all ethical grounds, but also any purpose at all. And yet, the scene with Kein initially presents what appears to be exactly this stable and traditional form of satirical critique: Kein, the unconscious imitator of Proust, is mocked by a satiric persona (Horace Zagreus), who then goes on to articulate a set of views virtually identical to those of his creator (Wyndham Lewis), which can be understood as the norms that motivate the satire itself. In such a reading, then, *The Apes of God*'s satire would critique a certain kind of "naïve" avant-gardism only to articulate a *rival* aesthetics, and Lewis's claims of a nonmoral satire would thus become a covert form of ethical satire, which claims to break from neoclassical traditions only to reassert them.

I will ultimately argue that *The Apes of God* employs recursive satire in a (not entirely successful) attempt to extricate itself from this double bind. Nonetheless, it is worth first skeptically examining Lewis's emphatic advocacy of purposeless satire. For one thing, there are obvious and inherent contradictions in the concept that must be registered. As I noted in the introduction, every satire—whether "purposeless" or not—is shadowed by its authors' tastes and proclivities, which manifest themselves in the *specificity* of the satiric targets selected. In the case of *The Apes of God*, the satire of individuals associated with the Bloomsbury Group, including more or less explicit parodies of Edith and Osbert Sitwell, inevitably reflects Lewis's own dim views of these writers' work. Nathan Waddell has noted the same problem in a different way, arguing that, despite claims of satiric objectivity, Lewis's "antipathy to specific political trends often spills through."[33] These residues of authorial intent, in indicating a specific and subjective point of view for satiric observation, appear hard to reconcile with claims of satire's objectivity and autonomy.

Moreover, there are good reasons to be suspicious of the various places where Lewis appears to articulate his aesthetic method in explicit terms. As I noted in the introduction, Waddell has demonstrated that Lewis's earlier arguments for "deadness"—which clearly influenced his notion of objective satire—are heavily ironized. Waddell has also pointed out that Lewis altered his views on satire in the late 1930s by suggesting that satire might have an "educative" purpose that is nonetheless "non-didactic" in refusing to offer a "tailor-made pathway" for social reform.[34] In this sense, Lewis's views on satire in *Men without Art* could well be ironic, and, at any rate, are inconsistent with his later views. While I agree that Lewis's views on satire did change later in his career, I nonetheless will attempt to demonstrate that *The Apes of God* treats the notion of a nonmoral, autonomous satire with high seriousness. Here, I am following Andrzej Gasiorek's assertion that "aesthetic autonomy and satire are closely woven together in Lewis's writing in the 1930s."[35]

While Lewis's theory does contain inconsistencies, I will argue that he nonetheless sought to undermine the authority of the satirist's position in *The Apes of God* through self-reflexive and recursive techniques. In undermining the specific norms articulated in "The Encyclical," the novel deactivates the grounds of what appears to be its explicit satirical critique. I will argue that this turn enables Lewis to harness the power of satire's critique for more open-ended aesthetic effects, which are intrinsically different from the ethical and instrumental purposes usually associated with satire. While this method does generate further inconsistencies, which I will discuss later, my suggestion is that these inconsistencies both are characteristic of aporetic modernist autonomy and are *productive contradictions* that Lewis valued in terms of their effects rather than their logical coherence.

The means by which the novel attempts to apply this unusual satirical method is prefigured in the scene with Kein, when he notices something about his conversation with Zagreus that is discomfiting—he has heard this diatribe before:

"My dear Zagreus, excuse me! But what you have just said is word for word what Pierpoint said the last time you were both here together—and about Proust—It was about Proust, if you remember that we were talking about at the time –"

The frown disappeared entirely from the face of Mr. Zagreus, and only the smile (but still held in leash by some other agency) remained.

"Well, what of it?" he asked.

Nothing at all. Noticing merely that you were *repeating*—. You remember that we disagreed with Pierpoint. . . . When that conversation you have been talking about occurred, it was you, Zagreus, who contradicted Pierpoint.[36]

Zagreus's repetition of Pierpoint's argument (whether it forms part of an elaborate joke or represents a genuine error on his part) underscores the fact that all of Zagreus's satirical attacks on the apes are themselves aped directly from Pierpoint (itself a winking acknowledgment that Pierpoint's views are virtually identical to Lewis's). Zagreus is revealed to be just as indebted and unoriginal as Kein, a point that another character states explicitly later in the novel: "All this taking you about to show you *The Apes!* Well of course they *are* Apes. What however in Jesus' name are you but an Ape and Horace Zagreus himself he is the worst Ape of the lot! Does he not take all of his ideas from Pierpoint?"[37] Here, the satirist is himself satirized, since Zagreus is reduced to an ape.

But Zagreus's unoriginality does not definitively undermine the satiric norms within *The Apes of God*, since his indebtedness does not undermine the legitimacy of either Pierpoint's arguments about satire or the larger critique of the apes expressed in "The Encyclical." As I will argue, however, *The Apes of God* enacts a larger, if heretofore unnoticed, staged reversal by intentionally copying the very premise of its satire from an earlier source text. In consciously repeating the ideas of another work, the novel renders its own satiric norms as unoriginal as Zagreus's claims of satiric objectivity.

3 Ape and original

The symbolism within *The Apes of God* suggests that the ape functions as the antithesis of the modernist avant-gardes, which sought to break with artistic paradigms of mimetically representing the world or copying from established traditions. This association, however, threatens to turn the text back into a classical satire with clear satiric norms—a situation the novel avoids by consciously modeling its satiric critique on E.T.A. Hoffmann's "Report of an Educated Young

Man," a text whose influence on Lewis's satire has not previously been noted. This appropriation problematizes the very basis of the novel's critique, which is revealed to be just as indebted and unoriginal as the art produced by avant-garde "apes."

Before examining Lewis's appropriation of Hoffmann's text, however, it is worth briefly examining the numerous, indirect allusions involving the ape that run throughout the novel, because, with certain notable exceptions,[38] both these simian allusions in particular and the rich intertextuality of *The Apes of God* in general have been largely overlooked in scholarly assessments of the novel. Even the lone monograph dedicated solely to Lewis's text, Mark Perrino's *The Poetics of Mockery* (1995), ignores the novel's references to texts employing the trope of apes and apery, despite its prominence in Lewis's title. Moreover, many of the possible sources for Lewis's employment of the phrase "ape of God," such as Karl Marx's early poem, "Scenes from Oulanem: A Tragedy," remain unexplored.[39] This omission reflects the generally negative critical reception that has plagued *The Apes of God* more or less since its publication—an unsurprising fact given the ambivalent reception of Lewis's work both during his life and posthumously. *The Apes of God* is an unabashedly "difficult" book, but, unlike Joyce's output of the same era, its difficulty has typically been chastised rather than praised.

There are a variety of reasons why Lewis work has had trouble finding a ready and receptive audience, and many are problems of his own making. For one, in his guise of "The Enemy," he often sought to put forward extreme positions for the purpose of being controversial. His 1931 political tract, *Hitler*, which praised the Nazi leader, irreparably damaged Lewis's reputation; especially following the publication of Fredric Jameson's *Fables of Aggression: Wyndham Lewis, the Modernist as Fascist* (1979), Lewis's relation to fascism has become, in Tyrus Miller's words, "*the* crucial question for Lewis criticism."[40] As a result, the complex textual features of Lewis's work have often been overshadowed by questions of their political significance.

Lewis's work from the 1920s and early 1930s also remains difficult to parse because of the sheer volume of material that Lewis published in this period, including *The Art of Being Ruled* (1926), *The Lion and the Fox* (1927), *Time and Western Man* (1927), *The Wild Body* (1927), *The Childermass* (1928), *Tarr* (revised edition, 1928), *Paleface: The Philosophy of the "Melting Pot"* (1929), and *The Apes of God* (1930), as well as the three volumes of his journal *The Enemy* (1927–29). This writing inhabited diverse genres, ranging from satire to cultural criticism. Moreover, even Lewis's polemical writings and essays tend to be difficult, indirect, allusive, and, as Reed Way Dasenbrock has noted, "constructed on principles closer to those of *The Waste Land* or *The Cantos*" than to "those of a conventional treatise on politics and society."[41] As a result, Lewis's arguments are often intentionally convoluted, suffused with irony, and even willfully contradictory. Critical appraisals of *The Apes of God* reflect this larger problem of reception, and often disapprovingly emphasize the novel's physical size ("a book of 625 pages,"[42] which is "three inches thick and weigh[s] just five pounds"[43]); its use of "lifeless" characters ("inanimate objects, chairs for example, seem more vital than people"[44]); and its accumulation of ornate detail that "makes the reader feel uncomfortable."[45] For these reasons, *The Apes of God* has been described as "often tedious,"[46] "no one's favourite book,"[47] or, in Fredric Jameson's words, "virtually unreadable for any sustained period of time."[48]

The Apes of God's many allusions to texts that depict artists as apes—itself part of the history of the trope of *ars simia naturae*—have evaded notice. And yet, Lewis saw this tradition as so central to the novel itself that the original design for the prospectus for *The Apes of God* (which was featured on the cover of the 1965 Penguin reprint of the novel) explicitly echoes Jean-Baptiste-Siméon Chardin's *Le Singe Peintre* (ca. 1740). Lewis's drawing (1929) is clearly a self-portrait, since the painting is signed "WL" and a book entitled *The Apes of God* is sitting next to the painter. From the outset, this self-portrait serves as a means of undermining the authority of the novel's satire, since it strongly suggests that Lewis, too, is an ape. Through this carefully constructed visual pun, Lewis attempts to acknowledge his debts in a fashion that ironically comments on the text accompanying Chardin's painting: "All painters imitate one another."[49] The outstretched hand of the painter in Lewis's prospectus perhaps also recalls the pose of John Wilmot, the second Earl of Rochester, in Jacob Huysman's famous portrait of him, in which he poses with his pet monkey. Wilmot's prominent inclusion of monkeys in many of his satirical works likely served as an influence for Lewis's satire.[50]

The novel's most important allusions to *ars simia naturae* come from other satirical texts. As Lewis was probably aware, satires employing the figure of the ape comprised "a literary genre of particular importance for the intellectual life of the eighteenth century."[51] H.W. Janson notes that this overlooked tradition of simian satire involved two possibilities for its dramatization: the satirist "could either construct a fully-fledged simian civilization in some remote corner of the globe and describe the adventures of a human visitor in such a setting, or he could show how a talented and properly instructed ape might become a respected member of contemporary human society."[52] Examples of this first type of satire, the "man in ape-land," can be seen in the final book of Swift's *Gulliver's Travels* (1726) in its depiction of the ape-like (but human!) Yahoos; Ludvig Baron Holberg's *Nicolai Climii Iter Subterraneum* (1741), which details the descent of Nicolai into a hollow-earth ruled by sapient apes; and Léon Gozlan's *Les Emotions de Polydore Marasquin* (1857).[53] The second tradition, that of the "intelligent" monkey introduced into society, perhaps first appears in Thomas Love Peacock's *Melincourt* (1818), in the character of Sir Oran Haut-ton, an orangutan to whom Mr. Forester provides a "philosophical education," before introducing him into polite London society.[54]

In *The Apes of God*, Lewis combines the two approaches under one umbrella. In the most literal sense, *The Apes* presents a tour of the "man in ape-land": Pierpoint's "Encyclical" instructs a naïve traveler, Dan, to survey the "apes" that comprise the artistic sectors of London. On the other hand, Dan is also the pet of Horace Zagreus; he is Zagreus's new "genius," the promising young outsider introduced by Zagreus into polite society. It is clear from Dan's demeanor and his inane inner monologue that Lewis intends to portray him as little more than another "ape." It is also telling that Lewis specifically chose to represent him as an Irish outsider. As L. Perry Curtis, Jr. notes, the late Victorian popular tradition in England consistently demeaned Irishmen by portraying them as simian.[55] Dan is, ambiguously, both the travelling "man in ape-land" (Gulliver) and the Irish "ape-man" brought into polite English society (Sir Oran). Given that the signal fixation of *The Apes of God* is the artistic indebtedness of its satiric targets, the specific references to other satires that employ the trope of the ape are important. Through its references to its own antecedents and influences, the novel begins to unravel its apparent satiric norms by suggesting that the novel's satirical critique as advanced in the "Encyclical"—that contemporary artists are unoriginal apes—is itself unoriginal.

As I noted earlier, *The Apes of God* owes its largest debts to one specific source: E.T.A Hoffmann's "The Report of an Educated Young Man." Hoffmann's story bears a close resemblance to Pierpoint's "Encyclical." Both employ an epistolary form and are presented as copies of an absent original: Pierpoint's missive is "a letter in duplicate," and "Report of an Educated Young Man" is not the original, but "a written copy of it."[56] The fact that both works are copies emphasizes the notion of indebtedness that each articulates.

Although the specific intertextual relation between "The Report of an Educated Young Man" and *The Apes of God* has thus far gone unnoticed, Hoffmann's influence on Lewis is already well documented. In Lewis's first novel, *Tarr* (1918), one of his protagonists, Otto Kreisler, is named after Johannes Kreisler, the protagonist of E.T.A. Hoffmann's *Lebensansichten des Katers Murr* (1820).[57] "Report of an Educated Young Man" comes from another E.T.A. Hoffmann's work about Kreisler, entitled the *Kreisleriana*, originally published as part of his four-volume *Fantasy Pictures in the Style of Callot* (1814–15). *Kreisleriana* offers a series of fragmentary reflections and essays "written" by Johannes Kreisler. That "Report of a Young Man" has never before been identified as the source for Lewis's *The Apes of God* is likely due to the relative obscurity of Hoffmann's work in the English-speaking world, as well as the fact that *Kreisleriana* was not available in English translation until the 1980s.

In the "Report of an Educated Young Man," Kreisler introduces a letter from his artist friend, Milo, who is "actually an ape."[58] Kreisler's introduction is then followed by Milo's letter, which recounts his early life in the African jungles, his capture, and subsequent education by "my dear teacher, the professor of aesthetics."[59] In a gesture similar to the notion of "aping" in *The Apes of God,* Milo associates imitation with the processes of aesthetic influence and judgment:

> The imitative instinct which is characteristic of our species . . . is nothing more than the irresistible urge not only to attain culture, but also to display that which we already possess. . . . Someone produces something, a work of art or whatever, and everyone cries "That's wonderful." The wise man, driven by his inner voice, immediately imitates it. Admittedly his version turns out differently, but he says "That is just as it should be, and the work you thought was wonderful merely gave me an incentive to bring forth the genuinely wonderful one I have so long been carrying in my head."[60]

Milo, for Hoffmann, is clearly a parody of the successful artist, and his views are held up as the objects of satire, but they afford an unusually close resemblance to Lewis's critiques of Bloomsbury artists, such as the "pseudo-Proust," Lionel Kein, or even Zagreus, in his "broadcasting" of Pierpoint's dictums, since both do little more than slavishly imitate their heroes. Milo, as an ape, embodies this unreflexive mimicry. His unusual definition of originality would likely have appealed to Lewis, since Milo attributes originality to an artistic *failure* to imitate another work; the original work thus becomes a bad copy.

As Milo continues in the letter, discussing his musical education and allegedly virtuosic mastery of the piano, he reveals the bourgeois-bohemian attitude that is precisely the psychological terrain of Lewis's own conception of modern ape-hood:

> For a genius, for a virtuoso, [composing] is all much too tedious and boring. In any case, if one wishes to command respect in every quarter . . . one need only be *thought* to be a composer, and that is enough. . . . Utter contempt for the exertions of others, the strength of mind to ignore totally all those who prefer silence and get on quietly without talking about it, overweening arrogance about all the seemingly effortless products of one's own brilliance—all these are unmistakable signs of the most highly cultivated genius.[61]

The consistent emphasis on "genius" is reflected in Lewis's own repeated use of the term in *The Apes*. Horace Zagreus is known for his interest in discovering young men of "genius," but his mentor, Pierpoint, makes clear that this epithet is applied in entirely ironic terms: "All are 'geniuses', before whose creations the other members of the Club, in an invariable ritual, must swoon with appreciation."[62] Moreover, for Milo, art is not a vocation or a necessity, but a lifestyle choice necessary to "command respect in every quarter." This resembles Pierpoint's critique in "The Encyclical," where he says, "Everyone able to afford to do so has become a 'bohemian' . . . [because] the well-off find the studio-café society the only one in which they are free to live as they chose."[63] Milo's hatred of "geniuses" is redescribed by Pierpoint as the "envy" of the "pseudo-artist" that inspires "the fervour of their caprice or ill-will to the 'professional' activities of the effective artist—that rare man born for an exacting intellectual task, and devoting his life unsparingly to it."[64] Milo is precisely the type that Pierpoint attacks, being one of "*those prosperous mountebanks who alternatively imitate and mock at and traduce those figures they at once admire and hate.*"[65] In the world of imitators that Lewis presents, it appears that Hoffmann's ape is, in a contradictory sense, the *original* ape of God.

By recycling the premise of E.T.A. Hoffmann's text (an indebtedness already acknowledged in the word "Encyclical," which suggests a cyclical repetition), the novel makes itself guilty of the very failings for which it attacks its satiric targets, thereby leveling the distinction between it and the objects of its satire. The implication is that, rather than making judgments from a privileged or objective viewpoint, Lewis himself is another ape of god, who has appropriated Hoffmann's hundred-year-old critique of pseudo-artists articulated in the *Kreisleriana*, rather than producing an original work of art. In foregrounding its own unoriginality, the novel attempts to deactivate its satiric critique, since its apparent satirical intent (the mockery of unoriginal artists) becomes an object of satire. Lewis's autocritical satire resonates with what Andrzej Gasiorek has termed the "self-deconstructive" tendency of Lewis's work more generally.[66]

In undermining these norms, the novel also problematizes its relationship to the claims that appear to comprise the authorial "intent" behind Lewis's satire. The autonomy of the text, here, is generated not by the reification of the specific authorial intent reflected in Lewis's various polemical texts, but rather by a complex and contradictory textuality that renders ambiguous its relationship to various claims made by Lewis, since the novel's indirect revelation of its own indebtedness ironizes the attack on an imitative modernism that Lewis undertakes in a variety of his polemical texts. Gasiorek has registered this tendency in Lewis's fiction, arguing that, for Lewis, the goal of the aesthetic is to attain "a universality that exceeds the particular," which produces a "radical de-individuation" of the artist.[67] In this process, Lewis's intention (as reflected in various published commentaries and essays) and authority are not reified but ramified; his "explicit" authorial intent is problematized in order to produce an autonomous and complete work of art that transcends such claims. Autonomy for Lewis is thus the product of an irresolvable contradiction—in this case the clash between the particularity of the satirist's viewpoint and Lewis's claim of satiric objectivity—which can only be resolved within an autonomous, totalizing work of art.

While this self-reflexivity does undermine the satiric norms expressed in "The Encyclical," which are now implicated as targets of Lewis's satire, the attempt to excise all instrumentality from satirical critique, however, is not entirely successful. In particular, the novel still generates two, implicit registers of unoriginality: a negative concept of slavish imitation and a positive notion of a productive, ironized, and self-conscious appropriation of tradition. *The Apes of God*'s indebtedness is thus not the same as that of the apes in the novel, because its appropriation of Hoffmann is a self-conscious, textual effect created through indirect allusion, rather than unconscious imitation. In this sense, while the novel does render ambiguous the grounds of satiric critique, a residue of traditional satiric judgment persists since there do appear to be some criteria that separate successful from unsuccessful works of art. It may well be that Lewis's later modifications to this theory of satire, which Nathan Waddell has noted, were motivated by an acknowledgment of this inherent contradiction.

Nonetheless, I would suggest that to focus unduly on this contradiction in Lewis's conception of autonomous satire, or even to view it as a flaw in his work, overlooks the aesthetic effects—some of which I have already noted—that are produced by Lewis's self-reflexive satire. Moreover, as Jodie Greenwood has argued, Lewis frequently produced works with irresolvable contradictions; the "inconsistent" nature of these texts—which is not accidental, but rather a provocation to readers—nonetheless presents a challenge to Lewis scholars, since it conflicts with literary criticism's "drive toward tidiness and completion."[68] Following this claim, I would suggest that the contradictions within Lewis's theory of objective satire—although important to note—are less significant than their productive effects. In particular, I want to suggest that the theory of objective satire shifted the emphasis within the genre of satire itself. Despite the residues of satiric instrumentality in *The Apes of God*, the satiric distinction between "good" and "bad" artists becomes, at best, a secondary concern in Lewis's satire, which, instead, now focuses on larger aesthetic questions: in particular, Lewis's theory of objective satire presents nothing less than an attempt to find an adequate aesthetic form for registering the contradictions of an overdetermined modernity by refashioning—rather than breaking with—literary tradition. This new orientation for satire—although "purposive" in a generalized sense—differs significantly from the means-end instrumentality traditionally associated with the satiric form.

4 Mimesis, humanism, and satire

Rather than merely serving to distinguish good from bad artists, *The Apes of God*, as I will argue, was meant to constitute an aesthetic response to the failure of the avant-garde. *The Apes of God* satirizes the modernist avant-gardes in order to establish the reasons for this failure, but its critique also ironically constitutes an extension of the avant-gardes' project in attempting to locate—albeit apophatically—an aesthetic form that could register the contradictions of an overdetermined modernity. At heart, then, *The Apes of God*'s critique examines the conceptual and methodological shortcomings of the modernist avant-gardes, particularly their presumption that traditional forms of mimetic representation could be transcended through formal experimentation. *The Apes of God* presents an alternate mode of avant-gardism through its autonomous, ironized, self-reflexive satire, which Lewis viewed as an elastic aesthetic form that would critically respond to tradition rather than transcending it.

Despite the modernist avant-gardes' attack on traditional aesthetics, Lewis argued in his expository prose that most avant-garde works unintentionally fell back into the mimetic paradigm they had sought to overcome. *Time and Western Man* (1927), for example, criticizes modernist authors—including such prominent figures as Gertrude Stein, James Joyce, and Ezra Pound—whose work, as Lewis argues, betrays an unconscious repetition of traditional aesthetics. This same critique is implicitly echoed in the title of *The Apes of God*, since the notion of "aping" suggests a mimetic "mirroring" of an absent original. Unconscious repetition of this sort, followed by the surreptitious reassertion of mimeticism, presented a danger for which the artist must be ever vigilant—a point underscored when a character in *The Apes of God* paraphrases Zagreus's explanation of how traditional forms inevitably survive "revolutionary" aesthetic movements: "By words, this is it seems the idea, we are handed over to the tender mercies of the Past. That is the parasitic no-longer-with-us class of has-beens, he cleverly calls it. In other words the dead."[69] For Lewis, the modernist avant-gardes failed precisely because their belief in their own transcendence of tradition ironically enabled a return of repressed mimetic tendencies.

Lewis sought a genuinely nonmimetic mode of art that would not rely on representing a "real-life" original. This goal is explicitly announced in *The Apes of God*, when Zagreus, quoting Pierpoint, argues for a fiction that, rather than mirroring the world, would emphasize its separateness from reality: "I think *the real* should not compete with creations of fiction. There should be two worlds, not one."[70] The crucial question for Lewis was how to establish a new approach to representation that would not unconsciously reproduce the unexpectedly resilient mimetic paradigm. Any solution to this problem, from Lewis's perspective, would require a rigorous self-reflexivity that would neutralize mimesis by wrestling with the dead weight of aesthetic tradition in an open and ongoing conflict. In other words, the answer, as Peter Nicholls has argued, was to employ the objective theory of satire, which enabled a "disruption of mimesis" by using mimesis against itself.

Self-reflexive satire, for Lewis, was not simply one form of literary modernism among a wider set of possibilities. Rather, as Fredric Jameson has argued, he believed nonmoral satire to be the only legitimate vehicle for a truly radical, modern art—"the very essence of art itself, vorticism or expressionism riding in the Trojan Horse of a generic designation, a style which is now in reality a whole world-view."[71] More recently, Jamie Wood has argued that Lewis's notion of satire presented a critical response to developing notions of literary theory in the work of T.S. Eliot, I.A. Richards, and F.R. Leavis.[72] Autonomous satire no longer represented its targets according to a set of ethical norms, but utilized satiric critique in the "external method" of objective observation, which redescribed the human in inherently inhuman terms. The external method enabled by this form of satire was key for Lewis, because it was simultaneously mimetic and anti-mimetic.

With that said, it is necessary to acknowledge Paul Edwards's point that Lewis's notion of the external method was a "retrospective" concept applied to earlier fiction, which also disregards the many depictions of internal psychology in Lewis's work.[73] David Bradshaw has argued that Lewis's reliance on stereotypes that are "anti-Black, anti-Semitic, and homophobic" undermines any claims to an external method, because his satire reflects "broader discourses of inter-war racial and homosexual intolerance."[74] As Jonathan Greenberg has pointed out, although Lewis consistently advocated for an ethic of "emotional coldness," the "unpredictable practice of novel-writing" meant that his work still often betrayed passionate, emotional, and even sentimental aspects which conflict with any pure notion of the external method.[75] As Greenberg argues, this tension between the desire for a pure, cold art and the inherent messiness of life, which makes such detachment impossible, is already a key theme in Lewis's *Tarr*, since the title character idealizes an "inhuman" artistic perspective, yet "never succeeds in extricating himself from the 'slop of sex.'"[76] As I will argue, the irreconcilability of the inhuman perspective of the satirist with the material fact of his humanity can only be resolved in *The Apes of God* through a strategy of absence, in which the satiric persona is never physically present. Although Lewis's external method may not be consistently applied, I would nonetheless argue that his employment of inhuman and external representations remain the most distinctive aspect of his aesthetics and thus constitutes his most singular contribution to literary modernism. As a result, the external method remains key for understanding Lewis's work.

At first blush, the "external method"—unlike much literature associated with the modernist avant-gardes—appears to be rigidly mimetic since it relies precisely on the re-presentation of carefully observed detail. As Douglas Mao has pointed out, Lewis's "radical insistence" on selecting his "*materica poetica*" from "the world as it is" actually "brings Lewis much closer than he had been to the procedures of the allegedly more purely empirical art that he had once abhorred."[77] In this sense, Aaron Matz is not quite correct in claiming that Lewis's satire represents "the flight of . . . satire to non-realist territory,"[78] since Lewis's work reengages with realism's mimetic impulse. This reengagement with aspects of a Victorian "satirical realism" also problematizes (again) the notion of the modernist avant-gardes as a rupture with past traditions, since Lewis draws directly on the tradition of Victorian satire in order to revise it: although the "external method" is rigorously mimetic, the content of this mimeticism is radically altered by Lewis's dehumanizing vision. This is so because traditional mimesis, unlike the "external method," was not an objective reproduction of "reality," but rather a representation of reality from a human perspective. Traditional mimeticism tacitly affirms an anthropocentric view of reality because it always presumes a human spectator, or—to rephrase the argument along a Kantian line of thinking—that the object of perception is created by the anthropomorphic contours of perception itself. In this sense, mimesis is an unacknowledged form of humanism.

But the form of representation that Lewis employs in his satire short-circuits the link between mimesis and humanism. This can be seen, to use one small example, in *The Apes of God*'s depiction of a woman getting up out of a chair: *Without fuss the two masses came apart. They were cut open into two pieces.*[79] An everyday act (a woman rising from a chair) is thus rendered in terms that strive to make the commonplace undeniably strange. Moreover, Lewis's description of this event undermines the humanism inherent in traditional mimesis, since people and objects are represented as being of the same order of *things;* both the chair and the woman are simply described as "two masses," as if there were no distinction between them.

Throughout *The Apes of God*, Lewis describes people and events in ways that are consistent with this dehumanizing vision. In the book's opening pages, for example, Lady Fredigonde is portrayed as if she were already one of the walking dead: "There was nothing left in her body. . . . Her arms were made of plaster. . . . She still would exercise her headpiece sharply, upon the ruined clock-work of her trunk."[80] Lewis's description of Fredigonde as a machine or a waxwork paints a thoroughly dehumanized portrait of her; even her internal monologue is lifeless, composed only of "patterns of conversations, with odds and ends from *dead* disputes, and cat's-cradles of this thing and that."[81] Virtually all characters within *The Apes of God* are portrayed as if they were dead objects or perambulating machines. When internal monologue occurs, it does not glorify the free association of the consciousness in motion, as so many other modernists (Joyce, Woolf) do, but focuses rather on the way that consciousness consists of clichéd and received language (as it does for Fredigonde). As the narrator of the novel notes: "This was an all-puppet cast."[82] Lewis's dehumanizing approach to representation (the "external method") critiques traditional mimesis by emptying the human content out of representation. But this critique is enacted through mimesis itself, since Lewis's description maintains a rigid adherence to the external qualities of objects (a tendency, as I mentioned earlier, that has often resulted in critics finding the novel tedious or boring).

Lewis's work thus constitutes a response to the provocations of the modernist avant-gardes, and his new theory of satire can be understood only within the context of the questions raised by the avant-gardes concerning mimeticism, humanism, and the role of art in modernity. Although Lewis called his response to these problems the "external method," in reality, it was something far more significant than a simple technique. Lewis's dehumanizing vision formed part of a larger project that could perhaps be best termed an aestheticized antihumanism (or an antihumanistic aestheticism). In Lewis's thought, art's transcendence appears only through a diminution of the human: art's sovereign position as the sole medium for "truth" derives from its *distance* from a flawed humanity, and art's power—and, indeed, the source of its "truth"—can be located precisely in its *inhumanity*. While presenting a simultaneous critique of mimesis and humanism was often a signal fixation of the modernist avant-gardes,[83] Lewis's re-deployment of mimesis as the "external method" presents one of the most virulent strains of modernist inhumanism in that its very goal becomes nothing less than the removal of the human from representation as such.

The goal of mimeticism in nonmoral satire, then, was to present things that were fundamentally marked by their emptiness and their *absence*. As Peter Nicholls has described it, Lewis enacts a mode of radical representation in which mimesis becomes "a process which somehow *supplements* its model" by means of making its own lack or emptiness part of its gesture.[84] Lewis had already made *absence* one of the bulwarks of his own avant-garde movement of Vorticism, whose aesthetic was perhaps best described (if also in a manner bordering on self-parody), by the character Tarr from the novel of the same name, as an "absence of *soul*, in the sentimental human sense."[85] Lewis's reconception of satire was itself fittingly marked by an absence or a lack, since its defining characteristic lay in being *nonmoral*.

It is thus perhaps unsurprising that *The Apes of God* renders absence as a palpable figure, not only in the absence of any moral grounds or satiric norms (which the novel intentionally undermines), but also in the all-important but forever-absent character of Pierpoint, who organizes all of the action of the plot, and yet is never presented directly to the reader. Pierpoint has all the substance of a rumor, and everything about him is either related secondhand by other characters or appears in "The Encyclical." Pierpoint's absence is necessary within the logic of autonomous satire; if Pierpoint had appeared physically in the novel, he, too, would be subjected to the withering objectification of the satiric eye, and thereby rendered yet another ape of God. It is only through his absence that he can retain his authority, a point he indirectly acknowledges by saying that "the supreme judge [i.e. God] is constantly absent."[86] For Lewis, human judgment, by nature of being embodied and inherently anthropomorphic, can never attain a truly authoritative status—a point reinforced by a marginal note in Lewis's incomplete novel entitled *Joint*: "GOD is NOT an individual. He is the IMPERSONAL impersonified. All definition is negation."[87] As this comment suggests, Lewis believed that human judgments cannot be reconciled with an objective or authoritative ground.

Thus, while satire could not produce definitive judgments of any type, satire could nonetheless be productively recast as an oblique strategy for evading capture by the logic of mimesis. And this is a radical transformation of the satiric tradition, since, for Lewis, satire in the twentieth century becomes the only form adequate for presenting—albeit obliquely—a legitimate alternative to traditional modes of mimetic representation. Satire's dehumanizing mode of representation and its negative self-referential critiques thus present a way of navigating between the Scylla and Charybdis of the views held by the modernist avant-gardes regarding the work of art: presenting neither a naïve belief in its own originality nor a conservative desire to return to a traditional mode of representation that has been superseded, Lewis's self-reflexive satire served as a means of both confronting and ultimately overcoming the linked traditions of humanism and mimesis.

At the same time, however, it is also worth emphasizing that even Lewis's self-reflexive, aesthetic antihumanism betrays elements of a romantic inheritance. As Manfred Frank has argued, romantic self-consciousness can be described as "the epistemic relation of a subject term to itself as an object term."[88] Lewis's dehumanizing vision, which relegates human beings to the status of physical objects, reconfigures this self-reflexivity to a new set of demands. In this sense, the antihumanism of Lewis's satire can be recuperated as a strange humanism, since it reduces the human to an object for the purpose of gaining greater insight into the human (which is precisely the kind of paradoxical reversal that is common in Lewis's thought). In his essay "Physics of the Not-Self" (1925), Lewis argues that all "ultra-human activity is really inhuman."[89]

For Lewis, it is only through an adherence to the notion of the inhuman (which requires the transcendence of the subject) that we can actually hope to become "ultra-human." The true goal of humanism can be achieved only through the *negation* of the human. While it is undeniable that Lewis's inhumanism deeply informed his interest in authoritarian politics,[90] it is also essential to note that an inhuman aesthetics needn't necessarily be authoritarian (nor were Lewis's politics always authoritarian). Such left-leaning theorists as Giorgio Agamben and Francois Lyotard have argued for inhumanism, and the Marxist critic Theodor Adorno noted that Art "is loyal to humanity only through inhumanity toward it."[91]

For Lewis, however, this inhumanist reconception of satire presented a third way of responding to modernity (an aesthetic maneuver perhaps not entirely divorced from Lewis's political interest in alternatives to capitalism and communism, and his shifting allegiances to various forms of radical politics): rather than presenting the universal progressivism of the modernist avant-gardes, or a conservative appeal to tradition, self-reflexive satire attempted both to deploy a radical aesthetics suited for the demands of modernity and to reveal the inadequacy of those very aesthetics through satiric critique. Lewis thus transformed satire from a primarily ethical genre into a self-reflexive genre that offered a preeminent position for thinking through the contradictions of the aesthetics of the modernist avant-gardes, and, as such, satire, for Lewis, became nothing less than the modernist genre par excellence.

At the same time, however, Lewis's theory of satire also inaugurated the subgenre of postromantic satire I have been calling avant-garde satires of the avant-garde. Lewis's satire carries over many attributes of postromantic satire, which were already visible in *Nightmare Abbey*—including a rejection of satire's traditional ethical grounds, a rigorous self-reflexivity, and a recursive satirical critique. But the self-reflexive recursion of postromantic satire is now applied directly to the modernist avant-gardes, which become the subject, object, and context of these satires. As a result, postromantic satire is recalibrated within the milieu of the modernist avant-garde, simultaneously examining the internal contradiction of avant-garde aesthetics while also taking up aspects of the avant-gardes' utopian project. From this point onward, avant-garde satires of the avant-garde will continue to explore and interrogate the aesthetics of the avant-garde throughout the twentieth century and beyond. In so doing, this new subgenre becomes an essential site for understanding both the avant-gardes' overdetermined aesthetics and their continuing influence.

At the same time, this reconfiguration of satire's goals seems to produce yet a final inconsistency in Lewis's notion of "satire for its own sake," since satire here—in attempting to register and respond to a contradictory modernity—can hardly be said to be a self-sufficient entity whose concerns are separate from any larger reality. There is little point in denying that Lewis's attempt to create an autonomous satire cannot be reconciled with his desire for a satire that more adequately responds to modernity. I would argue that this contradiction exemplifies my argument that modernist conceptions of autonomy are aporetic, since they always entail the simultaneous articulation of mutually exclusive claims. At the same time, however, it is worth distinguishing the "purpose" of Lewis's autonomous satire from the purpose behind more traditional satiric forms.

The various purposes that are indirectly advanced by Lewis satire—such as the formation of an alternate and perhaps more "authentic" (albeit ironized and self-reflexive) avant-gardism—do constitute aims that cannot be reconciled with a pure purposelessness. But these aesthetic aims are quite different in character from satire's traditional goal to offer moral inculcation through satiric critique, since the aesthetic purposes of Lewis's satire does not partake of the same means-ends rationality. Put more simply, the purposes behind *The Apes of God* are more open-ended than those of traditional satire, and thus of a different order. Moreover, while—as I have noted—there does remain an implicit register of distinction between good art and bad art in the novel, these distinctions are effectively subordinated to what appears to be a larger and more important series of aesthetic questions.

Whereas traditional satire used an ethical rule to illuminate specific instances of vice, Lewis's satire critiques individual artists *in order to make legible* a larger set of contradictions within the aesthetics of the modernist avant-gardes. In this sense, the procedure of Lewis's satire is essentially the opposite of traditional satire, since it uses the particularity of critique (which is always recursively undermined) as a way of moving toward aesthetic questions, rather than using specific examples to illustrate a normative rule for judgment. Lewis's revision of satire might therefore be considered as a form of purposive purposelessness (although not quite in the sense that Kant employed the term), since the assertion of a "purposeless" satire is used for ends that are *purposive* but also not entirely reconcilable with a didactic telos. While Lewis's satire does not purge itself of all vestiges of instrumentality, it nonetheless marks a stark departure from the normative rules and means-ends rationalism of traditional satire. In so doing, Lewis's satire increasingly orients itself with aesthetic judgments by mimicking their groundless and open-ended nature.

Notes

1 Although not simply reducible to each other, the avant-garde and modernism form a cultural matrix unified in its explicit rejection of traditional means of representation and its desire to locate innovative artistic forms adequate to the task of confronting a novel modernity. Following this logic, I have chosen to use the term "modernist avant-gardes" employed by Sascha Bru in *Democracy, Law, and the Modernist Avant-Gardes: Writing in the State of Exception* (Edinburg: Edinburgh University Press, 2009).

2 Matz, *Satire in an Age of Realism,* 35–36.

3 William Marx, "The Twentieth Century: The Century of the Arrière-Gardes?" *Europa! Europa?: The Avant-Garde, Modernism and the Fate of a Continent,* Eds. Sascha Bru et al. (Berlin: Walter de Gruyter GmbH & Co., 2009), 59.

4 Duve, *Kant After Duchamp,* 302–3.

5 For an excellent summary of this view, see Susan Stanford Friedman, "Definitional Excursions: The Meanings of Modern/Modernity/Modernism," *Disciplining Modernism,* Ed. Pamela L. Caughie (New York: Palgrave Macmillan, 2009), 11.

6 Hans Magus Enzensberger, "The Aporias of the Avant-Garde," 25–27.

7 Jo Anna Isaak, *The Ruin of Representation in Modernist Art and Texts* (Ann Arbor: UMI Research Press, 1986), 3. Peter Nicholls, in "Apes and Familiars: Modernism, Mimesis, and the Work of Wyndham Lewis," *Textual Practice,* 6.3, also notes that the "problem of mimesis appears as the founding condition for modernism itself" (434).

8 Hugh Kenner, in *The Pound Era* (Berkeley; Los Angeles: University of California Press, 1971), emphasizes that Imagisme's assertion of a "direct" connection between word and thing is different from mimetic "mirroring" (178).

9 Jeff Wallace, "Modernists on the Art of Fiction," *The Cambridge Companion to the Modernist Novel,* Ed. Morag Shiach (Cambridge: Cambridge University Press, 2007), 15.

10 Friedman, "Definitional Excursions," 12.

11 Greenberg, *Modernism, Satire, and the Novel,* 27.

12 Friedman, "Definitional Excursions," 24.

13 Brooker, *Bohemia in London,* 137.

14 Ibid., 15.

15 Ibid., 10–23.

16 Ibid., 8.

17 Ibid., 22.

18 Lewis, *Apes of God,* 122.

19 Wyndham Lewis, *Wyndham Lewis the Artist: From "BLAST" to Burlington House* (New York: Haskell House Publishers Ltd., 1939), 20.

20 Ibid., 74.

21 Wyndham Lewis, *Men Without Art* (Santa Rosa, CA: Black Sparrow Press, 1987), 109.

22 Aaron Matz, "The Years of Hating Proust," *Comparative Literature* 60.4 (2008): 355–69.

23 Lewis, *Apes of God,* 272.

24 Ibid., 257.

25 Lewis, *Men Without Art,* 87.

26 Ibid., 87.

27 Greenberg, *Modernism, Satire, and the Novel,* 27.

28 Lewis, *Men Without Art,* 103.

29 Ibid., 104–5.

30 Ibid., 93.

31 Wyndham Lewis, "The Meaning of the Wild Body," *The Complete Wild Body,* Ed. Bernard Lafourcade (Santa Rosa, CA: Black Sparrow Press, 1982), 158.

32 Greenberg, *Modernism, Satire, and the Novel,* 5.

33 Nathan Waddell, "Providing Ridicule: Wyndham Lewis and Satire in the 'Postwar-to-end-war' World," *Utopianism, Modernism, and Literature in the Twentieth Century,* Eds. Alice Reeve-Tucker and Nathan Waddell (London: Palgrave Macmillan, 2013), 59.

34 Ibid., 68.

35 Andrzej Gasiorek, "Wyndham Lewis on Art, Culture and Politics in the 1930s," *Wyndham Lewis and the Cultures of Modernity,* Eds. Alice Reeve-Tucker, Andrzej Gasiorek, and Nathan Waddell (Surrey, England: Ashgate, 2011), 214.

36 Lewis, *Apes of God,* 271.

37 Ibid., 481.

38 Antonio Feijo, *Near Miss: A Study of Wyndham Lewis (1909–1930)* (New York: Peter Lang Publishing, Inc., 1998), 184. Andrzej Gasiorek, *Wyndham Lewis and Modernism* (Horndon, UK: Northcote House Publishers, 2004), 74. Paul Edwards, "*The Apes of God* and the English Classical Tradition," *Wyndham Lewis the Radical: Essays on Literature and Modernity,* Ed. Carmelo Cunchillos Jaime (Bern, Switzerland: Peter Lang AG, 2007), 91–108.

39 Karl Marx, "Scenes from Oulanem: A Tragedy," *The Unknown Karl Marx,* Ed. Robert Payne (London: University of London Press, 1971), 83. Specifically, one character refers to "we Apes of a cold God" (83). Marx's poem has not been previously identified as an intertext in Lewis scholarship. Lewis's allusion to Marx appears to have a dual resonance: not only does *The Apes of God* end with the General Strike of 1926, but also Marx's (very, very bad) poem is heavily indebted

to German Romanticism—which is to say that the young Marx was also an "ape of God" in Lewis's sense. Even more topically, the poem contains multiple references to humans as puppets and machines, and the notion of deadness, which further suggests it as a likely intertext: "Ourselves being clockwork, blindly mechanical . . ./ So Death becomes alive, wears shoes and hose" (81).

40 Tyrus Miller, *Late Modernism: Politics, Fiction, and Arts between the World Wars* (Berkeley: University of California Press, 1999), 236–37. Jameson describes Lewis as a "proto-Fascist." My preference is for the more neutral term "authoritarian." Lewis's early interest in fascism predated any knowledge of the Holocaust and he later renounced any association with German fascism, although he continued to be interested in radical (and often right-wing) politics. It is also true that many assertions in Lewis's writing would, by contemporary standards, rightly be deemed anti-Semitic, sexist, homophobic, and racist. These problematic aspects of Lewis's writing have been extensively critiqued in David Ayers, *Wyndham Lewis and Western Man* (New York: St. Martin's Press, 1992), and in Andrea Freud Lowenstein, *Loathsome Jews and Engulfing Women: Metaphors of Projection in the Works of Wyndham Lewis, Charles Williams, and Graham Greene* (New York; London: New York University Press, 1993), among others. More recent scholarship has examined how Lewis's critique of liberalism resonates with contemporaneous radical, left-wing movements. David Wragg, in *Wyndham Lewis and the Philosophy of Art in Early Modernist Britain* (Lewiston, NY: Edwin Mellon Press, 2006), examines the similarities between Lewis and Theodor Adorno. Alan Munton, in "Wyndham Lewis: From Proudhon to Hitler (and Back): The Strange Political Journey of Wyndham Lewis," *E-rea: Revue Electronique d'Etudes sur le Monde Anglophone*, 4.2 (2006), details Lewis's close and long-running political allegiances with anarchism—which contradict claims that Lewis's politics were essentially or straightforwardly fascist.

41 Wyndham Lewis, *The Art of Being Ruled*, Ed. Reed Way Dasenbrock (Santa Rosa, CA: Black Sparrow Press, 1989), 436.

42 Toby Avard Foshay. *Wyndham Lewis and the Avant-Garde: The Politics of the Intellect* (Montreal: McGill-Queen's University Press, 1992), 81.

43 Hugh Kenner, *Wyndham Lewis, 1886–1957* (London: Methuen, 1954), 100.

44 Timothy Materer, *Wyndham Lewis the Novelist* (Detroit: Wayne State University Press, 1976), 84.

45 Ian Patterson, "Apes, Bodies and Readers," *Volcanic Heaven: Essays on Wyndham Lewis's Painting and Writing*, Ed. Paul Edwards (Santa Rosa, CA: Black Sparrow Press, 1996), 127. See also Daniel Schenker, in *Wyndham Lewis: Religion and Modernism* (Tuscaloosa; London: University of Alabama Press, 1992), 77.

46 Reed Way Dasenbrock, *The Literary Vorticism of Ezra Pound and Wyndham Lewis: Towards the Condition of Painting* (Baltimore: Johns Hopkins University Press, 1985), 169.

47 Scott W. Klein, *The Fictions of James Joyce and Wyndham Lewis: Monsters of Nature and Design* (Cambridge: Cambridge University Press, 1994), 21.

48 Fredric Jameson, *Fables of Aggression: Wyndham Lewis, the Modernist as Fascist* (Berkeley: University of California Press, 1979), 5. See also Martin Puchner, *Poetry of the Revolution: Marx, Manifestos and the Avant-Garde* (Princeton, NJ: Princeton University Press, 2006), 130–31.

49 Thierry Lenain, *Monkey Painting* (London: Reaktion Books, 1997), 47.

50 For more on the use of simian symbolism in Wilmot's satire, see Keith Walker, "Lord Rochester's Monkey (Again)," *That Second Bottle: Essays on the Earl of Rochester,* Ed. Nicholas Fisher (Manchester: Manchester University Press, 2000), 81–88. See also Peter De Gabriele, "Clothes Make the Ape: The Satirical Animal in Rochester's Poetry," *Early Modern Literary Studies* 18.1/2 (2015): 1–15.

51 H.W. Janson, *Apes and Ape-Lore in the Middle Ages and the Renaissance* (London: Warburg Institute, 1952), 338.

52 Ibid.

53 Ibid., 338–42.

54 Thomas Love Peacock, *The Works of Thomas Love Peacock: Headlong Hall, Melincourt, Nightmare Abbey, Maid Marian* (London: George Routledge and Sons, Ltd.), 125.

55 L. Perry Curtis, Jr., *Apes and Angels: The Irishman in Victorian Caricature* (Washington, DC: Smithsonian Institution Press, 1971), 2.

56 Lewis, *Apes of God,* 116. E.T.A. Hoffmann, "Report of an Educated Young Man," *E.T.A. Hoffmann's Musical Writings: Kreisleriana, The Poet and Composer, Music Criticism,* Trans. Martin Clarke (Cambridge: Cambridge University Press, 1989), 136.

57 Robert Currie, "Wyndham Lewis, E.T.A. Hoffmann, and *Tarr,*" *Review of English Studies,* 30.188 (1979): 169–81.

58 Hoffmann, "Report of an Educated Young Man," 136.

59 Ibid., 139.

60 Ibid., 140.

61 Ibid., 142–43.

62 Lewis, *Apes of God,* 123.

63 Ibid., 119.

64 Ibid., 122.

65 Ibid., 123. Lewis's emphasis.

66 Gasiorek, *Wyndham Lewis and Modernism,* 129.

67 Gasiorek, "Wyndham Lewis on Art," 219.

68   Jodie Greenwood, "The Crisis of the System: *Blast's* Reception," *Wyndham Lewis and the Cultures of Modernity,* Eds. Andrzej Gasiorek, Alice Reeve-Tucker, and Nathan Waddell (Surrey, England: Ashgate, 2011), 92.

69   Lewis, *Apes of God,* 20.

70   Ibid., 271.

71   Jameson, *Fables of Aggression,* 136.

72   Jamie Wood, "Lewis, Satire, and Literature," *Wyndham Lewis: A Critical Guide,* Ed. Andrzej Gasiorek and Nathan Waddell (Edinburgh: Edinburgh University Press, 2015), 83.

73   Paul Edwards, "Lewis, Satire, and Portraiture," *The Cambridge Companion to Wyndham Lewis,* Ed. Tyrus Miller (Cambridge: Cambridge University Press, 2015), 80.

74   David Bradshaw, "*The Apes of God,*" *Wyndham Lewis: A Critical Guide,* Ed. Andrzej Gasiorek and Nathan Waddell (Edinburgh: Edinburgh University Press, 2015), 104.

75   Greenberg, *Modernism, Satire, and the Novel,* 31.

76   Ibid., 30.

77   Douglas Mao, *Solid Objects: Modernism and the Test of Production* (Princeton, NJ: Princeton University Press, 1998), 96.

78   Matz, *Satire in an Age of Realism,* 175.

79   Lewis, *Apes of God,* 22.

80   Ibid., 10.

81   Ibid., 13. My emphasis.

82   Ibid., 81.

83   Giorgio Agamben, *Stanzas: Word and Phantasm in Western Culture,* Trans. Ronald L. Martinez (Minneapolis: University of Minnesota Press, 1993), 50. See also Stephen Sicari, *Modernist Humanism and the Men of 1914* (Columbia, SC: University of South Carolina Press, 2011).

84   Nicholls, "*Apes and Familiar,*" 430.

85   Wyndham Lewis, *Tarr: The 1918 Version,* Ed. Paul O'Keefe (Santa Rosa, CA: Black Sparrow Press, 1990), 299–300.

86   Lewis, *Apes of God,* 118.

87   Edwards, *Wyndham Lewis,* 320.

88   Manfred Frank, *The Philosophical Foundations of Early German Romanticism,* Trans. Elizabeth Millan-Zaibert (Albany, NY: SUNY University Press, 2004), 63.

89   Wyndham Lewis, "Physics of the Not-Self," *Collected Poems and Plays,* Ed. Alan Munton (New York: Persea Books, 1979), 198.

90   Lewis, in "Physics of the Not-Self," suggests that strong and wise leaders were marked by their ability to employ the *not-self,* a principle that, among the masses,

"awaken[s] suspicion instead of trust" and acts as "a radio-active something in the midst of more conservative aggregations" (198). A good political leader, employing the not-self, would "be a philosopher" and "dispose of what he rules over, as though he were an indifferent god" (202). For Lewis, the not-self was thus fundamentally incompatible with the democratic belief in popular governance.

91 Theodor Adorno, *Aesthetic Theory,* Trans. Robert Hullot-Kentor (London: The Athlone Press Ltd., 1997), 197.

4

Exhausting Modernism: Satire, Sublimity, and Late Modernism in William Gaddis's *The Recognitions*

1 Satire and late modernism

While Wyndham Lewis viewed self-reflexive satire as a means of revivifying a failed avant-garde, William Gaddis, by the time he published *The Recognitions* in 1955, had good reasons to be more skeptical about the capacity of satire—however radical its form—to enact such cultural change. This ambivalence is reflected at the formal level: whereas Lewis employed a recursively self-ironizing satiric judgment to revise the avant-garde, *The Recognitions* amplifies the indeterminacy of its satiric judgment for the purpose of generating a prolonged textual uncertainty that, in many cases, cannot be decisively resolved. The novel presents a wearied disinclination to disambiguate these indefinite judgments. I will also argue that *The Recognitions* attacks exhausted, modernist concepts in order to reassert them apophatically in a purified form. Such apophasis produces what I will call an "ambivalent sublime" that implicitly posits the superiority of art over logical discourses—a gesture that both intensifies and attenuates the effects of avant-garde satire. Before making these claims, however, I will argue that the novel's reticence to clarify its own judgments is linked to a set of aesthetic practices that are constitutive of "late modernism."[1] In making this connection, I am following Lisa Siraganian's argument that Gaddis should be considered an exemplary late modernist.[2]

Late modernism is a term that accounts for those works produced from the 1930s to the 1970s (and possibly beyond),[3] which simultaneously perpetuate and critique various aspects of the modernist avant-gardes' aesthetic project. Late modernism is crucial for understanding both *The Recognitions'* satire and its relation to the modernist avant-gardes, because late modernism refers to the fraught cultural contradictions that appeared once the modernist avant-gardes had been absorbed into European and Anglophone high culture and began to exert an important, and arguably dominant, influence over the elites in control of large cultural institutions, such as universities, museums, galleries, and both public and private funding bodies.[4] As Jeremy Braddock has argued, the modernist avant-gardes entered the literary canon through the work of academic scholars associated with the "New Criticism,"[5] as well as the efforts of public-sphere critics like T.S. Eliot (an exemplary modernist himself). But such success created an intolerable contradiction: as standard-bearers of elite culture, the modernist avant-gardes could no longer claim to be "outsiders" rebelling against tradition—the oppositional critique that had initially provided their (false) justification. As Peter Bürger has argued, the avant-gardes' institutional triumph effectively led to their exhaustion, because they had absorbed into the aesthetic traditions they had sought to overturn.

This exhaustion produced a variety of effects, but two are particularly important for understanding *The Recognitions'* relation to the modernist avant-gardes. First, the increased prominence of avant-garde artists, led to the commodification of the avant-garde persona, which, as Robert Genter notes, had been "quickly absorbed by the culture industry" as the "image of the chain-smoking, half-drunk, romantic artist slinging paint across canvases . . . even before the suicidal gestures of Pollock and Kerouac."[6] The prevalence of this caricature threatened to reduce the avant-garde artist to little more than the cliché of the enfant terrible, whose "rebellious" gestures were merely the performative expression of the artist's ego. Unlike the earlier modernists who wished to distance themselves from the clichéd image of the Victorian dandy, late modernists wished to preserve many of modernism's aesthetic goals, while resisting popular portrayals of modernist artists as romanticized outsiders. As a result, late modernist texts, in general, and *The Recognitions,* in particular, disparage the figure of the artist, whose persona threatens to overshadow the work of art.

This contradiction also created a double bind for those following in the modernists' footsteps. Gaddis belongs to this generation for whom, as Jonathan Greenberg notes, "modernism had already happened."[7] Born in 1922, the year when both Joyce's *Ulysses* and Eliot's *The Waste Land* were published, Gaddis was keenly aware that the avant-gardes had not overturned tradition and had been appropriated by cultural institutions. On one hand, the attempt to perpetuate the avant-garde project of rupture thus seemed doomed in advance. On the other hand, appropriating avant-garde techniques as the basis of a new literary tradition seemed equally problematic, since this appropriation conflicted with the avant-garde imperative for radical originality. Avant-garde aesthetics thus appeared to be a dead end, which produced a sense of desperation among late modernists: "As Henry Green noted, Joyce and Kafka were for his generation 'cats who ha[d] licked the plate clean.'"[8] Late modernist authors thus worked within a fundamentally unresolvable contradiction: they desired to continue the project of the modernist avant-gardes, while also believing such a project to be fundamentally unrealizable.

Late modernism, with its fixation on belatedness and exhaustion, is born out of this contradictory position: it reflects the desire to reappropriate, continue, or surpass the work of the modernist avant-gardes while simultaneously acknowledging that these goals can't be reached. As Cheryl Hindrichs notes, "It is the historical context of 'lateness,' of an awareness of being at a moment of ending and judgment, that most reshapes the topography of modernism in late modernism. The 'new' that underwrote high modernism had become by the thirties and forties impossible or repugnant."[9] Thus, while late modernist works retain the formal innovation, obscurity, and difficulty that are typically associated with the modernist avant-gardes, late modernism nonetheless differs from its immediate precursor (although many exemplary avant-gardists subsequently produced paradigmatic examples of late modernism) in its skepticism of originality, novelty, or rupture with tradition. As Jonathan Greenberg notes, "For the late modernists, sexual transgression had lost its shock, revolutionary manifestoes had lost their urgency, and innovation had lost its originality"; as a result, late modernists also tended to be far more pessimistic about the ability of art to instigate meaningful social change or attain a state of radical originality.[10] Late modernist works reflect the fraught inheritance of an exhausted avant-garde, by counterpoising the avant-garde desire for transcendence with an overwhelming sense of the impossibility of achieving such transcendence. The result is a deeply ambiguous body of literature that pursues oblique and self-reflexive strategies to prolong and sustain this ambiguity rather than resolving it.

I will follow Lisa Siraganian in classifying *The Recognitions* as a novel whose thematic fixations and unusual formal techniques mark it as an exemplary work of late modernism.[11] Like most late modernist works, the novel signals its debts to the modernist avant-gardes at a formal level, through its length, density, allusiveness, and nonlinear composition. The sheer accumulation of details that recur in subtle variations across the text's 956 pages produces a "difficulty" also characteristic of the modernist avant-gardes: jokes may not receive their punch-lines for hundreds of pages; party scenes sprawl with unattributed dialogue and little discernible advancement of the plot; the narrative is swollen with digressions on obscure topics, such as Christian theology, the processes used to counterfeit money, and the painting technique of Flemish masters. But these displays of encyclopedic knowledge and formal inventiveness are accompanied by a deep ambivalence about the kind of virtuosic, avant-garde technique that the novel itself employs. Various characters in the book are skeptical as to whether twentieth-century art—for all of its formal achievement—can attain the lofty goals that it sets for itself. And the novel returns again and again to themes—unoriginality, appropriation, mimicry, plagiarism, and counterfeiting—that resonate with the late modernist view that the modernist avant-gardes had exhausted in advance the work of their successors.

It is appropriate, therefore, that *The Recognitions* largely follows the life and career of the art forger, Wyatt Gwyon. After the death of his mother, Camilla, Gwyon is raised by his father, who is a preacher, and by his Aunt May in a strict, Puritan household. Despite his exceptional artistic talent (evident in his ability to copy great works), Wyatt is prepared by his parents for entry into the seminary; rather than following this path, he counterfeits a Hieronymus Bosch painting in his father's possession, which he then sells to fund a trip to study art in Europe. When his first art exhibition fails because he refuses to bribe a critic in exchange for a positive review, Wyatt returns to America, where he meets a shady art dealer, Recktall Brown, with whom he strikes a Faustian bargain to forge Flemish paintings. After suffering a crisis of conscience, Wyatt attempts (and fails) to expose his own fraud, and then flees to Europe where he (ambiguously) either goes mad or departs for an unknown destination in an attempt to start a new life. The last section of the novel follows various other characters in the book, a great many of whom die in bleakly comic ways. Rife with seemingly "original" art that turns out to be anything but, the novel is preoccupied by the aesthetic problems that the late modernists inherited from the modernist avant-gardes.

But while late modernist works problematize their relation to the modernist avant-gardes, late modernism (as its name suggests) also continues the avant-garde project in an altered form. Late modernism thus presents a strange survival of the modernist avant-gardes; as Anthony Mellors argues, "If modernism dissolved, its solution was more modernism."[12] If *The Recognitions* simply rejected avant-garde aesthetics by revealing their groundlessness, it would be more correctly characterized as a *postmodern* novel, rather than a late modernist one. As I will argue, one of the most effective ways to understand late modernism is to contrast it with postmodernism. While both respond critically to the modernist avant-gardes, late modernism reaffirms elements of this earlier project, but postmodernism rejects most (if not quite all[13]) of the foundational principles of the modernist avant-gardes—especially their assertion of aesthetic autonomy.

The term postmodernism was hotly debated within the academy for several decades. The canonical texts on the subject—such as Jean-Francois Lyotard's *The Postmodern Condition: A Report on Knowledge* (1979) and Fredric Jameson's *Postmodernism, or the Cultural Logic of Late Capitalism* (1991)—not only disagree on key points, but also have inspired an extensive secondary literature that continues the debate. Although a definitive account of postmodernism is beyond the scope of my argument, a discussion of several of its key features is necessary to conceptualize late modernism. As is well known, postmodernism presents as an "incredulity toward metanarratives" that seek to legitimate themselves through "an explicit appeal to some grand narrative, such as the dialectics of Spirit, the hermeneutics of meaning, the emancipation of the rational or working subject, or the creation of wealth."[14] The result of this incredulity is the "displacement of the 'grand narratives' of history" with "multiple language games,"[15] which is to say that postmodernists view grand theories as the products of complex discursive systems. By thus drawing attention to "the constructedness of social reality,"[16] postmodern works of art deny the authority once assumed by traditional social institutions.

Postmodernism critiques modernist aesthetics by attacking the relationship between this aesthetic discourse and the "truths" that are their authorizing grounds. While this postmodernist critique comprises more than an aesthetic shift (postmodern aesthetics have typically been linked to the changed modes of economic production and consumption under late capitalism[17]), it produced new aesthetic preferences: postmodern works display certain stylistic tendencies—such as a preference for pastiche and the play of surfaces that reflect a variety of experiences or "intensities,"[18] including fetishization, "schizophrenic" euphoria, and the waning of affect.[19] These tendencies are starkly different from the aesthetics of modernism, which sought to shock and provoke its audiences (still clinging to a Victorian moralism) by being "dissonant, obscure, scandalous, immoral, subversive, and generally 'antisocial.'"[20] This provocation was, as Jameson argues, "hermeneutical": modernist works encouraged their audience to view the work of art itself "as a clue or a symptom for some vaster reality which replaces it as its ultimate truth."[21] Postmodernism overturned modernist aesthetics by eschewing "ultimate truth" for the exploration of surface effects that were unique to the experience of a hyper-commodified late capitalism, upon which modernist art could no longer gain critical purchase.

If postmodernism overturns or repudiates modernism, then late modernism critiques the modernist avant-gardes in order to refine and revise their central aesthetic concepts. While late modernist works like *The Recognitions* reject modernist accounts of originality and authenticity, they still view the aesthetic as a privileged site for representing and contesting social, political, and philosophical problems.[22] As Fredric Jameson has argued, late modernists preserve modernism's key feature: the notion of art as a wholly autonomous space. The ideology of modernism "is first and foremost that which posits the autonomy of the aesthetic," and what this autonomy does is "endow the aesthetic with a transcendental value which is incomparable (and indeed which does not need to be completed with descriptions of the structure of other kinds of experience, social or psychological; which stands on its own and needs no external justification)."[23] My argument is that *The Recognitions* preserves this notion of aesthetic autonomy—especially in the sense of the aesthetic being a *totalizing* experience that "does not need to be completed" by "other kinds of experience" or discourses. Later, I will examine how the novel's employment of an unusual form of the sublime reaffirms the exceptional nature of aesthetic works through their capacity to exceed the binaries of formal logic.

Nonetheless, aesthetic autonomy in *The Recognitions* is always affirmed indirectly, in a typically late modernist gesture also bound up with the novel's self-reflexive satire. Rather than producing grounded judgments, *The Recognitions* creates radical indeterminacy around the objects of its satire by rehearsing a series of claims and counterclaims that simultaneously support and undermine the novel's satiric critique. As a result of this contradictory evidence, the validity of satiric judgment is rendered indeterminate; *The Recognitions*' ambiguous method of undermining satiric judgment presents as an intensification of the "staged reversals" already deployed in *The Apes of God*. At the same time, this critique of satiric judgment spills over into a critique of aesthetic judgment, which is revealed to operate on similarly faulty premises. In so doing, the novel reveals the groundless nature of a variety of the modernist avant-gardes' key aesthetic principles, including notions of originality and novelty. But these critiques paradoxically enable the novel to reaffirm modernist aesthetic autonomy through apophatic methods. Once again, modernist autonomy is the product of logically contradictory claims.

Through this apophatic reaffirmation, *The Recognitions* purifies the modernist avant-gardes' aesthetics by excising their exhausted content, a process I will demonstrate in relation to two concepts—genius and aesthetic autonomy—central to the novel's concerns. In both cases, the novel attacks these notions to reassert them in a form purged of exhausted content. Finally, I will argue that the novel's apophatic affirmation culminates in the production of the "ambivalent sublime"—an overdetermined sublimity that both prolongs the ambiguity typical of late modernism and affirms the aesthetic as a privileged locus of meaning.

2 Indeterminacy and judgment

Like Lewis's *The Apes of God, The Recognitions* consciously undermines the validity of its own satiric judgment (and, ultimately, as I will argue, its satiric authority). But it achieves this end by different means. Rather than overturning prior satiric judgments in a series of "staged reversals," *The Recognitions* places the reader in a zone of indistinction, in which the legitimacy of satiric judgment remains unknowable. This textual production of radical uncertainty is typical of late modernist works, and reflects their own overdetermined aesthetics. As Tyrus Miller has noted, late modernism's characteristic gesture is the leveling of seemingly opposed qualities: "The vectors of despair and utopia, the compulsion to decline and the impulse to renewal are not just related; they are practically indistinguishable."[24] *The Recognitions* participates in this same project because its satiric judgments render ambiguous the act of judgment itself.

While the novel's satire might ultimately produce this uncertainty, its initial satiric targets—much like in *The Apes of God*—seem relatively clear. *The Recognitions* targets avant-garde and bohemian artists of New York's Greenwich Village "scene" of the 1950s. The novel's targets—and, indeed, the trans-Atlantic jump in my analysis of self-reflexive satire—reflect the fact that, by the 1950s, the center of gravity of avant-garde production had shifted from European capitals to the United States in general and New York City in particular. As Lisa Siraganian notes, this cultural shift reflected an economic one, as the New York art market rapidly expanded to become the most significant global site of art consumption, due both to the rise of a new generation of "super-rich collectors" and a popular demand for reproductions of classic artworks.[25]

The Recognitions stages this shift by setting its narrative in both New York and—at important points in the story—Paris and other European centers of culture; one of the novel's wry observations is that the bohemian elites of Greenwich Village travel overseas en masse, replicating their cultural surroundings abroad. The novel includes two montage-like depictions of US cultural tourists in Paris toward the beginning and the end of the novel.[26] In so doing, the novel reflects an awareness of how bohemian cultures tapped into transnational networks connecting both old and new urban centers of cultural production. As Richard Miller argues, these networks—which connected both major metropolitan US centers like New York and San Francisco, as well as international locales like Paris and Tangiers—were greatly expanded by the Beat writers, whose privileging of "the road" and a vagabond existence encouraged the establishment and maintenance of informal connections between local cultural scenes; as he describes through a somewhat unfortunate metaphor, the Beat network was "an underground railroad connecting a series of stations and terminals . . . through which hitching, driving, riding in boxcars, the same population flowed."[27] *The Recognitions*' satire suggests that the modernist avant-gardes—rather than bequeathing a revolution of art—produced a jet-setting, cultural elite, which increasingly imposed their particular tastes and fashions on the broader world. This critique further reveals Gaddis's allegiances to late modernism, since, as Greenberg has noted, "Late modernism . . . turns modernist skepticism against modernism's own revolutionary and romantic tendencies."[28]

The Recognitions also directs its satire toward specific, contemporaneous avant-garde movements, such as Abstract Expressionism. To take one key example, which Lisa Siraganian has also analyzed at length, many of the characters attend a party thrown in honor of a new "painting" that appears to be a parody of this contemporary avant-garde:

> No one was looking at [the painting]. The unframed canvas was tan. Across the middle a few bright spots of red lead had been spattered. The spots in the lower left-hand corner were rust, above them long streaks of green paint, and to the upper right a large smudge of what appeared to be black grease. It looked as though the back of an honest workman's shirt had been mounted for exhibition, that the sleeves, collar, and tails might be found among the rubble in the fireplace.[29]

Several aspects of the painting, particularly the "spattered" spots of paint mixed with "long streaks," explicitly recall abstract expressionism.[30] Moreover, the painting—which appears to be composed of a workman's shirt[31]—rearticulates a link between avant-garde gestures and fashion, since the painting is made from a piece of clothing that represents the affected, hypermasculine, working-class sensibility associated with abstract expressionism.[32] The suggestion, then, is that the painting is ephemeral and fashionable, invoking a set of trendy signifiers that indicate the work's cutting-edge aesthetics. This fashionable, intellectual posturing is also reflected by the painting's viewers, who respond to it with a mishmash of art-world jargon.[33]

As the reader soon learns, this fraudulent work of art was produced by Max, who seems to be the ultimate artist manqué. In Max's first appearance in the novel (which is mediated through the consciousness of the character Otto, an outwardly sympathetic if ironized self-portrait of Gaddis as a young man[34]), his smile is described as the product of "disarming calculation," which mimics openness in order to gain the "confidences" of those he intends to manipulate; Otto "mistrusts him accordingly" and wishes "to carry a gun, not to flourish, certainly not to fire, simply to feel it heavily protective under his arm."[35] This perspectival introduction has a palpable effect on the reader who is induced to view Max as a manipulator and fraud.

This initial impression of Max is fleshed out through a series of fragmented anecdotes, rumors, and snatches of conversation, which, taken in concert, build a circumstantial, but compelling case that Max is, if anything, worse than Hoffmann's Milo or the Bloomsbury Apes. Whereas Lewis's apes were unaware of their indebtedness, Max is simply a plagiarist. Of his book, *Wild Goose Chase,* his publisher remarks that "the whole God-damned novel is lifted."[36] Max also publishes a poem under his own name in a literary journal, which turns out to be a translation of one of Rilke's *Duino Elegies.*[37] Max's visual art is similarly cribbed; one character notes that his abstract paintings are "all fragments lifted right out of Constable canvases."[38] Another claims that Max obtains his artwork from his mistress, the wife of a famous painter, who gives Max "her husband's unfinished canvases that he's discarded and forgotten about, and Max touches them up and sells them as originals."[39] These slowly accruing anecdotes depict Max as a fraud and perpetual borrower of ideas, whom one character in the novel names "Max Rilke Constable"[40] in honor of the artists he steals from.

Although this portrayal is consonant with the late modernist tendency to view contemporary art as exhausted and hopelessly unoriginal, it also seems to present a stable, ethically grounded satire, in which explicit satiric targets are held up for mockery as a result of specific vices (i.e., engaging in fraud and plagiarism). But this satiric portrait of Max is contradicted by other evidence within the novel. In a gesture characteristic of *The Recognitions'* satire, every damning anecdote about Max is contradicted elsewhere in the book.

While Max's publisher seems to think his novel is plagiarized, another character recognizes the story as a thinly veiled fictionalization of his friend's real-life experiences, noting, "You could sue that wise bastard."[41] Max's plagiarism of Rilke was also probably unintentional; another character claims it only occurred because Esme gave Max the poem and "asked him to have it published under his name . . . in case people didn't like it" (although this story is not wholly accurate, either).[42] The claim that Max has plagiarized Constable appears to be one character's attempt to sound intelligent by regurgitating elements of an overheard conversation.[43] As to Max stealing canvases from a better-known artist, we are later told that Max actually paints pictures for a famous painter who then sells them as his own.[44] Even the seemingly unimpeachable claim that Max is a fraudulent and second-rate artist is open to question; Max's art may not be very original, but virtually everyone acknowledges that he is not without talent and actually possesses a good understanding of composition, space, and form.[45] While Max is initially depicted as a fraudulent artist, the criteria for judging him thusly is undermined by this wealth of contradictory information, making it difficult to form a confident judgment of him as an artist or as a person.

What had previously been a satiric judgment of a vicious character now appears as an irresolvable indeterminacy. Instead of presenting definitive satiric judgments, *The Recognitions'* satire produces a complicated web of claims and counterclaims that positions its apparent satiric targets in a zone of indistinction where they are simultaneously portrayed as blameworthy and innocent. Since judgments are not definitive, it is left up to the reader to assess their validity in the face of contradictory evidence. While this strategy resembles Wyndham Lewis's staged reversals of satiric norms within *The Apes of God*, Gaddis's undermining of satiric judgment in *The Recognitions* intensifies Lewis's method: not only are apparent norms revealed as illusory, but also readers are presented with excessive information that both supports and contradicts the satiric judgments.

This indeterminacy levels the distinction between seemingly praiseworthy characters and the targets of satire. Traditional satires make sharp distinctions between the virtuous and the vicious, but *The Recognitions* strategically sets up such distinctions only to subvert them. For example, by introducing Max to the reader from Otto's perspective, Otto and Max appear to be established as foils for each other: the virtuous but naïve Otto (an explicit avatar of Gaddis) is contrasted with Max, who possesses a cynical desire to attain worldly success by any means, no matter how immoral. But these differences erode over the course of the book. Max, for example, points out that Otto has plagiarized long sections of a play he is writing from Henry de Montherlant.[46] As the character Herschel notes, "Nobody's named Otto any more, he must be an imposter."[47] And, in a sense, Herschel is right: having just returned from Central America where he worked on a banana plantation, Otto has donned a fake sling, claiming his arm was injured in a civil war. Later in the novel, Otto mimics Wyatt's unusual mannerisms, repeats Wyatt's insights and ideas as if they were his own, and even beds Wyatt's estranged wife, all of which emphasizes Otto's status as a copycat.[48]

The uncertainty of these satiric judgments also implicitly registers a more generalized critique of judgment in all of its forms. As the contradictory information about Max indicates, judgment in *The Recognitions* manifests itself as a binary oversimplification of a complex reality that is distorted by the process of judgment itself. In so doing, *The Recognitions* foregrounds the limitations of satiric judgment, which can register only virtue and vice, and is therefore powerless to make finer distinctions than its either/or logic allows. The ethical judgments of traditional satire, in which characters are deemed malicious or honorable, are thus revealed as a fictitious construct rather than the revelation of a deeper reality. The goal of *The Recognitions'* satire, then, is not to reveal the vice and folly of its satiric targets, but to throw light onto the practice of satiric judgment itself by showing that the binary outcomes of such judgments are a product of the process of judgment itself. While this goal constitutes a "purpose," this purposiveness is, once again, quite different from the means-ends rationality associated with the didacticism of traditional satire.

This uncertainty is not limited to satiric judgments: the flawed nature of aesthetic judgment in *The Recognitions* is also revealed when Wyatt Gwyon's forgeries of Flemish masterpieces are accepted as the "real" thing. Wyatt's work corrodes the grounds of both subjective and theoretically objective judgments, since his forgeries have managed to pass all available scientific tests.[49] Once again judgment becomes the fictitious result of a bifurcating logic: just as characters in the novel are deemed to be either virtuous or immoral, paintings are forgeries or originals. Such outcomes in the novel do not really pertain to reality, but are the product of a language game whose result must always be unambiguous. By representing judgment in this way, *The Recognitions* inverts its traditional relationship with authority: judgments are not authorized through reference to a stable or absolute ground, such as the ethical authority of the satirist or the aesthetic expertise of the critic, but, instead, it is the very act of judgment that produces authorization.

In *The Recognitions,* authorization reflects a human consensus rather than an objective reality. What counts in the modern world of *The Recognitions* is not the true provenance of Wyatt's paintings, but only what they are *judged* to be (forgeries or originals). In this sense, judgment and authorization become mutually reinforcing concepts that rely on each other—rather than a stable ground—to produce their effect. This implicit critique of judgment is then re-marshaled as a means to satirize aspects of the modernist avant-gardes' aesthetics, such as originality and authenticity, which are unveiled as epiphenomena of authorized judgment rather than qualities inherent to the work of art.

Max explicates the problematic relationship between authenticity, originality, and authorization in a conversation about "'the first *authorized* Sherlock Holmes story to appear' since Arthur Conan Doyle died"—a story not written by Doyle but rather by two men who have studied "Doyle's sentence rhythms, his use of the comma, the number of words in the average Holmes sentence."[50] While Otto and Stanley express concern over these stories being passed off as the "real" thing, Max states that you can make a new Dürer painting "by taking the face from one and turning it around, the beard from another, the hat from another"; what matters, according to Max, is not the provenance of the work, but whether or not it's been "authorized."[51] Max's critique assumes that neither originality nor artistic style are intrinsically meaningful. As Max suggests—in an anticipation of Foucault's concept of the author-function[52]—an artist's individual style (which comprises an artist's originality and authenticity) is only a series of signifiers that have been collected and *authorized* under a specific name. As a consequence, Max argues there is no contradiction in having new, "authorized" Sherlock Holmes stories. It is Stanley and Otto's nostalgia for originality that seems atavistic.

At this moment, *The Recognitions'* critique of judgment appears to attack the modernist avant-gardes' privileged aesthetic notions, such as originality, formal innovation, personal style, and authenticity. As Max suggests, these aesthetic concepts—put forward as objective or transcendental qualities—are grounded in arbitrary social practices derived from a contingent, historical tradition. Just as satirical judgments derive from the language game of judgment, judgments regarding originality have no meaning outside of the context of Western aesthetics, and thus are a product of this discourse, rather than external to it. In revealing originality and judgment as convenient and contingent social fictions, *The Recognitions* appears to offer an unhedged critique of the modernist avant-gardes.

But if *The Recognitions* wholeheartedly embraced this critique of the aesthetic, it would become a postmodern text because this critique—and the implicit relativist attitudes toward art and culture accompanying it—would resonate with postmodernism's suspicion of metanarratives and rejection of grounded discourses, such as aesthetic autonomy. Instead, *The Recognitions*—as a late modernist text—peers over the abyss of relativism, only to pull back from the edge and reaffirm autonomy at the last second. Because of the strange form of *The Recognitions*' satire, however, this reaffirmation cannot be straightforwardly explicated, but must take an apophatic form.

3 Apophaticism and self-reflexive satire

Despite *The Recognitions*' apparent attack on the aesthetics of modernism, the novel reaffirms several of the modernist avant-gardes' key aesthetic concepts through an oblique strategy of radical negation that draws, as Christopher J. Knight has noted, on the tradition of negative theology.[53] But the novel's apophaticism can be understood only in relation to its self-reflexive satire as a tactic for both critiquing and reappropriating the aesthetics of the modernist avant-gardes—an intentionally contradictory, late modernist gesture. Apophaticism presents a method for ambivalently acknowledging and overcoming exhaustion, which recalls Derrida's conception of the rhetorical significance of apophasis: "Negative Theology means (to say) very little, almost nothing, perhaps something other than something. Whence its inexhaustible exhaustion."[54] Since the relentless negation of postromantic satire precludes any positive program that might establish explicit satiric norms, *The Recognitions* deploys apophatic gestures to reassert the modernist avant-gardes' notion of aesthetic autonomy obliquely.

As Christopher J. Knight has pointed out,[55] the novel indicates its apophaticism when Wyatt (the novel's protagonist and an art forger) states that he has "been trying to make negative things do the work of positive ones."[56] The novel even acknowledges the resonance between its self-reflexive satire and the oblique strategy of a *via negativa* by mocking its own apophatic tendencies: in a running gag that recurs over the first half of the novel, an unnamed character refers to himself variously as a "negative positivist" and a "positive negativist."[57] Elsewhere, both Wyatt and Stanley describe their notions of the "true" purpose of art in an apophatic mode, saying only that it should aim for "something higher."[58]

The Recognitions' apophaticism constitutes a two-step process in which the novel 1) relentlessly satirizes a variety of the modernist avant-gardes' key aesthetic concepts, such as originality, genius, and autonomy, and then 2) undermines this satiric critique through a dialogic indeterminacy in order to reassert indirectly this same aesthetic concept in a "purified" fashion. *The Recognitions'* satirical negations thus serve a "positive" function, since its self-reflexive satire tears down the aesthetics of the modernist avant-gardes, removing the contradictions of an earlier modernism, in order to assert a pure art. I will illustrate this phenomenon by examining how the novel indirectly reasserts two "exhausted" aesthetic concepts: genius and autonomy.

These two concepts are intimately linked, since genius forms the groundless ground from which the autonomous work of original art springs.[59] Although characters within *The Recognitions* appear to be obsessed with the *concept* of genius (and the word appears in the book more than twenty times), most dismiss it as naïve romanticism. Recktall Brown says, "Most of what we call genius around us is simply warped talent"; he accordingly dismisses the possibility of genius in a fallen modernity, although he describes Wyatt's forged paintings as "damn near . . . genius."[60] In perhaps the most important critique of genius within the novel, Wyatt argues that the concept fundamentally misapprehends the relationship between the work of art and the artist who created it:

> This passion for wanting to meet the latest poet, shake hands with the latest novelist, get hold of the latest painter, devour . . . what is it? What is it they want from a man that they didn't get from his work? What do they expect? What is there left of him when he's done his work? What's any artist, but the dregs of his work? the human shambles that follows it around. What's left of the man when the work's done but a shambles of apology.[61]

Instead of viewing genius as the grounds of the work of art, Wyatt reduces the figure of the genius to something like the precipitate left by an alchemical reaction—"the dregs" of the work. What we are left with is not the figure of the artist as genius, but of the artist as human, all too human. On the face of it, then, Wyatt's claim presents a strident rejection of the grounds of both originality and autonomy.

But this denigration of genius indirectly reaffirms the transcendent capacities of the autonomous work of art. Wyatt's critique suggests that, in modernity, the transcendent capacity of the work of art has been conflated with the human "genius" who created it. For Wyatt, genius presents a threat to aesthetic autonomy because the artist becomes more important than the work itself. Wyatt's critique of genius, then, apophatically reasserts the value of the autonomous work, as this exchange between Esther and Wyatt suggests: "—Genius in itself is essentially uninteresting. —But the work of genius . . ."[62] From Wyatt's perspective any truly autonomous aesthetics must denigrate the human figure of the artist in order to valorize the transcendent *work* of genius (and it is in this gesture that Gaddis's aesthetics also partake of an inhumanism, which Wyatt succinctly sums up by saying, "All of our highest goals are inhuman ones."[63]). The novel's approach to genius offers a glimpse of the purpose behind its relentless negation: a concept like genius is reduced to absurdity so that it can be indirectly affirmed in a form purged of its exhausted historical connotations.

The novel approaches aesthetic autonomy through this same apophatic method—albeit in a more complicated fashion. On a surface level, *The Recognitions* savagely denigrates the notion of aesthetic autonomy: the character Anselm parodies art for art's sake as "Arse gratias artis,"[64] and Recktall Brown states baldly, "Art today is spelled with an *f*. You know that. Anybody knows that."[65] In the novel's most extensive attack on aesthetic autonomy, the composer Stanley argues that autonomous art is little more than a symptom of a "diseased"[66] and fallen modernity. He claims that, in classical times, the work of art had to "fit into one whole, and express an entire perfect action, as Aristotle says," but this approach is "impossible now," because we live in an accelerated modernity so fragmented that "we can't even conceive of a continuum of time."[67] For Stanley, modernity's temporal fragmentation has deleterious effects on both artists and audiences: because bodies of work require a continuous sense of time (which no longer exists), modern artists have created autonomous, individual works that "try to get all the parts together into one work that will stand by itself and serve the same thing a lifetime of separate works does, something higher than itself."[68] Stanley thus suggests that, instead of constituting a heroic and decisive break with tradition, autonomous works produced by the modernist avant-gardes derive from modernity's flawed relationship to temporality. The modernist avant-gardes were thus not radically innovative, but rather the product of a modernity incapable of comprehending itself, resulting in "the great disease, this plague of newness."[69]

Worse still, aesthetic autonomy, for Stanley, contributes to the sense of alienation experienced under modernity; art's claims to "originality" and "self-sufficiency" turn it into a "religion of perfect form and beauty,"[70] which produces a "gulf" between the public and professional artists.[71] In extricating themselves from the everyday world, autonomous artworks also isolate themselves from their potential audience. Stanley views aesthetic autonomy as a self-defeating concept, because, in asserting its independence from social institutions and legitimizing discourses (such as religion or artistic tradition), art only reveals its emptiness, its lack of content: "Nothing is self-sufficient, even art, and when art isn't an expression of something higher . . . it breaks up into fragments that don't have any meaning."[72]

Despite its vehemence, Stanley's critique constitutes a reactionary desire for grounded certainties, as evidenced by his belief that "some transcendent *judgment* is necessary."[73] But Stanley's desire for objective or transcendent judgment contradicts *The Recognitions*' satirical unveiling of judgment as a contingent process without legitimizing ground. What Stanley desires is the very thing that the novel presents as impossible. Stanley's lament expresses what Lyotard calls a "nostalgia for presence,"[74] which views modernity as fallen and corrupt rather than a progressive rupture with tradition. Lyotard argues such nostalgia is the opening gesture of a modernist sublime: the lost "presence" of modernity constitutes the negative moment of sublimity which is then reconciled through the sensual pleasures of style and form that continue "to offer the reader or spectator material for consolation and pleasure."[75] Stanley's critique invokes a modernist aesthetics of nostalgia, and covertly rearticulates modernist sublimity.

This nostalgic mode of the modernist sublime appears in what is usually considered one of the novel key scenes, involving Wyatt—who has a "recognition" in front of a Picasso painting. Wyatt shares Stanley's belief that modernity is fallen and degraded and also desires grounded certainties[76]—a point Wyatt emphasizes when he states that he desires recognition for his work, "but not from you, and not from them, from the thing itself."[77] Wyatt's later sublime "recognition" is a particularly fraught moment in the novel: there are good reasons to suspect that Gaddis even intended this scene to depict a privileged or "pure" encounter with a work of art. If nothing else, it certainly presents the most detailed account of one of the "recognitions" to which the novel's title refers. Richard Eldridge and Paul Cohen have read Wyatt's encounter in exactly these terms, arguing that "Gaddis appears to be suggesting that art can sometimes reveal truths to us all, and it looks as though engaging with genuine art will allow us to grasp a higher reality, despite whatever conditions surround us."[78]

Nonetheless, I will argue that the novel's later deployment of a different form of sublimity—which I am calling the "ambivalent sublime"—undermines the notion that Wyatt's experience constitutes an aesthetic ideal. This conflict between Gaddis's apparent intent and the novel's internal logic, however, is not surprising. Many of the sentiments expressed in Gaddis's interviews, essays, and letters suggest an affinity for the nostalgic aesthetics advocated by Stanley and Wyatt, such as when Gaddis states that "the process of art is the artist's working out of his own redemption."[79] Whatever Gaddis's stated beliefs, however, I will seek to demonstrate how the novel inverts and undermines Stanley and Wyatt's claims. This contradiction between Gaddis's apparent "intent" and the effect of the novel serves as yet another reminder that modernist autonomy is generated through a contradictory transcendence of authorial intention, rather than its straightforward enactment.

Wyatt's experience in front of Picasso's *Night Fishing at Antibes* draws heavily on the "plot" of the Kantian sublime. The Kantian sublime is typically seen to comprise three stages. First, the subject is confronted with a sublime object whose "magnitude" cannot adequately be established by the "aesthetic estimation" of the imagination in a manner that corresponds with reason's own estimation of the sublime object's magnitude; this disagreement between reason and the imagination produces a "a feeling of pain" in the subject, but this feeling of pain is accompanied "at the same time [by] a pleasure thus excited," because this disagreement accords with reason's own "judgment of the inadequacy" of the faculty of the sense to "strive after" ideas.[80] These conflicting feelings of pleasure and pain produce an oscillation, characterized by "a quickly alternating attraction towards, and repulsion from" the sublime object.[81] Secondly, this oscillation creates an indeterminacy that enables the sublime object to "transport"[82] the subject beyond his or her "determinate" or "habitual"[83] relation to the world. Thirdly, through this encounter with the sublime object, the subject comes to understand that reason is both greater than the faculty of the senses and greater than nature itself, producing an inflation or affirmation of the subject[84] that is nonetheless different from the subject's self-understanding prior to the encounter with the sublime object. This stage completes the "plot" of the Kantian sublime.

Wyatt's experience, which, as I will argue, is characteristic of the modernist sublime, differs from the Kantian sublime in a number of ways. First, rather than beginning with the disruption of a habitual, comfortable relation between mind and object, Wyatt's encounter with the sublime begins with an experience of extreme disconnection: "In the street everything was unfamiliar, everything and everyone I saw was unreal, I felt like I was going to lose my balance out there, this feeling was getting all knotted up inside me."[85] Seeking a reprieve from the unreality of the real, Wyatt enters a gallery where he sees a work of art (the sublime object, which in this case is a Picasso painting) that so defies description that he can only say, "And then I saw this thing."[86] In Wyatt's account, the feeling inspired by the painting then yields to a sense of transport, which enables him to overcome the sense of alienation that preceded the sublime encounter: "Everything was freed into one recognition, really freed into reality that we never see, you never see it. You don't see it in paintings because most of the time you can't see beyond a painting. . . . They become familiar and then it's too late."[87] In keeping with the modernist sublime, Wyatt's encounter is mediated not by nature, but by the work of art (although the work of art can also mediate the Burkean, Kantian, and romantic sublime).[88] The mediation of the modernist sublime through the work of art is essential, because the "positive" resolution of the modernist sublime is first and foremost an *aesthetic* experience,[89] in which "reality" is revealed as essentially fictitious (indeed, as Wyatt says, "everything and everyone I saw was *unreal*") while the aesthetic experience (Wyatt's recognition) partakes of a "deeper" reality. This is a key distinction between the modernist sublime and other forms of the sublime: rather than being grounded in reason, the imagination, or God, the modernist sublime takes the form of a subjective aesthetic experience. Although the modernist sublime may gesture toward some "deeper" reality or grounds, these grounds are never named in explicit terms.

But despite these differences between the modernist and Kantian modes of sublimity, what's notable is how the logic of the Kantian sublime remains largely intact in Wyatt's experience: through the sublime encounter, the severed connection between mind and the object of perception is restored through *anagnorisis*[90]—a point underscored by Wyatt's own description of the moment as a "recognition." Moreover, Wyatt's *anagnorisis* is nostalgic to the point of being conservative, since the visionary moment provided by the work of art serves as an affective means to combat modern alienation. Here we see an unexpected resonance between the modernist sublime and a Victorian aesthetic paradigm associated with Matthew Arnold's claim that art could serve as both a salvific and ethical guide in a modernity no longer legitimated by religious tradition.[91] Wyatt's idealized aesthetic experience thus threatens to reground the work of art within the very ethical framework that *The Recognitions*' satire has evaded.

But, as I will argue, this sublime *anagnorisis* is not the privileged experience it might appear to be: although Wyatt's recognition is powerful and sincere, this only means that Wyatt believes in the legitimacy of his experience. The dialogical indeterminacy within *The Recognitions* means that no single character's perspective can be viewed as authoritative or definitive—and Wyatt is no exception; his experience is just one among the many (and emphatically plural) recognitions signaled by the novel's title. In fact, *The Recognitions* satirizes Wyatt's sublime desire to "see beyond a painting," when he later attempts to "restore" a series of paintings by scraping them back down to a blank canvas, thereby destroying them.[92] Wyatt's valorization of the sublime transport enabled by the work of art ironically diminishes the value of the work itself, whose sensuous surface is dispatched in favor of a "deeper" experience. Just as the elevation of the figure of genius threatens to obscure the work of genius, so, too, does valorizing transport make the work of art ancillary to the experience of sublimity. As I will argue, *The Recognitions* apophatically asserts the unique and autonomous value of the work of art above all else through a very different and overdetermined form of sublimity, which I have called the ambivalent sublime.

4 Late-modern satire and the ambivalent sublime

Although Wyatt's aesthetic recognition cannot be read as an exemplar of the novel's late modernist aesthetics, my argument is that *The Recognitions'* self-critical satire does affirm art's autonomy through a sublime encounter. But this moment of sublimity (and its accompanying affirmation of aesthetic autonomy) differs markedly from the modernist sublime that Wyatt experiences. *The Recognitions'* sublime must operate within the parameters of the novel's apophatic satire in which no position can be advanced without being criticized or negated. For this reason, *The Recognitions*—if it is to be true to its own methods—cannot explicitly present the positive moment of the sublime without undoing the logic of its satire. Instead, *The Recognitions* recuperates the sublime within its apophaticism by emphasizing the negative moment of sublimity. As I have noted earlier, the negative is an essential aspect of the sublime, and as Thomas Weiskel has noted, the sublime moment "is phenomenologically a negation, a falling away from what might be seized, perceived, known."[93]

The Recognitions appropriates this negative moment within its apophatic logic in order to produce a sublime that hovers between vertiginous collapse and affirmation, creating an irresolvable tension between the negative and positive poles of the sublime. This tension characterizes the ambivalent sublime. As I will argue, *The Recognitions'* deployment of this sublime is important for two reasons: 1) the sublime moment within the novel becomes paradigmatic of late modernism, and 2) the goal of *The Recognitions'* satire becomes the production of a sublime, aesthetic moment, which represents a significant intensification of the aestheticist turn in satire I have noted in Wyndham Lewis's *The Apes of God*.

It's also worth briefly examining how the ambivalent sublime diverges from the postmodern sublime, which Fredric Jameson has termed the "Hysterical Sublime."[94] The hysterical sublime consists first and foremost of a moment of "derealization" in which "the world . . . momentarily loses its depth and threatens to become a glossy skin, a stereoscopic illusion, a rush of filmic images without density."[95] But this derealization ambiguously presents as both a vertiginous, overwhelming experience and an exhilarating rush; in the postmodern sublime, the negative and affirmative moments of the sublime coincide. The postmodern sublime resembles the late modernist sublime insofar as both blur the boundaries between the sublime's negative and positive moments, and thus constitute what Cliff McMahon calls "negative modes of the sublime."[96] But there is an essential distinction between the ultimate referent of the late modernist and postmodern sublime. As Jameson argues, the irresolvable "hysterical sublime" refers to the unrepresentable complexity of the "whole world system of multinational capitalism,"[97] and thus resituates the work of art in the context of the cultural and material networks that have made it possible. The postmodern sublime thus undermines the work of art's autonomy by returning to the complexity of relations that enabled its becoming.[98] The referent of the postmodern sublime—which emphasizes art's lack of autonomy—differentiates it from the late modernist sublime, which reasserts aesthetic autonomy at precisely the moment it threatens to disappear.

An exemplary moment of the late modernist sublime occurs in *The Recognitions'* final scene in which the church in Fenestrula collapses. The composer Stanley has long been planning to play his magnum opus—a requiem mass for his mother—on the pipe organ in this small church in a fictional, Italian town. But the performance proves fatal: Stanley is told by a monk (in Italian, which Stanley does not speak) not to pull out all the stops of the organ or play any odd chord-voicings, because the church is structurally unsound. Unable to understand this warning, Stanley—in a gesture that makes the cliché literal—pulls out all the stops and plays his masterwork, a dense and dissonant modernist piece, resulting not only in the annihilation of both church and composer, but also in the partial fragmentation of Stanley's masterwork: "Afterward, *most of his work* was recovered too, and it is still spoken of, when it is noted, with high regard, though seldom played."[99]

On the face of it, this might appear to be an example of the "mock sublime"—a mode traditionally associated with "mockery in ancient Menippean satire, and in literary forms such as the mock encomium and mock epic."[100] The mock sublime, according to McMahon, is presented either for the purposes of ridicule, or else to advance a vague or tenuous concept, such as "the artist as a new priest of the imagination,"[101] a position similar to Wyatt's sublime anagnorisis mediated by the work of art. Many aspects of the crash clearly register as essentially ridiculous. The very notion that Stanley's performance causes the collapse is intentionally absurd, as is his inability to understand the monk's warning.

Furthermore, the collapse comprises an elaborate joke that begins with Stanley's first appearance in the novel some 600 pages earlier, when he sees a crack in the ceiling of his apartment, and thinks about how flimsy, modern buildings will collapse long before "the cathedral at Fenestrula, centuries in building, and standing centuries since."[102] The obvious irony is that it is precisely the church at Fenestrula that will bury Stanley. He also develops a phobia of being buried alive, which results in his carrying around a hammer and chisel, which he describes as "escape tools."[103] Stanley's escape tools—the hammer and chisel—are also the implements of a sculptor, which links the future collapse directly to the work of art. Moreover, Stanley describes his own composition using sculptural—and, indeed, sepulchral—analogies: he describes his work as being like a church-commissioned tomb from the Middle Ages, in which artists were kept busy with "a succession of fireplaces and doorways, the litter of this life, while the tomb remained unfinished."[104]

While these comic aspects of *The Recognitions'* final scene cannot be ignored, I would argue that it moves beyond the parameters of the "mock sublime." This is so because Fenestrula's collapse draws together a variety of themes that have run through the entire novel relating to art, religion, and the problem of traditional institutions' "shaky" foundations in modernity. In this sense, the collapse of Fenestrula cannot be exhausted by one reading, despite the humorous and absurd aspects of this scene. That the "meaning" of the collapse is impossible to capture in a single, discrete reading[105] is characteristic of authentic (rather than "mock") forms of the sublime.[106] While the collapse remains irreducibly polysemous, I nonetheless want to focus on one aspect of it, which explains its relationship to the novel's broader aesthetic anxieties and oblique strategies.

The collapse of Fenestrula can be read as a synecdoche for the collapse of modern aesthetic discourse, which has been delegitimized and separated from any transcendent authorizing grounds. In other words, the collapse of Fenestrula is linked to the disappearance of any "transcendent judgment," as Stanley terms it, for assessing the work of art. The name of the church helps establish this connection: Fenestrula is Latin for "little window"—an allusion to Leon Battista Alberti's *De Pictura*, in which he famously argued for conceiving of the painting as an "open window" (*fenestra aperta*), a metaphor that has been repeated as a trope throughout Western art.[107] This traditional conception of the painting as a window is directly referenced in *The Recognitions* when the novelist Ludy watches two birds trying (and failing) to escape from his room through *trompe l'oeil* paintings of windows.[108] But the novel's implicit link between the collapse of Fenestrula and the delegitimation of the work of art is no surprise given that Fenestrula's collapse is caused by the performance of Stanley's masterwork. Moreover, the novel repeatedly links the figure of the window (which I am reading as a synecdoche for art) with destruction and collapse: Stanley's mother kills herself by jumping out of a window; Stanley's occasional lover, Agnes Deigh, also attempts defenestration; and Arny Munk is killed in the collapse of a hotel as the result of opening a window that, ridiculously, was structurally supporting the building's façade.[109] Thus, while this event may be framed by comic gestures, its content rehearses the same (and very serious) issues of art, legitimation, and autonomy that have been raised throughout the novel. The novel's ending seems both sublime and comic, without one aspect being reducible to the other.

The signal feature of *The Recognitions'* sublime, as exemplified by this scene, is that the vertiginous, overwhelming, "negative" aspect of the sublime coincides with the restorative, positive pole of sublimity. Further, as the impressionistic language used to describe the moments leading up to the collapse suggests, these contradictory aspects of sublimity seem to be indistinguishable from each other:

> The music soared around him . . . and even as he read the music before him, and saw his thumb and last finger come down time after time with three black keys between them, wringing out fourths . . . wringing that chord of the devil's interval from the full length of the thirty-foot bass pipes, he did not stop. The walls quivered, still he did not hesitate. Everything moved, and even falling, soared in atonement.[110]

Paradoxically, this event is rendered as both a collapse and a moment of transcendence—thereby repeating the oscillation of pleasure and pain that characterizes the subject's response to the sublime object in the first stage of the Kantian sublime. But rather than moving past this oscillation, as the Kantian sublime does, *The Recognitions* restages the sublime as a liminal event, prolonging this moment of oscillation without any clear resolution. It is for this reason that I have termed the novel's sublime an ambivalent sublime, because it offers these conflicting sensations from the first stage of the sublime without definitively privileging either one.

One curious result of this unusual form of the sublime is that—in a certain sense—it is not really an instance of the sublime at all, because it does not result in the progression that has been associated with the sublime since Kant. Instead of the plot of the Kantian sublime that I outlined earlier, *The Recognitions* employs only the oscillation between pleasure and pain that occurs within the first stage of the sublime, producing an indefinite and circling suspension of polarities—a static structure that carefully balances opposing qualities without producing a resolution. *The Recognitions* borrows from the structure and symbolism of the sublime in order to short circuit the traditional logic of sublimity. The key word in the passage concerning the collapse of Fenestrula is *atonement*, which signals the static or totalizing nature of these carefully balanced antipathies. Earlier in the novel, the narrator refers to the "etymology of 'atonement'" as meaning "at-one-ment."[111] This is the figure that the end of the novel attempts to enact: the paradoxical motions of falling and soaring suggest a resolution of contrary positions, an identity that moves beyond binary oppositions, an "at-one-ment." Destruction and creation are inextricably bound together in the paradoxical logic of the ouroboros (and, as Jung says, the ouroboros is "the One and All, the union of opposites during the alchemical process"[112]) that graced the cover of the first edition of *The Recognitions*.

Moreover, this sublime suspension of contraries—which marks the uniqueness of late modernism's ambivalent sublime—constitutes the goal of *The Recognitions*' satire. *The Recognitions*' recursive satire, which undermines the possibility of directly asserting its legitimating grounds, results not in the re-presentation of a new legitimating discourse, but rather the indirect (or apophatic) suggestion of transcendence, which is, paradoxically, also a collapse. The resolution of *The Recognitions*' satire reflects a paradigmatically late modernist disposition, which Tyrus Miller has described as "an aesthetic on the threshold of dissolution" that has not forsaken transcendence entirely, since late modernist authors prepare "themselves, without hope, to pass over to the far side of the end."[113] The ambiguous sublime presents an ideal figure for maintaining this liminal position between hope and despair. But *The Recognitions*' production of sublimity through its self-reflexive satire is not simply—or at least not entirely—a stylistic quirk, since the production of the ambivalent sublime has other important consequences.

The ambivalent sublime of *The Recognitions'* final scene constitutes nothing less than an apophatic reaffirmation of the autonomy of art. In order to understand why this is so, we must turn to the ultimate referent of the ambivalent sublime. Unlike Jameson's postmodern hysterical sublime, which uses a similar ambiguity to refer outward to the material networks of late modernity that present the conditions of possibility for the work of art, late modernism's ambiguous sublime refers to itself. The key referent of the ambiguous sublime is the work of art—or, in the case of *The Recognitions,* the novel itself—because it is only in the work of art that these binary oppositions can be overcome by being held in a suspension that constitutes an identity. For late modernists, the work of art remains a privileged site precisely because it is only within the work of art that, to appropriate a phrase of Joseph Campbell's, "the logic of Aristotle fails, and what is *not-A* can indeed become *A*."[114] While *The Recognitions* cannot, and does not, reaffirm art as the mediator of sublime *anagnorisis*, it indirectly posits the work of art as the heterocosmic space in which binaries can be suspended in an identity—which registers as a form of transcendence. To transpose this argument back into Fredric Jameson's terms, the ambivalent sublime reaffirms the autonomy of art precisely because it "endow[s] the aesthetic with a transcendental value which is incomparable," resulting in a totalizing experience that "stands on its own and needs no external justification."[115] If anything, the ambivalent sublime attempts something more ambitious, because it unifies opposed concepts in a manner that transcends logical thought: not only is the ambivalent sublime an affirmation of art's autonomy, but also it suggests that the work of art is superior to other forms of discourse that rely on logic.

The paradoxical sublime of *The Recognitions* attempts to recover one specific trajectory from the many that comprise the utopian project of the modernist avant-gardes. As many theorists, including Peter Bürger, have noted, a defining feature of the avant-gardes was their adherence to a utopian aesthetico-political project[116] (although this utopianism could be of the right—as in the case of Futurism—as well as of the left). Although *The Recognitions* does not attempt to reclaim that utopianism in its entirety, it does present what Andreas Huyssen has termed the "utopia of aesthetic transcendence," a utopianism often associated with a modernist aesthetics, and represented by, for example, "the discovery of that other language that Rilke phantasized about, that other music which Gregor Samsa in Kafka's *Metamorphosis* desires to hear, or that purity of vision which only abstract art has been said to be able to even aspire to."[117] *The Recognitions* clings to this utopia in depicting the work of art as a privileged space in which such "otherness" can manifest—even though, given the apophatic nature of the novel, it cannot state this project openly.

In *The Recognitions*, the production of a certain kind of aesthetic experience—the ambivalent sublime—becomes the *telos* of its satire. On one level, this represents an intensification of the aesthetic turn in satire that was already apparent in Wyndham Lewis's *The Apes of God*, since satire becomes almost solely directed toward the aesthetic. But the aestheticized telos of *The Recognitions* also means that its satire is deployed for distinctly different ends than those of *The Apes of God*. Lewis used the recursion inherent in satire to examine the contradictions of modernist aesthetics, with the goal of establishing a more authentic modern art. But *The Recognitions* deploys its satire to purify and enliven a seemingly dead and exhausted tradition of the modernist avant-gardes. Here, satire's aesthetic project—like the project of late modernism more generally—hovers between the reactionary and the utopian, seeking to locate a space of open potentiality by reclaiming an aspect of an older aesthetics. *The Recognitions'* satire simultaneously navigates and preserves this limbo.

But *The Recognitions'* reinvigoration of modernism is also, perhaps inevitably, an attenuation that preserves some elements of the modernist project (such as notions of aesthetic autonomy and transcendence) while ignoring many others. This loss can be seen in the different goals of Lewis's and Gaddis's satire. Lewis saw in self-reflexive satire a means for wrestling with aesthetic traditions and critiquing the unconscious repetition of much modernist art. Satire therefore became a fundamentally diachronic form that could make explicit a series of historical tensions, which other forms of modernism had unconsciously sought to repress. While Lewis's satire was aesthetic (rather than ethical), its aestheticism could not easily be disentangled from a set of historical, political, and social concerns. But Gaddis's work is synchronic in the sense that all of the (copious) historical and political material in the novel is directed toward the production of a self-sufficient moment that sits outside of temporality as such. The ambivalent sublime that occurs at the novel's end is, above all else, a static figure that carefully balances opposites into a fixed unity, rather than a dynamic reaction to an unfolding historical process. Instead of serving as a means to confront history, *The Recognitions'* aestheticism seeks to evade or transcend its own contexts. In this sense, while intensifying satire's aesthetic commitments, *The Recognitions* nullifies the more radical possibilities that Lewis thought satire could realize.

Notes

1   Charles Jencks, in *Late Modern Architecture and Other Essays* (New York: Rizzoli, 1980), coins the term "late modernism" to describe an architectural style. Tyrus Miller, in *Late Modernism*, provides the most comprehensive account of the term in relation to literature. Fredric Jameson, in *A Singular Modernity: Essay on the Ontology of the Present* (London: Verso, 2002), also presents an account of late modernism as occurring at the moment when modernism exhausts itself (164–200). For a considered history of the development of the term late modernism within the scholarly literature, see Cheryl Hindrichs, "Late Modernism, 1928–1945: Criticism and Theory," *Literature Compass*, 8. 11 (2011): 840–55.

2   Siraganian, *Modernism's Other Work*, 115.

3   The dating of "late modernism" remains contentious. Miller, in *Late Modernism*, argues that "late modernism" occurs during "the late 1920s and 1930s" (5). David G. Farley, in *Modernist Travel Writing: Intellectuals Abroad* (Columbia, MO: University of Missouri Press, 2010), uses the term "to describe the literature written up to and during the Second World War" (194). Jameson, in *A Singular Modernity,* rejects any attempt to date late modernism, stating baldly that "one cannot periodize" (94). Jonathan Greenberg, in *Modernism, Satire, and the Novel*, registers the tension between the desire to define late modernism either in "a narrow chronological sense" or "a formal and nonhistorical one" (40). Anthony Mellors, in *Late Modernist Poetics: From Pound to Prynne* (Manchester; New York: Manchester University Press, 2005), views late modernism as being "contemporary with the emergence of anti-modernist tendencies after 1939," and argues that late modernism "can be said to refer to the continuum of modernist writing into the war years and until at least the end of the 1970s" (19). I will ultimately follow Greenberg and Mellors's suggestion that late modernism is a broader tendency that continues to exert an influence on contemporary literary production.

4   Fredric Jameson, "Postmodernism and Consumer Society," *Postmodern Culture,* Ed. Hal Foster (London: Pluto Press, 1985), 111. Jeremy Braddock, in *Collecting as Modernist Practice* (Baltimore, MD: Johns Hopkins University Press, 2012), describes this stifling institutionalization of modernism in the visual arts, stating that from "1939, MoMA drew authority both from its iconic and centrally located museum building and from its permanent holdings, which canonized modernism primarily as both *field* and *period,* not as an ever-renewing and evolving set of aesthetic and cultural practices" (213). Nonetheless, the claim that modernism was a "cultural dominant" has been disputed. Lawrence Rainey, in *Institutions of Modernism*, argues that such accounts have "distilled" the "material complexity"

of culture, producing "fairy tales of good and evil . . . garbed in academic diction"
(7). Astradur Eysteinsson and Vivian Liska, in "Approaching Modernism,"
Modernism Vol. 1 (Amsterdam; Philadelphia: John Benjamins Publishing Co.,
2007), argue both that modernism was never a cultural dominant and that it has
not been exhausted (1).

5 Braddock, *Collecting as Modernist Practice,* 213. See also Hugh Kenner, "The
Making of the Modernist Canon," *The Chicago Review,* 34.2 (Spring, 1984): 49–61.

6 Robert Genter, *Late Modernism: Art, Culture, and Politics in Cold War America*
(Philadelphia: University of Pennsylvania Press, 2010), 313.

7 Greenberg, in *Modernism, Satire, and the Novel,* states that, for "this later
generation, modernism had already happened" (43).

8 Ibid.

9 Cheryl Hindrichs, "Late Modernism," 850.

10 Greenberg, *Modernism, Satire, and the Novel,* 43–44.

11 Siraganian, in *Modernism's Other Work,* has suggested that *The Recognitions*
be viewed as a late modernist work (115). John Johnston, in *Carnival of
Repetition: Gaddis's The Recognitions and Postmodern Theory* (Philadelphia:
University of Pennsylvania Press, 1990), argues that it is a "Janus-faced" novel,
which sits between modernism and postmodernism (2). Hindrichs, in "Late
Modernism," notes that the quality of being "transitional" or "Janus-faced"
is common among late modernist works (850). At the same time, Mellors,
in *Late Modernist Poetics,* points out that late modernism is "antithetical to
postmodernism, which discloses myth as ideology and treats the 'self' as a
construct, not as an organic unity" (23).

12 Mellors, *Late Modernist Poetics,* 23.

13 Jameson, in *Singular Modernity,* notes the continuing "dependence of the
Postmodern on what remain essentially modernist categories of the new" (5).

14 Jean-Francois Lyotard, *The Postmodern Condition: A Report on Knowledge,*
Trans. Geoff Bennington and Brian Massumi (Manchester: Manchester University
Press, 1979), xxiii–xxiv.

15 Jameson, *Singular Modernity,* 3.

16 Ibid., 7.

17 Fredric Jameson, "Postmodernism, or the Cultural Logic of Late Capitalism," *New
Left Review.* 1:146 (1984): 56.

18 Ibid., 76.

19 Ibid., 59–64.

20 Ibid., 56.

21 Ibid., 59.

22 Genter, *Late Modernism,* 321.

23 Jameson, *Singular Modernity,* 161–62. It's worth noting that, for Jameson, this
    is a misperception on the part of late modernists, who have sought to purge
    the political from modernism, which they have misinterpreted as an apolitical
    formalism. This claim, however, does not account for the deeply held political
    commitments (on both the Right and the Left) of a variety of late modernists,
    including, for example, Wyndham Lewis, Charles Olson, and even William
    Gaddis, whose attempt to offer a systematic account of a variety of social systems,
    such as art in *The Recognitions,* economics in *J R* (1975), and the legal system in *A
    Frolic of His Own* (1994), cannot be characterized as apolitical.

24 Miller, *Late Modernism,* 14.

25 Siraganian, *Modernism's Other Work,* 117–18.

26 Gaddis, *Recognitions,* 63 and 938.

27 Richard Miller, *Bohemia: The Protoculture Then and Now* (Chicago: Nelson Hall,
    1977), 227–28.

28 Greenberg, *Modernism, Satire, and the Novel,* 44.

29 Gaddis, *Recognitions,* 176.

30 Siraganian, in *Modernism's Other Work,* notes that the painting recalls abstract
    expressionism, and points out that, even if no particular artist seems directly
    signaled, the intent is critical, since Gaddis's "allusion is not flattering" (119).

31 Gaddis, *Recognitions,* 623. One character notes the work's title is "The Workman's
    Soul."

32 Michael Leja, *Reframing Abstract Expressionism: Subjectivity and Painting in the
    1940s* (New Haven: Yale University Press, 1993), 256.

33 Gaddis, *Recognitions,* 182–3.

34 The name "Otto," which appears to be a pun on the prefix *auto* (meaning "self"),
    suggests that he is an ironic self-portrait of Gaddis. Fittingly, both share a variety
    of autobiographical details: they grew up estranged from their fathers, labored on
    banana plantations in Central America while working on creative works, and later
    (fraudulently) claimed to have taken part in military struggles during their travels.

35 Gaddis, *Recognitions,* 190.

36 Ibid., 350.

37 Ibid., 622.

38 Ibid., 623.

39 Ibid., 940.

40 Ibid., 623.

41 Ibid., 609.

42 Ibid., 746. This claim appears to be incorrect; see Gaddis, *Recognitions,* 299.
    Max secretly takes a piece of paper, which appears to contain the Rilke poem,
    from Esme's apartment. It remains an open question, however, whether Max's

publication of this poem under his own name is a plagiarism or else a misguided attempt to impress Esme.

43 Ibid., 185.

44 Ibid., 944.

45 Ibid., 184, 306, 577.

46 Ibid., 530.

47 Ibid., 173.

48 Ibid., 122–3. Johnston, in *Carnival of Repetition,* also discusses this resemblance (12).

49 Gaddis, *Recognitions,* 872.

50 Ibid., 464. My emphasis.

51 Ibid.

52 Michel Foucault, "What is an Author?" *The Foucault Reader.* Ed. Paul Rabinow (New York: Pantheon Books, 1984), 101–20.

53 Christopher J. Knight, *Omissions Are Not Accidents: Modern Apophaticism from Henry James to Jacques Derrida* (Toronto: University of Toronto Press, 2010), 6.

54 Jacques Derrida, "Post-Scriptum: Aporias, Ways and Voices," *Derrida and Negative Theology.* Eds. Harold Coward and Toby Foshay (Albany, NY: SUNY University Press, 1992), 295.

55 Christopher J, Knight, "Trying to Make Negative Things Do the Work of Positive Ones: Gaddis and Apophaticism," *William Gaddis: "The Last of Something,"* Ed. Crystal Alberts, Christopher Leise, and Birger Vanwesenbeeck (Jefferson, North Carolina; London: McFarland & Company, Inc., 2010), 51–68.

56 Esther levels this accusation against Wyatt on two occasions in *The Recognitions* (590, 621).

57 This joke recurs four times in *The Recognitions* (178, 185, 194, 306).

58 The invocation of "something higher" forms something like a *leitmotif* throughout *The Recognitions* (32, 488, 616, 617, 632, 713, 878, and 929).

59 As Kant, in *Critique of Judgment,* notes, "Genius is the talent (or natural gift) which gives the rule to art" (112). David Wellbery, in *The Specular Moment: Goethe's Early Lyric and the Beginnings of Romanticism* (Stanford: Stanford University Press, 1996), argues that genius becomes the central principle of artistic production in the second half of the eighteenth century (121). Ken Frieden, in *Genius and Monologue* (Ithaca; London: Cornell University Press, 1985), also offers a good, brief summary of the development of the concept of genius (66–83).

60 Gaddis, *Recognitions,* 229.

61 Ibid., 95–96.

62 Ibid., 81. Extreme suspicion of the cult of personality surrounding authorship is common in late modernist works, which often therefore seek to denigrate the

figure of the author in explicit terms. Thomas Bernhard, in *Extinction,* Trans. David McLintock (New York: Vintage, 1995), presents another example of this suspicion:

> I can't imagine anything worse than meeting a writer and sharing a table with him. I'm prepared to accept his works, but not their producer. Most of them are bad characters, if not positively repulsive, no matter who they are, and if you meet them they ruin their work for you—they simply extinguish it. People jostle to meet some writer whom they love or admire—or even hate—and this completely ruins the work for them (309).

63 Gaddis, *Recognitions,* 589. This statement of Wyatt's is reported by his wife, Esther.

64 Ibid., 633.

65 Ibid.

66 Ibid., 615.

67 Ibid., 616.

68 Ibid.

69 Ibid., 318.

70 Ibid., 632.

71 Ibid., 632.

72 Ibid., 617. Note that Stanley's speech is itself fragmented by ellipses.

73 Ibid. My emphasis.

74 Jean-Francois Lyotard, *The Postmodern Explained: Correspondence 1982–1985* (Sydney: Power Publications, 1992), 13. Cliff McMahon, in *Theory of the Sublime: Pillars and Modes* (Lewiston, NY: Edwin Mellen Press, 2004), states that two "marks of modernity are postulated by Lyotard: a passive nostalgic mode of melancholic regret for the absence of significant presence, and a zestful *novatio* mode of bold experiment, the former seen in Proust and German expressionism, the latter in Joyce, Braque, Picasso" (68). Knight, in *Omissions Are Not Accidents,* notes that Stanley and Wyatt "turn their backs on the present, seeking refuge in the perfections of the past" (133), which would seem to be characteristic of modernist nostalgia in Lyotard's account.

75 Lyotard, *The Postmodern Explained,* 14. While I believe that Lyotard's account captures *one* aspect of the modernist sublime, I will argue that the modernist sublime is actually more complicated than Lyotard's binary would suggest. See Endnote 94 in this chapter.

76 Knight, in *Omissions Are Not Accidents,* notes "both [Wyatt's] serious need for a Truth that transcends contingencies and his hitherto repressed doubts regarding the surety of such a search" (125).

77 Gaddis, *Recognitions,* 362. It's worth noting that Wyatt, himself, later disagrees with this position: "It's never the thing itself, it's always the possibility that . . . . So then you have to look up, and look for something bigger. See?" (814).

78 Richard Eldridge and Paul Cohen, "Art and the Transfiguration of Social Life: Gaddis on Art and Society," *Powerless Fictions? Ethics, Cultural Critique and American Fiction in the Age of Postmodernism,* Ed. Ricardo Miguel-Alfonso (Amsterdam: Rodopi, 1996), 46. See also David Wyatt, *Secret Histories: Reading Twentieth-Century American Literature* (Baltimore: Johns Hopkins University Press, 2010), 258.

79 Quoted in Christopher J. Knight, *Hints and Guesses: William Gaddis' Fiction of Longing* (Madison: University of Wisconsin Press, 1997), 49.

80 Kant, *Critique of Judgment,* 72.

81 Ibid.

82 Alan Richardson, *The Neural Sublime: Cognitive Theories and Romantic Texts* (Baltimore, MD: Johns Hopkins University Press, 2010), 25.

83 Thomas Weiskel, *The Romantic Sublime: Studies in the Structure and Psychology of Transcendence* (Baltimore, MD: Johns Hopkins University Press, 1976), 23–24.

84 Ibid.

85 Gaddis, *Recognitions,* 92. Weiskel, in *The Romantic Sublime,* argues that the concept of alienation is integral to the dialectic of sublimity and a signal fixation of the romantic sublime, as well (36).

86 Gaddis, *Recognitions,* 92.

87 Ibid.

88 Donald Pease, in "Sublime Politics," *The American Sublime,* Ed. Mary Arensberg (Albany, NY: SUNY University Press, 1986), states that in "modernism, the sublime does not move from nature to culture . . . but from culture to a 'neonature' where differentiation, the very mode of being of modern culture, can become itself and be experienced as authentic" (39).

89 Nicholas Brown, *Utopian Generations: The Political Horizon of Twentieth-Century Literature* (Princeton; Oxford: Princeton University Press, 2005), 20.

90 Weiskel, *Romantic Sublime,* 37. Weiskel articulates the relation between sublimity and anagnorisis.

91 Terry Eagleton, *Literary Theory: An Introduction* (Minneapolis, MN: University of Minnesota Press, 2008), 21. Eagleton offers a brief gloss on Arnold's notion of literature as a new legitimating ground for modernity.

92 Gaddis, *Recognitions,* 868–75.

93 Weiskel, *The Romantic Sublime,* 24. See also Jean-Francois Lyotard, *Lessons on the Analytic of the Sublime,* Trans. Elizabeth Rottenberg (Stanford, CA: Stanford

University Press, 1994), 152. Lyotard argues that the sublime aims at the negative presentation of the absolute.

94　Jameson, "Postmodernism," 76. Lyotard, in *The Postmodern Explained,* also provides an account of the postmodern sublime (13–15). Lyotard's account, from my perspective, is problematic for the reason that it elides the postmodern with the project of the historical avant-gardes. As I have already argued in the previous chapter, I see the historical avant-gardes as comprising *part of* the larger modernist project, rather than being in opposition to it. In this sense, I see Lyotard's notion of the postmodern sublime of *novatio* as another version of a modernist sublime, in which the cognitive dissonance produced by the Modern work of art's novelty serves as the negative moment of the sublime. J.M. Bernstein, in *Against Voluptuous Bodies: Late Modernism and the Meaning of Painting* (Stanford: Stanford University Press, 2006), provides a description of the modernist sublime that supports my argument: "The idea of the 'modernist sublime' tokened the moment of dissonance in autonomous art, the moment of negativity through which such art declared its departure from the cannon of the harmonious, the beautiful, the tasteful" (159). Brown, in *Utopian Generations,* articulates a similar position (15–17). In my reading, then, the modernist sublime possesses two polarities—one that is nostalgic and one that is enthralled by the new—but these are two sides of the same coin that result in the same affirmative moment with art/culture as the locus of a sublime visionary moment that affirms the ego of the viewer. As I will argue, both the postmodern and late modernist sublime re-deploy these same polarities, but to very different ends.

95　Jameson, "Postmodernism," 76–7.

96　Cliff McMahon, *Reframing the Theory of the Sublime,* 136.

97　Jameson, "Postmodernism," 79.

98　As John Frow has argued, "'Postmodernism' . . . is the self-fulfilling prophecy of its own impossible autonomy." "What Was Postmodernism?" *Time and Commodity Culture: Essays in Cultural Theory and Postmodernity* (Oxford: Oxford University Press, 1997), 63.

99　Gaddis, *Recognitions,* 956. My emphasis.

100　McMahon, *Reframing the Theory of the Sublime,* 138–39. For more on the relationship between neoclassical satire and the sublime, see Weiskel, *The Romantic Sublime,* 20–1.

101　McMahon, *Reframing the Theory of the Sublime,* 139.

102　Gaddis, *Recognitions,* 319.

103　Gaddis, *Recognitions,* 319.

104　Ibid., 323.

105 Stephen J. Burn, in "The Collapse of Everything," *Paper Empires: William Gaddis and the World System*, Eds. Joseph Tabbi and Rhone Shavers (Tuscaloosa: University of Alabama Press, 2007), argues that the "collapse of the church at Fenestrula symbolizes the crushing weight of information" (57). Other notable readings of the collapse include Johnston, *Carnival of Repetition*, 106; Knight, *Hints and Guesses*, 33; and Gregory Comnes, *Ethics of Indeterminacy in the Novels of William Gaddis* (Gainesville: University Press of Florida, 1994), 75.

106 Weiskel, *Romantic Sublime*, 28.

107 Leon Battista Alberti, *On Painting*, Trans. Cecil Grayson (Penguin, 2005), 54. Anne Friedberg, in *The Virtual Window from Alberti to Microsoft* (Cambridge, MA: MIT Press, 2006), traces the influence of Alberti's metaphor of the painting as a window on subsequent Western art (26–48).

108 Gaddis, *Recognitions*, 900. This scene also alludes to the ancient Greek painter Zeuxis (to whom Alberti also refers), whose paintings, according to Pliny, were so lifelike that the birds tried to eat the grapes off of his painted vines. Elizabeth Mansfield, in *Too Beautiful to Picture: Zeuxis, Myth, and Mimesis* (Minneapolis, MN: University of Minnesota Press, 2007), offers a brief account of these and other myths about Zeuxis (26–9).

109 Gaddis, *Recognitions*, 561, 740, 942.

110 Ibid., 956.

111 Ibid., 828.

112 Carl Jung, *Alchemical Studies, The Collected Works of Carl Jung*, Vol. 13, Eds. Herbert Read, Michael Fordham, and Gerhard Adler (New York: Pantheon Books, 1953), 232.

113 Miller, *Late Modernism*, 14.

114 Joseph Campbell, *The Mythic Image* (Princeton, NJ: Princeton University Press, 1981), 8.

115 Jameson, *Singular Modernity*, 162.

116 This notion has become more or less a commonplace in avant-garde and modernist studies. For one recent example, see Andreas Huyssen, *Twilight Memories: Marking Time in a Culture of Amnesia* (New York: Routledge, 1995), 98.

117 Huyssen, *Twilight Memories*, 99.

5

Aporia and the Satiric Imagination:
The Limit-Modernism of Gilbert Sorrentino's
Imaginative Qualities of Actual Things

1 Satire without content

Gilbert Sorrentino's *The Imaginative Qualities of Actual Things* (1971) openly denies a connection between its satire and any legitimating grounds. Whereas Wyndham Lewis's *The Apes of God* and William Gaddis's *The Recognitions* evoke stable conceptions of ethical satire and then undermine them through elaborate formal devices that reveal the groundless nature of judgment, *Imaginative Qualities* begins with this premise. As the novel's narrator and satiric persona, who very much resembles Gilbert Sorrentino,[1] asserts, "I have a certain story, or tale. But there is no point to that. I have certainly no moral to draw."[2] In what constitutes probably the best-known quotation from the novel, the narrator explains that—because of fiction's groundless nature—it cannot be used for didactic ends:

> Such the perfections of fiction, as well as that honed cruelty it possesses which makes it useless. Everything it teaches is useless insofar as structuring your life: you can't prop up anything with fiction. It, in fact, teaches you *just* that. That in order to attempt to employ its specific wisdom is a sign of madness. . . . There is more profit in an hour's talk with Billy Graham than in a reading of Joyce. Graham might conceivably make you sick, so that you might move, go somewhere to get well. But Joyce just sends you out into the street, where the world goes on, solid as a bus. If you met Joyce and said "Help me," he'd hand you a copy of *Finnegans Wake*. You could both cry.[3]

Although this quotation is sufficiently complex to evade a simple reading (and I will consider it in more detail later), its basic argument is clear: *Imaginative Qualities* does not, and, indeed, cannot, make ethical or any other instrumental claims about ordinary reality for the reason that, as a "useless" work of autonomous art, it opposes such instrumentality. But the narrator's articulation of this strong claim of aesthetic autonomy has significant repercussions for the novel's satire, which must renounce any claim to an ethical basis for its judgment.

The novel undermines conceptions of grounded satiric judgment in its opening pages by presenting a hypothetical scenario addressed directly to the reader. "You" are engaged in the seduction of the bad "avant-garde" poet Sheila Henry, who has given "you" one of her poems and is awaiting "your" judgment: "The most subtle relaxation of critical acumen, will hasten you to bed with her. . . . Is seeing, finally, the hair glossy between her thighs so important that you will lie? About art?"[4] Not only does the narrator's direct and confrontational language turn this banal scenario into a parody of a more serious ethical quandary, but also it emphasizes that satire cannot be grounded in objective discourses precisely because there is no such thing as disembodied judgment. Bodily desire warps judgment—a point underscored by a crass allusion to the material fact of the sexual arousal of this theoretical (and clearly male) judge, whose "penis [is] a bar of steel."[5] The narrator implies that—because we are self-interested and embodied beings— human judgment can never be detached, objective, or ethical, and will always be influenced by factors more immediate and less rational than logic.

Through these gestures, *Imaginative Qualities* appears to empty its satire of any content, since satirical critiques—which can no longer be justified as an ethical "corrective" to vice and folly—maintain their rhetorical force even though they lack ethical significance. What remains is indiscriminate critique, which has become a corrosive agent dissolving whatever it touches. Satiric judgment now becomes performative—its harsh invective is reduced to a generic convention that can now be amplified and exaggerated for aesthetic ends. While satire has often been described as a textual form of "symbolic violence,"[6] the vindictive mockery within *Imaginative Qualities* reads as excessive even within the context of satire's aggressive tendencies. Of the character Horace Rosette, for example, the satiric persona states, "Some people would call him a sycophant, but I prefer to think of him as an ass-kisser."[7] He calls Sheila Henry "a particular kind of modern-day whore" who has "none of the whore's finesse about her."[8] He paints an abject portrait of Anton Harley, who combines the glutinous devouring of pizza with sexual perversity and abuse:

> From the look of things, it seems as if Anton has been—fucking—some of the pizza. There is a banging from the bathroom, and muffled shouts. That is his latest girl, whom he has locked in so that she can't share any of the pie. He'll let her out soon and let her eat the pizza that he came over, if she wants.[9]

Here, the novel's satire becomes grotesque invective, a transformation that has significant ramifications for the *meaning* of such critique, which has already divested itself of any claim to a normative basis. Gerhard Hoffmann has noted that "satire relies on a 'realistic' base for its critique," but the excessiveness of *Imaginative Qualities'* satire renders any relationship to "reality" ambiguous,[10] since its critique is too ridiculous to be believed, and thus disavows a connection to any "real" object.

Even when the novel does mock satiric targets for what—in traditional satire—would be clear vices, the narrator explicitly dissociates his attacks from an ethical framework. While the novel satirizes a wide array of "perverse" sexual acts, including sodomy, adultery, sadomasochism, group sex, and fetishes, as well as intercourse with a variety of inanimate objects, including trees, pizza, and, in one case, a copy of Nabokov's *Lolita* (1955), the narrator repeatedly emphasizes that "perversity," rather than being a vice, is a universal condition: "Shall we then select the 'perverse' for our observation? We shall select then, it would seem, much of our world."[11] While the narrator finds a great deal of vicious humor in the sex lives of his characters, he emphasizes his own similarity to these satiric targets by acknowledging his fetishistic sexual desires: "I would prefer a maid in the shortest of skirts, wearing black nylons and high heels. But I am not writing pornography, so I'll have to save the maid (Annette)."[12] This represents a decisive break with traditional satire, which establishes sharp distinctions between the virtuous outrage of the satiric persona and the vices of his satiric targets.[13]

In the various explicit ways that it denies the ethical and didactic grounds of traditional satire, *Imaginative Qualities of Actual Things* appears to be a very different kind of satire than the other self-reflexive satires I have examined. Without any recourse to ethics, Sorrentino's satire can be performative and playful, experimenting with the genre's tropes rather than moving toward the production of a moral judgment. More importantly, *Imaginative Qualities* shows no nostalgia for the now absent grounds of traditional satire, preferring to revel in the possibilities available to satire after it has renounced them. In these gestures, the novel embraces aesthetic methods closely associated with textual forms of postmodernism. Its rejection of transcendent grounds, for example, recalls Lyotard's argument that postmodernism's essential feature was its "incredulity toward metanarratives" (its rejection of appeals "to some grand narrative").[14] Moreover, the novel's playful experimentation with the traditional generic markers of satire evokes the Derridean conception of the "free play of signifiers," which is also typically seen as a key element of postmodern aesthetics.[15] As a result of these tendencies, *Imaginative Qualities* (like Sorrentino's work more broadly) is often viewed as an exemplar of postmodernism, which would also suggest that the novel presents a postmodern revision of self-reflexive satire.[16]

While *Imaginative Qualities* displays some characteristics commonly associated with postmodernism, this classification ignores the fact that Sorrentino viewed postmodernism skeptically—a position that was hardly uninformed given his involvement in the academy during the heyday of the so-called "postmodernism debates."[17] In a 1994 interview with Alexander Laurence, for example, Sorrentino pointed out that the criteria used to describe his work as postmodern could just as easily be applied to the work of many modernists:

> [Postmodernism is] a really imprecise term, despite the work of Lyotard, Jameson, Guattari, etc. I tend to think of it as an extension of the problems of unresolvability, indeterminacy and fragmentation proffered in the texts of high modernism. What is more "postmodern" than *Finnegans Wake* or *Watt* or *At Swim-Two-Birds*? Yet they are all arguably modern texts. Borrowings, quotations, inter- and intratextualities, references, collage, fragmentation, indeterminacies, ambiguities—they're all present in these texts. Yet they are all present in "postmodern" texts as well. One can't even mention irony, since modernist texts are full of it and some postmodern texts, like Creeley's late prose, reveal no irony at all. Maybe a better term would be late-late modernism, or contemporary modernism.[18]

Here, Sorrentino simultaneously affirms and denies his own affiliation with postmodernism. On the one hand, he acknowledges the resemblance between his work and other "postmodern" texts. On the other hand, by denying that postmodernism "breaks" with modernism, Sorrentino argues that his own work presents an "extension of the problems of unresolvability, indeterminacy and fragmentation" that were already inherent to modernism—a reconfiguration of standard critical conceptions of postmodernism and modernism. This reconfiguration produces two key effects that, as I will argue, are visible in Sorrentino's satire.

First of all, recategorizing postmodernism and modernism as a continuous tradition sidesteps the problem of exhaustion that—as I discussed in the previous chapter—typically haunted works of late modernism. If postmodernism is an extension of modernism, then modernism is neither exhausted nor relegated to history, but a contemporary and ongoing aesthetic that has maintained its vitality. It is in this sense that Sorrentino proposes the apparent pleonasm "contemporary modernism," which signifies the continuing significance of modernism itself. Secondly, the notion of a "contemporary" modernism attempts a radical reenvisioning of modernism. In viewing the postmodern as an "extension" of modernism, Sorrentino invokes an inherently dynamic conception of modernism that is not (or, at least, not entirely) beholden to the aesthetic principles associated with high modernism. In this sense, "contemporary modernism" presents a postmodern reframing of an earlier modernism.

Sorrentino's refiguring of the relation between postmodernism and modernism thus serves as a means of simultaneously reaffirming and revising a modernist aesthetics, resulting in an ambiguous form that could be read as a modernism inflected with elements of postmodernism, a postmodernism that reclaims aspects of an earlier modernism, or an altogether "new" hybrid of the two. For these reasons, *Imaginative Qualities* provides a key textual site from which to reexamine postmodernism's alleged "break" with modernism. In drawing postmodernism and modernism together, *Imaginative Qualities* calls into question the validity of these categories, which now appear, not as clearly demarcated traditions, but literary tendencies that can be extended, adapted, revised, and even productively subverted. This notion of tradition as both determining and elastic allows Sorrentino to signal his allegiance to modernism without being hemmed in by a static set of aesthetic practices associated with a canonical and historically reified modernism—an evasion of the claustrophobic aesthetics that haunted *The Recognitions'* late modernism.

Imaginative Qualities enacts this simultaneous assertion and revision of the modernist tradition by taking its title and opening and closing epigraphs from poems by William Carlos Williams and Ezra Pound. This final epigraph, from Pound's "Canto CXV," is particularly significant because it signals Sorrentino's awareness of earlier models for a nonmoral satire; Pound's poem is an elegy for Wyndham Lewis. As Sorrentino himself admitted, *Imaginative Qualities of Actual Things* "was directly influenced by" *The Apes of God*, which had already delineated "this morass of phony artiness that exists in New York and other places."[19] Here, the influence of modernism is clear, even though *Imaginative Qualities* pronounces the groundlessness of its satire in an eminently postmodern fashion.

In my view, the novel's imbrication of modernism and postmodernism serves a function similar to *The Recognitions'* attempt to reassert modernist aesthetics through apophatic means. *Imaginative Qualities* "postmodern" characteristics—particularly its open admission of its lack of any legitimizing grounds—rearticulate (indirectly) a notion of aesthetic autonomy that is heavily indebted to modernism. In the following pages, I will illustrate the novel's linked alternation of a postmodern antifoundationalism and a modernist concept of autonomy by examining the key rhetorical figure that enables the novel's antifoundationalist satire: the aporia. The figure of the aporia in *Imaginative Qualities* resonates with Jacques Derrida's description of the "*negative form (aporia)* . . . to designate a duty that, through the impossible or the impracticable, nonetheless announces itself in an affirmative fashion."[20] I will argue that, in *Imaginative Qualities,* the aporia presents this negative affirmation through a two-step process: 1) the aporia dissolves the ties between the satire and any grounded discourse or metanarrative through the intentional deployment of a logical contradiction, and 2) the text posits its own isolation from such discourses as a form of radical autonomy, albeit an autonomy considerably more complex than in most accounts of modernist autonomy.

While the use of aporia in *Imaginative Qualities* resembles *The Recognitions'* apophaticism, in that both marshal the negativity of satiric critique to indirectly express positive concepts, *Imaginative Qualities* advances a very different notion of aesthetic autonomy that cannot be viewed as either escapist or a reconfigured aestheticism. Whereas *The Recognitions* reclaims autonomy in order to purify an exhausted modernist understanding of the term, *Imaginative Qualities* attempts to recontextualize and reframe modernist autonomy to emphasize a different set of qualities already latent in the concept itself—using modernist autonomy for the postmodern end of revealing the constructed and arbitrary nature of the actual.

While these gestures—including the text's explicit denial of ethical intent, its willful emptying out of satire's traditional content, its antifoundationalist tendencies, and its implicit critique of reified notions of the actual—resonate with what I will describe as "weak" notions of postmodernism, *Imaginative Qualities'* satire remains incompatible with "strong" forms of postmodernism that undermine or disavow aesthetic autonomy. As I will argue, the desire to reaffirm autonomy (albeit indirectly or apophatically) becomes an essential attribute of the subgenre that I have termed "avant-garde satires of the avant-garde," which are thus incompatible with "strong" modes of postmodernism.

2 Satire and aporia

Imaginative Qualities of Actual Things is full of apparently contradictory assertions, which have typically been read by critics as examples of either authorial error or simple inconsistency.[21] In contrast, I will argue that the satiric persona of the narrator willfully and repeatedly juxtaposes mutually exclusive logical propositions to produce aporias. The exemplary aporia within *Imaginative Qualities'* satire concerns the question of whether or not the characters in the novel indirectly refer to "actual" people, in the tradition of the roman à clef. As Sean Latham has noted, while the roman à clef does constitute a "conditional fictionality,"[22] it differs from other forms of fiction because it "does not insist on the full autonomy of its characters from the world of historical fact."[23] For Latham, the roman à clef is a remnant of an eighteenth-century literary tradition that predates the (modern) novel and is in many ways inhospitable to postromantic notions of literature; the roman à clef presumes a direct tie to an outside reality in the same way that older conceptions of satire presumed a grounding in external ethical discourses. As Brian McHale notes, however, contemporary authors have often "exploited the ontological potential of the roman à clef" to blur the real and the fictional, since the roman à clef preserves "the ontological force" of the actual models for its characters "*without* reproducing their real-world proper names."[24] *Imaginative Qualities* pushes the inherent ambiguity of the roman à clef even further, since it asserts both that its characters are based on real-world figures *and* that they are purely fictional, despite the fact that "logically [they] cannot be both."[25]

There is a strong argument for viewing *Imaginative Qualities* as a roman à clef in the traditional sense: its "imaginary" characters clearly resemble actual people. As David Andrews states, "Lyman Gilmore, [Joel] Oppenheimer's biographer claims that 'Joel and his friends recognized the thinly disguised portraits as Fee Dawson, Joe and Anna Early, Tony Weinberger . . . Basil King, John Chamberlain, and Joel.'"[26] Oppenheimer believed himself to be the model for the fictional Leo Kaufman, a failed poet and dipsomaniac, and this portrait so infuriated him that "not only did he never speak with Sorrentino again (refusing even to acknowledge him as they passed each other in Westbeth halls and on neighborhood streets), he avoided even mentioning Sorrentino's name."[27] In truth, Sorrentino did very little to disguise the alleged targets of his attack, and, in many cases, textually encouraged such identification. For example, Fee Dawson—whose full name is Guy Fielding Lewis Dawson—is rather unambiguously portrayed in the novel as a character named "Guy Lewis."

All of these writers were associated with the literary bohemian cultures of New York in the late 1950s. Although the novel more or less picks up just after the publication of *The Recognitions* in 1955, Sorrentino now portrays New York City as the center of bohemian culture, rather than as a hub in a larger global network, as Gaddis did. At the same time, though, the novel depicts a self-contained literary bohemia just before bohemian cultures would undergo a massive expansion through the youth culture of the 1960s. Richard Miller has termed the years 1955–65, which are principally those that *Imaginative Qualities* covers, a "bohemia in transition" because many bohemian notions—of open sexuality, communal living, and the value of altered modes of perception—were becoming "mainstream" through rock music and drug culture.[28] In this sense, the novel critiques a literary scene that, by the time of its publication in 1971, had been absorbed into a broader counterculture.

But despite the novel's focus on this identifiable literary bohemia during a specific time period, the narrator denies that he has any interest in examining, mythologizing, or critiquing this literary scene. After listing twenty of Leo's experiences in late 1950s New York, the narrator states, "If the reader will take these things, and imagine for himself the events leading up to them . . . he will have a general picture of the hip New York scene during these years": the narrator encourages the reader to do this, because he doesn't "give a damn about the scene during those years" and has "no interest in writing" about it.[29] The disavowal of any interest in discussing the bohemian culture of 1950s New York contrasts with the novel's recurrent focus on precisely these aspects.

Like his disavowal of any interest in the "literary scene," the narrator—despite references to specific, recognizable people—insists that the characters he's writing about are entirely fictional, with no connection whatsoever to any real-life counterpart: "These people aren't real. I'm making them up as I go along."[30] The contradiction between the narrator's claims for his characters' absolute fictionality and the evidence that links them to a series of "real" writers and artists has remained particularly vexing for critics.[31] Instead of attempting to "resolve" this conundrum, I want to suggest that this contradiction has remained problematic precisely because of critics' desire for such resolution. Instead, I want to take the narrator's mutually irreconcilable statements at face value by reading this aporia as an essential and intentional element of the text, which refuses logical coherence. If the novel's contradictions are viewed as a key to its structure, then the larger stakes of its satire become clear.

For example, the narrator's aporetic assertion and denial of a specific "actual" reference for these characters enables the preservation of the generic form of satire without retaining the ethical significance attributed to traditional satire. In order for satire to be satire, generically speaking, it must have satiric targets, and, more importantly, these satiric targets cannot be chosen at random: they must be specific, representing either real people or a class of people that actually exist; as Edward Rosenheim argued, satire is an "attack on *discernible, historically authentic particulars*" and objects of satire "must be, or have been, plainly existent in the world of reality."[32] More generalized forms of critique (which rely on types or common traits) are traditionally associated with comedy rather than satire.[33] By ensuring that its targets refer to "actual" people, *Imaginative Qualities* fulfills satire's generic requirement of specificity. But this requirement clashes with the narrator's claim that art must be "useless insofar as structuring your life."[34] Modeling characters on specific people implies the direct relation between fiction and reality that the narrator attacks when he describes his novel as a "useless" work of autonomous art. By denying the actuality of the satiric targets and emphasizing their fictionality, however, the narrator can maintain his claim that there is no "actual" significance to his critiques (because his satiric targets are not real), while also maintaining the specificity of reference characteristic of satire (since the characters clearly correspond to real-life figures). This aporia thus enables the narrator to have it both ways, and navigate the inherent conflict between his commitment to aesthetic autonomy and the generic constraints of satire.

Considering the aporia only in this light, however, threatens to turn it into little more than a suspect logical move in the service of maintaining an ambit claim of aesthetic autonomy. Equally, one could simply dismiss the satiric persona's assertion of the characters' fictionality as a self-protective gesture, an intentionally ironic claim, or a patently false statement meant to be understood as such by readers. Rather than viewing its contradictory nature as a blemish or a self-protective maneuver, however, I want to focus on what happens when the force of the aporia's illogic is unleashed within the text. By simultaneously asserting and denying these characters' connection to "reality," this aporia creates an uncertainty about their ontological status—a gesture that undermines the text's capacity to place them in relation to a grounded discourse. These competing claims undermine each other, making it impossible to abstract a coherent critique from the text's satire. Through these mutually exclusive claims, the text renders the grounds of its satire inherently illogical—a gesture that recalls the practices of many of the historical avant-gardes who sought to create art that defied standard conceptions of logic and sense, whether in the form of Tristan Tzara's "word salads" or Alfred Jarry's 'pataphysics. Lacking any logical grounding, *Imaginative Qualities'* satire cannot produce the satiric norms—which by their nature must be both logical and universalizable—required for traditional forms of satiric judgment. Aporias thus represent another intensification of the methods used by self-reflexive satires to evade capture by grounded discourses: *The Apes of God* employs staged reversals of what initially appeared to be its satiric norms; *The Recognitions* creates an irresolvable uncertainty about essential facts regarding its satiric targets; and *Imaginative Qualities* takes such measures a step further by intentionally deploying contradictions that cannot be reconciled with a grounded, logical discourse.

In this sense, *Imaginative Qualities'* use of aporia is radically antifoundationalist in a way that distinguishes it from the other satires I have examined, and also resonates with postmodernism's "incredulity toward metanarratives."[35] As I noted earlier, however, *Imaginative Qualities'* relationship to postmodernism is complicated by the indirect reassertion of a modernist aesthetic autonomy, which these aporias enable. This assertion of autonomy, as I will argue, clashes with "strong" assertions of postmodernism. While I already provided a brief sketch of postmodernism in the previous chapter, it is necessary to clarify my usage and briefly survey some of the key literature from the postmodernism debates in order to understand in what sense *Imaginative Qualities* might be claimed as a "postmodern" work.

Although the postmodernism debates feel less urgent than they did twenty years ago,[36] it remains important to understand what postmodernism *was*—a point that Julian Murphet has recently emphasized.[37] Not only are many contemporary works still indebted to postmodernism, but also the questions raised by these debates still matter: Did a new form of art arise after modernism? Was it a coherent aesthetic movement? If so, what were its characteristics? Why did these forms arise, and what did they signify? In retrospect, the answers to these questions seem different from when they were first posed. Recent scholarship[38] highlights continuities between modernism and postmodernism, rather than their antagonism, and modernist studies increasingly examines works straddling this division. My analysis is influenced by this turn in modernist studies, and examines the ways in which postmodernism and modernism are imbricated, rather than presenting another account of literary postmodernism as such. Following Julian Murphet's recent claims, I want to suggest that the distinction between modernism and postmodernism remains useful, and that the latter should not simply be subsumed by an expanded conception of the former.

Nonetheless, defining postmodernism continues to be problematic,[39] given the different ways that the term has been applied across diverse fields of inquiry to describe a mode of cultural production, an economic system of distribution, a coherent aesthetic movement, a set of critical and theoretical texts ("postmodern theory"), and a specific historical era, among others.[40] Even when limited to aesthetics, the term can be understood in a variety of ways. Gerhard Hoffman and Andreas Huyssen have noted two historical usages of the term, the first in its tentative theorization in the 1960s and early 1970s (by critics like Susan Sontag, Ihab Hassan, and Leslie Fiedler[41]), and the second from the more rigorous postmodernism debates that occurred from the late 1970s until the early 1990s (in the work of such critics as Brian McHale, Linda Hutcheon, and Huyssen himself), but even this historicized approach does not capture all meanings of postmodernism.[42]

Consider the accounts of postmodernism by the three later theorists I just mentioned—none of whom agree on whether postmodernism can even be considered an internally coherent object of study. McHale, in *Postmodernist Fiction* (1987), argues that postmodernism presents a decisive shift from a modernist "epistemological dominant" to a postmodern "ontological one."[43] Hutcheon, in contrast, argues that postmodernism should "probably not be considered a new paradigm,"[44] but rather a historical assemblage of concerns (self-reflexivity, fictionality, historicity) that constitute a postmodern sensibility. Huyssen is also skeptical of postmodernism as a discrete concept and argues for multiple *postmodernisms*, but he nonetheless claims that postmodernism differs from modernism by embracing a "new creative relationship between high art and certain forms of mass culture."[45] Therefore, there is no consensus over whether literary postmodernism constitutes a historical movement, a new paradigm, or a set of linked artistic responses to modernism that resemble one another.

I will therefore approach the concept of postmodernism in a provisional and pragmatic manner, viewing it as a spectrum of interrelated (though divergent) theories. These theories will be classified variously as "weak" and "strong" accounts of postmodernism.[46] I classify as "weak" those accounts that—as in Hutcheon's case—view postmodernism as a matter of family resemblances or shared sensibility. I describe as "strong" those theories—like McHale's and Huyssen's[47]—that posit an essential difference between postmodernism and modernism. Finally, following Fredric Jameson, I contend that strong accounts of postmodernism always undermine or overturn modernist conceptions of aesthetic autonomy that view the work of art as a privileged discursive site.[48] While suspicion of autonomy is not constitutive of postmodernity, aesthetic autonomy presents an essential point of difference between "strong" postmodernism and both modernism and late modernism.[49] Whereas modernist and late modernist works ultimately reaffirm autonomy (although often in a complicated, conflicted, or oblique manner), strong postmodern works are either indifferent to autonomy or undermine it. Jennifer Ashton's description of modernist autonomy serves as an exemplary "strong" account of postmodernism: for Ashton, modernist works present an autonomy determined by strong authorial intention, whereas postmodern works display a heteronomy characterized by an authorial "attention" that makes the reader a cocreator of the work itself.[50]

While *Imaginative Qualities* can be considered postmodern in a "weak" sense, it indirectly reaffirms autonomy in a manner that clashes with strong postmodernism. The novel's aporias, which ensure that its satire cannot be abstracted or mapped onto a logically coherent discourse, display antifoundationalist characteristics, but this disconnection from grounded discourses serves as an indirect means of asserting the novel's "uselessness." This assertion of uselessness paradoxically forms the grounds for claiming a special status for literature that is indebted to modernist notions of autonomy—although the autonomy that the novel articulates is a critical one that seeks to reframe the relation between art and life rather than denying such a connection altogether.

In using aporias to disrupt the connection between the work of art and grounded discourses for the purposes of reasserting its aesthetic autonomy, *Imaginative Qualities* occupies a threshold between modernism and postmodernism—a liminal space already implicit in Sorrentino's self-description of his work as a "contemporary modernism." But it's crucial to register that the text's "contemporary modernism" conflicts with strong postmodernism, because of their incommensurate approaches to autonomy. The subgenre of avant-garde satires of the avant-garde always opposes strong postmodernism, because it perpetuates the aesthetic autonomy inaugurated by romanticism and transformed by modernism and late modernism.[51] The inaugurating gesture of these satires is to enact an autonomous separation from ethical discourses to assert their legitimacy as aesthetic objects. In this sense, it is impossible to separate avant-garde satires of the avant-garde from notions of aesthetic autonomy.

Avant-garde satires of the avant-garde also present a counter-narrative to traditional histories that see modernism ceding to postmodernism as a cultural dominant. These satires represent another trajectory out of literary modernism: although they critique and complicate many aspects of modernism and adopt the ironic and self-reflexive tropes characteristic of postmodernism, they nonetheless retain a conception of aesthetic autonomy indebted to modernism in its various forms. This subgenre of satire is therefore not an escape from modernism, but rather a revision or reengagement with the fundamental questions that motivated modernism in the first place. In simple terms, this subgenre presents modernism as *contemporary* rather than as an exhausted, historical tradition—and this may be why Sorrentino describes his own work as "contemporary modernism." As I will argue, Sorrentino's contemporary modernism reengages with the question of autonomy in novel ways: *Imaginative Qualities'* assertion of radical autonomy serves as an indirect means of recalibrating the relation between art and life, rather than rejecting the realm of the actual altogether.

3 Satire, autonomy, imagination

Unlike *The Recognitions'* conception of autonomous art as a static and atemporal utopian sublimity, aesthetic autonomy in *Imaginative Qualities* is used to reconceptualize the relation between the actual and the fictional, so that it does not result in either the utilization of art or the aestheticization of life. To do so, *Imaginative Qualities* returns to the foundational aesthetic question of mimesis, with the intent of recasting art's relation to the world. But this also necessitates the recasting of the world's relationship to art in a manner that is ultimately utopian, albeit not in an explicit or programmatic way. Moreover, the text's engagement with autonomy and anti-mimeticism results in a mode of satire that, rather than being an ethical or instrumental discourse, is now directly linked to a theory of the creative imagination in terms that constitute a postromantic refiguring of satire itself. This new approach to satire both explicates many of the novel's apparently contradictory assertions and constitutes a major revision of satire, which becomes a literary form for exploring the relation between the actual and the imaginative.

As I have noted, the narrator of *Imaginative Qualities* views the autonomous work of art as fundamentally "useless." For satire to be "useless," its grounds must be undermined through aporia, which renders its norms incoherent, producing ungrounded satiric judgments. But in asserting the uselessness of its satire, the novel appears to articulate a notion of autonomy very similar to Theophile Gautier's *l'art pour l'art* aestheticism, which was subsequently taken up by the French Symbolist poets and British decadent writers, such as Oscar Wilde. As Matei Calinescu has argued, the form of autonomy advocated by *l'art pour l'art* is not the philosophical autonomy of "disinterest" already established by thinkers like Kant, but an "aggressive assertion of art's total gratuitousness"[52] that defines art in contradistinction to both the actual and the "good taste" of bourgeois lovers of art (hence the rallying cry of *épater le bourgeois*). It would seem that the provocative rhetoric of *Imaginative Qualities'* satiric persona produces exactly the shock associated with this form of autonomy.

Moreover, like advocates of art-for-art's sake aestheticism, the narrator of *Imaginative Qualities* suggests that fiction's power results from its opposition to the actual. The narrator presents the actual (which he calls "the Rock"[53]) as a set of immutable givens. Life on the "Rock," in the novel's terms, consists of the facts about the world that exist "solid as a bus," which are beyond human control. This is why the narrator claims Joyce's work could be of no practical use, because fiction cannot alter the bare facts of life. Fiction, unlike the "solid" world, is flimsy, since you "can't prop anything up with" it. Unlike the immutable actuality of "the Rock," fiction remains a space of pure, unmitigated potential that partakes of the infinite faculty of the imagination. The narrator of *Imaginative Qualities* appears to conceive of the work of art as an ontologically separate fictional "world," which is to say a heterocosm that constitutes a self-sufficient *doubling* of the actual.[54] The heterocosm would seem to be a superior order of reality precisely because it can transcend the limitations of the actual. But fiction's superiority can only be established if the work of fiction remains "useless" and utterly detached from the actual.

Although Sorrentino's aesthetics have often been identified with art-for-arts' sake aestheticism,[55] I will argue that, despite surface similarities, they respond to very different contexts and conceive the relation between the actual and the imaginative in very different ways. Although the division between life and art suggested by some of the narrator's comments seems stark, *Imaginative Qualities* presents a far more nuanced conception of this relation. Rather than simply reasserting a doctrine of art for art's sake, *Imaginative Qualities'* declaration of autonomy reimagines the correlation between these categories. The intricacy of the relation between the actual and the imaginary is foregrounded by its title *Imaginative Qualities of Actual Things,* which suggests a complicated interpenetration of these categories, rather than a stark separation between them. The title derives from a longer passage in William Carlos Williams's early work *Kora in Hell: Improvisations* (1920), which also comprises the epigraph of the book.

I will argue that this passage from *Kora in Hell* is the key context for understanding *Imaginative Qualities'* approach to the (linked) issues of autonomy and mimesis, and that the novel imports Williams's complicated account of the relation between the actual and the imaginary—which has important implications for understanding how the novel reshapes satire. As Williams's passage suggests, attempts to understand the creative process need to consider the manner in which "reality" is mediated by phenomenal processes:

> In the mind there is a continual play of obscure images which coming between the eyes and their prey seem pictures on the screen at the movies. Somewhere there appears to be a mal-adjustment. The wish would be to see not floating visions of unknown purport but the imaginative qualities of the actual things being perceived accompany their gross vision in a slow dance, interpreting as they go. But inasmuch as this will not always be the case one must dance nevertheless as he can.[56]

Perhaps the two best-known models of aesthetic representation are the mimetic and meontic, which M.H. Abrams associates with classical and postromantic conceptions of representation. As Abrams argues, classical representation relies on a mimetic paradigm, in which art holds up a mirror to the world, whereas postromantic representation employs a meontic paradigm, in which the creative object shines like a radiant lamp, its meaning self-sufficient and separate from direct representations of the actual.[57] Williams's passage offers a third model, which, although it recalls the opposition between meontic and mimetic representation, resituates them in the context of the phenomenological processes of human consciousness. For Williams, phenomenology is essential for grasping the interrelation of the actual and the imaginary, since, as he notes elsewhere in *Kora in Hell,* "the relation between thing and idea" occurs within "the maelstrom of the perceptual or imaginative process itself."[58]

Williams thus recasts the real-imaginary relation in a post-Kantian consciousness, wherein things-in-themselves (noumena) cannot be accessed directly, but rather are experienced through the veil of perception as *phenomena*—a mediated form of "reality" that is experienced as the actual. In this sense, the relation between thing and perception—and, by extension, between the real and the imaginary—is always already an *aporetic* one, since the gap between things-in-themselves and perception can never be entirely bridged. The result of this for Williams is that consciousness becomes not a simple matter of processing sense perception in a stimulus-response framework, but rather a heavily mediated process that appears as something more like "a continual play of obscure images which coming between the eyes and their prey seem pictures on the screen at the movies."

In this process, the mediated form of the actual comprises both what is perceived through sense experience and sensations that are the product of consciousness itself. Pure sense perceptions (or what Williams describes as the "gross vision") are actively and imaginatively interpreted by the consciousness in a complicated interpretive "dance." The realm that we perceive as the *actual* (which is different from the reality of things-in-themselves) is thus experienced as the "imaginative qualities of actual things." The "qualities" of the imaginative refer to those aspects of perception reconfigured in the transformative imagination, while the "actuality" of things serves to emphasize that we do not experience things-in-themselves, but rather things as they have been mediated by perception.

These imaginative qualities are products of consciousness without being manifestations of pure fancy (or in Williams's terms, are "not floating visions of unknown purport"), because they transfigure the phenomena of sense perception through a process of creative interpretation. It is, therefore, neither the case that the mind generates "imaginative qualities" without any reference to "real" things, nor that sense perception determines the internal process of the mind. But despite the imbrication of the imaginative with the actual, neither can be reduced to the other, nor do the two form a straightforward logical relation. What Williams envisions is a threshold where the actual and the imaginative are entangled in a complicated feedback loop, while nonetheless remaining in separate and distinct spheres. The "imaginative qualities of actual things" thus map out two distinct categories: the "imaginative," on one hand, and "actual" things, on the other hand, which are both surrounded by liminal zones.

By mapping out this complicated interrelation of reality, perception, and imagination through this allusion to Williams, Sorrentino is thus able to claim a radical difference between the products of imagination and reality, while nonetheless arguing that these imaginative products are not entirely divorced from reality. The creation of the imaginative work of art, however, introduces yet a further complication into this process, since it involves the actual only insofar as the material of perception has been radically transformed through an imaginative process. The imagination echoes the actual while simultaneously transforming the data of perception into a heterocosmic work of art that is distinct from the actual.

This notion of creative imagination articulated by Williams and Sorrentino thus recalls and revises Coleridge's romantic conception of the primary and secondary imagination in the *Biographia Literaria*.[59] As is well known, Coleridge describes the primary imagination as "the living power and prime agent of all human *perception*."[60] At this level, the imagination constitutes the phenomenological experience of the actual (but not, of course, the "reality" of noumena, which for Coleridge is the work of God's "imagination") through a simultaneous process of perception and imagination. The primary imagination appears to correspond to Williams's conception of an actual that is created half through perception and half through an imaginative faculty.[61]

But the secondary imagination—while being "an echo" of the primary imagination that is "identical . . . in the *kind* of its agency"[62]—differs in that it "co-exist[s] with the conscious will,"[63] rather than being an apparently fixed quality as is the case with sense perception mediated through consciousness (which constitutes the *actual*, but not "reality"). The secondary imagination employs the products of the primary imagination, but is not beholden to them, and has the capacity to transform this perceptual data. As Coleridge explains it, the secondary imagination "dissolves, diffuses, dissipates" the perceptual data of the primary imagination (which constitutes the actual) in order to "re-create."[64] The product of this process of re-creation enacted by the secondary imagination is the work of art, which uses the materials of the primary imagination, but, in so violently transforming them, produces a heterocosm that is not only distinct from the "actual," but also constitutes a self-sufficient alternate reality in its own right. It is for this reason that Coleridge describes the imagination as an "esemplastic power,"[65] or a "power of coadunation" that "forms the many into one,"[66] since the imagination's ideal product is the creation of a unified heterocosm.

Williams's conception of the "imaginative qualities of actual things" formally resembles Coleridge's account of the primary and secondary imagination, since both view the work of art as a heterocosm produced out of an imaginative transfiguration of the actual. But Williams's account also retains an essential difference. For Coleridge, the real (the world created by God), the primary imagination (the subjective perception of the world that constitutes the actual), and the secondary imagination (the individual capacity of intentional, imaginative creation) all derive from the same source, which he describes as the

"the eternal act of creation in the infinite I am."[67] This divine source grounds both the mediated process of perception and the heterocosmic work of art that springs from it, with the result that the secondary imagination and the work of art continue to speak about things that are real, because they echo the primary imagination, which is a repetition of the power of divine creation.

But Williams and Sorrentino's conception of the imaginative qualities of actual things contains no such grounding. An obvious effect of this difference is that, for Williams and Sorrentino, the imaginative work of art now appears entirely contingent, lacking any direct or essential connection to either the actual or things-in-themselves. Yet it is not just the imaginative that is affected by this lack of grounds: the actual, in Williams's account of the "imaginative qualities of actual things," has no intrinsic or transcendent qualities, but is rather an effect produced by the comingling of perception and imagination. The actual—and, thus, what is perceived as "reality" (although still distinct from the reality of things-in-themselves)—is entirely contingent. Rather than being an echo of the actual, the imaginative (and, by extension, the work of art) is its ontological equal, since both are contingent and ungrounded states that exist in discrete but parallel spheres.

In removing these grounds, Williams and Sorrentino invert the traditional, hierarchal relation between the actual and the imaginative work of art. Under the mimetic paradigm, for example, the work of art, in "mirroring" the world, was frequently seen as a false or bad copy of a superior "reality."[68] But in Williams and Sorrentino's account, both actual things and imaginative works of art are contingent—meaning that neither can claim an ontological primacy. And yet, there is a sense in which the work of art can claim superiority over the actual. The work of art has been shaped and molded by the conscious activity of the imagination, which imbues it with a significance (and, presumably, an intent) absent from the actual, which in its comingling of perception and imagination is taken as read by the perceiving subject. The subjective force of perceptual phenomena, in fact, masks the contingency of the actual. But the imaginative work of art admits its own contingency, and, in so acknowledging its fictitious nature, ironically produces a "truth" that the actual cannot equal. It is in this sense that the narrator of *Imaginative Qualities* simultaneously claims that fiction is an "overwhelming lie" and "a realm of total truth."[69] But, since transcendent or grounded truths remain unavailable, the truth of fiction does not derive from an external source; instead, it is an internal effect produced by the work of art (and in this sense remains a "lie").

In asserting the superiority of art over the actual, Sorrentino's aesthetics resemble *l'art pour l'art* aestheticism, but where aestheticist notions tend to valorize the imaginative work of art at the expense of the actual, Sorrentino employs the unique capacities of the work of art to blur and complicate what had appeared to be sharp or stable distinctions between these two categories. In this sense, the leveling of the ontological difference between the actual and the imaginary—which is made possible through the notion of the imaginative qualities of actual things—profoundly transforms satire, which now becomes a literary form for exploring the complicated relation between the actual and the imaginary.

This new trajectory for satire can be seen in the narrator's playful slippage between the categories of the real and the actual in regard to the novel's satiric targets, who, as I discussed earlier, appear to be actual persons even though the narrator claims they are entirely fictional. This destabilization becomes explicit in the section concerning Leo Kaufman (who appears to have been modeled on Joel Oppenheimer). The narrator invokes the relation between the actual and the imaginative when he says, "Leo, Leo, leave me alone. We are not friends any more. Tell it to the Marines . . . tell it to Joel Oppenheimer, who knows more about baseball than you'll ever learn."[70] This statement evokes the referential mode of the roman à clef, since the allusion to Oppenheimer furtively suggests that he is the model for Leo. But in the very process of invoking the "real" Kaufman, the novel problematizes the traditional relation between the actual and fiction, since Oppenheimer and Leo, despite their apparent similarity, possess different qualities (specifically their respective levels of knowledge about baseball). The concept of the imaginative qualities of actual things undermines the hierarchy of original and copy in the mimetic paradigm, which has traditionally applied to satiric targets.

The novel's satire complicates this relation between the actual and the imaginary still further. Consider, for example, this description of Lou Henry, who is imagining what would happen if he caught his wife in the act of adultery with Dick Detective: "If he were there, he would masturbate in a frenzy of voyeurism. . . . That's what *this* Lou would have done anyway. A real Lou, i.e. like the friends you may have, might have been sick or angry."[71] The narrator calls attention to the fictionality of this character by underscoring the difference between the fictional Lou (who would masturbate) and the real Lou (who would be angry). But, as is almost always the case with Sorrentino's satire, there is an ambiguity in the satiric attack that undermines this simple distinction. Part of the joke seems to be that the reader would refuse to believe that a "real" person would have the "perverse" response that the fictional Lou does. But, as the narrator has argued all throughout the novel, perversity is normal. This raises an unanswerable question: is Lou's voyeurism abnormal and, thus, unrealistic, as the narrator states, or is the narrator poking fun at an imaginary reader who is in denial about what his or her "friends" are really like? Attempting to determine which Lou is more realistic depends upon the intentionally unresolved and unresolvable answer to this question. The comparison between the actual and the imaginary results in the (possible but not definite) suggestion that the fictional Lou's response may be "real," while the actual Lou's imagined response might be fictitious. Rather than creating a stable relation or hierarchy between the real and the imaginative, this comparison problematizes both categories, which, lacking any absolute ontological difference, come to resemble each other, even though they remain distinct.

This erosion of ontological difference, which is enabled by the conception of imaginative qualities of actual things, thus makes comprehensible (without entirely resolving) the narrator's aporetic assertions that the novel's characters are both real and entirely fictional. In acknowledging the groundlessness of both the imaginative and the actual, this aporia loses much of its force: following the narrator's logic, it doesn't really matter whether the characters are "actual" or not, ontologically speaking. The narrator chooses to underscore this point by resorting to an absurd argument that the characters in the novel are based on other characters within *Imaginative Qualities* itself:

> Now I have this character. This "character." You can think he's real, i.e., representative of someone who is alive (outside of this book). . . . What if I were to tell you that Anton is a character in this book, based on a character in this book? That is, Anton is "really" Lou Henry. It seems complicated, but it isn't, because it wouldn't change the book at all. There is *no* character development whatsoever (I hope) to Lou Henry, so if Anton is Lou, it means nothing. But what is nice about making fiction is that I can do this.[72]

Previously, the narrator's aporetic assertions had counterpoised the existence of "actual" models for the novel's characters with a claim of their radical fictionality, but this new argument recasts the aporia by suggesting that what appears to be external reference to an "actual" person could just as easily be an internal reference to another fictional entity within the novel. This revision of the aporetic claim inverts the presumed relation between the actual and the fictional, since the work of fiction creates the external reality to which it is seemingly opposed. It is in this sense that the narrator can claim that "people who 'recognize' themselves in books are never in the books. It is the meticulously woven fabric of the ruthless imagination that makes them think they did what the artist said they did."[73] The result of the Sorrentino's account of the real and the actual is that it becomes increasingly difficult to locate the axis of difference between these categories.

Paradoxically, then, the novel's strident assertion of the radical autonomy of the work of art undermines what had previously been a stable and clear distinction between the actual and the imaginary. Throughout *Imaginative Qualities*, the narrator often asserts that there is a "fictional" aspect of the actual, such as when he argues that even "the most suave man, the woman of unbelievable chic, may have in their lives somewhere, the most putrescent garbage, safely hidden."[74] The "unbelievable chic" of these actual people masks another reality. At the same time, as I have already argued, literature, despite being fictional and thus "unreal," frequently presents truth that is more "true" than the actual. Satire, for Sorrentino, thus becomes the literary form that can most effectively reveal this paradoxical relation between the actual and the fictional. Satire is uniquely positioned to register this complicated relation because of its generic tendency toward specific reference, which I discussed earlier. But this tendency is productively exploited by Sorrentino, who, by employing a nonmoral, imaginative satire, is able to use satire's demands for specific reference to reveal the tensions that underlies the process by which imaginative works of art "reference" the actual. Once again, the novel reveals its mixture of postmodern and modernist elements, since a modernist claim of autonomy is applied to the seemingly postmodern end of generating indeterminacy about the status and relation of the actual and the imaginary, which now lack any essential difference.

Satire, here, has moved far away from its traditional conception as form of critiquing vice and folly for the purposes of upholding ethical standards. In Sorrentino's reconception of the form, satire investigates the aporetic relation between the actual and the imaginative work of art. This revision of satire fits in with Sorrentino's broader aesthetic program, which he has elsewhere described as comprising "a dislike of the repetition of experience," a "great pleasure in false or ambiguous information," and a "desire to invent problems that only the invention of new forms can solve."[75] This nonmoral, imaginative satire presents the form that can "solve" the problem of the relation between the actual and the imaginative. While the novel invokes a claim of radical autonomy, it does not seek to create a transcendental and organic work of art hermetically sealed from an "other" reality. *Imaginative Qualities'* autonomy does undermine utilitarian and aestheticist conceptions of art, but its revised conception of the romantic imagination (in the notion of the imaginative qualities of actual things) reveals the essentially groundless nature of the actual itself. Here, the work of art is not a form of escapism, but a utopian desire to recalibrate the relation between art and the actual world. Satire, a genre which traditionally has a fixed relationship between its internal textual dynamics and the external grounded order imposed by ethics, becomes the ideal form for this revision of the relation between the actual and the fictional. In this sense, *Imaginative Qualities'* satire has come full circle, in that its undermining of its own authority and its articulation of a notion of art as radically separate from life forms the means by which it can claim to reconfigure, critically and imaginatively, the relationship between fiction and the actual.

Notes

1   The satiric persona of the narrator appears to be what Wayne Booth, in *The Rhetoric of Fiction* 2nd Ed. (Chicago: University of Chicago Press, 1983), has termed the "implied author," a fictionalized avatar that is similar to, but distinct from the "actual" author (71).

2   Sorrentino, *Imaginative Qualities,* 70.

3   Ibid., 215.

4   Ibid.

5   Ibid., 4.

6   Jones, *Satire and Romanticism,* 18. See also Rene Girard, *The Scapegoat,* Trans. Yvone Freccero (Baltimore: Johns Hopkins University Press, 1986).

7   Sorrentino, *Imaginative Qualities,* 120. Horace Rosette is almost certainly based on Barney Rosset, founder of the avant-garde publisher Grove Press, where Sorrentino worked as an editor in the 1960s. The first name Horace refers to Horace Liveright, who was renowned for publishing works by such prominent members of the modernist avant-gardes as T.S. Eliot, William Faulkner, Ernest Hemmingway, and Hart Crane.

8   Ibid., 8.

9   Ibid., 167.

10   Gerhard Hoffmann, *From Modernism to Postmodernism: Concepts and Strategies of Postmodern American Fiction* (Amsterdam; New York: Rodopi, 2005), 290.

11 Ibid., 9. For more on the importance of perversity in *Imaginative Qualities*, see Tyrus Miller, "Fictional Truths: *Imaginative Qualities of Actual Things* between Image and Language," *Review of Contemporary Fiction* 23.1 (Spring 2003): 59–67.

12 Sorrentino, *Imaginative Qualities,* 107.

13 Bogel, *The Difference Satire Makes,* 42.

14 Lyotard, *The Postmodern Condition,* xxiii–xxiv.

15 Alexander Laski, "The Politics of Dancing—Gay Disco Music and Postmodernism," *The Last Post: Music after Modernism,* Ed. Simon Miller (Manchester: Manchester University Press, 1993), 110–11.

16 Some scholars have viewed *Imaginative Qualities'* employment of metacommentary, self-reference, irony, indeterminacy, allusion, and collage as representative of a set of concerns shared by other "postmodern" novelists (usually authors like John Barth, Thomas Pynchon, and Donald Bartheleme). McHale, in *Postmodernist Fiction,* adduces Sorrentino's *Imaginative Qualities* as an exemplar of postmodern fiction (58). Hoffmann, in *From Modernism to Postmodernism,* similarly classifies Sorrentino's work as postmodern (67). Tyrus Miller, in "Fictional Truths," however, views Sorrentino's work as a continuation of a strand of reflexive modernism, and specifically notes the debt *Imaginative Qualities* owes to Wyndham Lewis's *Apes of God* (49).

17 Despite lacking a higher degree or a formal qualification, Sorrentino taught in a variety of universities from the 1970s until the 1990s, including seventeen years as a professor at Stanford (from 1982 to 1999). He was very much aware of contemporary critical and theoretical debates over postmodernism, and refers to them at various points throughout his work. Sorrentino, in *Mulligan Stew* (New York: Grove Press, 1979), presents a fictitious "Reader's Report" by Horace Rossette (who also appears in *Imaginative Qualities*). Rossette describes the text of what appears to be *Mulligan Stew* as part of the "un-defeated rear guard of the Late-Post-modern movement" (viii). A fictitious interview with the avant-garde author Antony Lamont later in *Mulligan Stew* mentions the "power of the post-modern," and the interviewer responds by saying, "Your command of the critical vocabulary is stunning. I must admit that I was not quite prepared for your subtleties" (349). Sorrentino in "Post-Modernism Explained," *Mississippi Review* 8.1 (Winter/Spring 1979), responds to the notion of postmodernism in verse. Although gnomic, the poem seems to treat the concept with a healthy dose of irony.

18 Gilbert Sorrentino, "Interview with Alexander Laurence," *The Write Stuff: Interviews,* http://www.altx.com/int2/gilber.sorrentino.html, accessed on November 7, 2011. Sorrentino ends his comment with some revealing skepticism about the vogue for postmodernism, as well: "You know that you're in terminological trouble when you hear . . . movie reviewers blather about 'deconstruction' when you realize that they mean satire."

19 Gilbert Sorrentino, "A Conversation with Gilbert Sorrentino by John O'Brien," http://www.dalkeyarchive.com/a-conversation-with-gilbert-sorrentino-by-john-obrien/, accessed on December 3, 2013. See also Gilbert Sorrentino, *Something Said: Essays* (San Francisco: North Point Press, 1984), 7. Sorrentino quotes Lewis in attempting to articulate how the creative process functions for the artist.

20 Jacques Derrida, *Aporias,* Trans. Thomas Dutoit (Stanford: Stanford University Press, 1993), 19.

21 Stacey Olster, in "Gilbert Sorrentino's Problematic Middle Child: *Imaginative Qualities of Actual Things,*" *Review of Contemporary Fiction* 23.1 (Spring 2003), argues that the "problem with *Imaginative Qualities . . .* is that it frequently lapses into the kind of disquisitions on the state of the world beyond its own covers that its narrator repeatedly renounces" (76).

22 Sean Latham, *The Art of Scandal: Modernism, Libel Law, and the Roman á Clef* (Oxford: Oxford University Press, 2009), 58.

23 Ibid., 27.

24. McHale, *Postmodernist Fiction,* 206.

25 Ibid., 207.

26 David Andrews, "Of Love, Scorn, and Contradiction: An Interpretive Overview of Gilbert Sorrentino's *Imaginative Qualities of Actual Things,*" *The Review of Contemporary Fiction* 23.1 (2003): 17.

27 Ibid.

28 Richard Miller, *Bohemia,* 243.

29 Sorrentino, *Imaginative Qualities,* 122.

30 Ibid., 27.

31 Joseph Tabbi, "Matter into Imagination: The Cognitive Realism of Gilbert Sorrentino's *Imaginative Qualities of Actual Things,*" *Review of Contemporary Fiction* 23.1 (Spring 2003): 90. See also Andrews, "Of Love, Scorn, and Contradiction," 12.

32 Edward W. Rosenheim, Jr., *Swift and the Satirist's Art* (Chicago: University of Chicago Press, 1963), 25.

33 Gary Dyer argues that "when satire becomes less specifically personal, it moves closer to comedy," because the "targets become more general," evoking "widespread tendencies in human behaviour" that are "more prevalent, more resistant to correction, and more befitting the absolution and reintegration into the community that is essential to comedy." *British Satire and the Politics of Style, 1789–832* (Cambridge, UK: Cambridge University Press, 1997), 106.

34 Sorrentino, *Imaginative Qualities,* 215.

35 Lyotard, *The Postmodern Condition,* xxiii–xxiv.

36 Bran Nicol, in *Postmodernism and the Contemporary Novel* (Edinburgh: Edinburgh University Press, 2002), argues that "the moment when postmodernism was at the forefront of academic analysis—as is inevitably the case with all era-defining concepts—has passed" (2).

37 Julian Murphet, "Introduction: On the Market and Uneven Development," *Affirmations: Of the Modern* 1.1 (2013): 1–20.

38 Examples of this turn include Siraganian, *Modernism's Other Work,* and Lecia Rosenthal, *Mourning Modernism: Literature, Catastrophe, and the Politics of Consolation* (New York: Fordham University Press, 2011).

39 For example, Simpson, in *The Academic Postmodern*, states that "I am not sure what *postmodernism* is, although I do know a good deal about the arguments around the term" (1).

40 Hoffmann, in *From Modernism to Postmodernism*, notes "the multifariousness of the *conceptualizations* of postmodernism" (19). Simpson, in *The Academic Postmodern,* argues that the definition of the postmodern (about which "there is no substantial consensus") "depends on whether one thinks one is defining a postmoder*nism*" as an aesthetic break, or "postmoder*nity*, a break from the entire culture of modernity and modernization in place since at least the Enlightenment" (15).

41 Susan Sontag, *Against Interpretation and Other Essays* (New York: Farrar, Straus, and Giroux, 1966). In particular, the essays "Against Interpretation" and "Notes on Camp" are frequently seen as early accounts of a postmodern aesthetic sensibility. Ihab Hassan, "POSTmodernISM: A Paracritical Bibliography," *Paracriticisms: Seven Speculations of the Times* (Urbana, IL; Chicago: University of Illinois Press, 1975), 39–62. Hassan's approach to postmodernism became more systematic in his later work. Leslie Fiedler, "The Death of Avant-Garde Literature," *The Collected Essays of Leslie Fiedler* Vol. 2 (New York: Stein and Day, 1971), 454–60. It's also worth noting that these early periodizing accounts clash dramatically with Lyotard's influential account of postmodern aesthetics. Lyotard, in *Postmodernism Explained,* argues that postmodernism is "undoubtedly part of the modern" but represents the "nascent state" of modernism's aesthetic development, before novel experimentation hardens into set traditions, schools, or movements; in Lyotard's sense, postmodernism is thus a "recurrent" or transhistorical sensibility, which privileges the search for "new presentations" over a nostalgia for tradition (13–15).

42 Hoffman, *From Modernism to Postmodernism,* 35–36. See also Andreas Huyssen, *After the Great Divide: Modernism, Mass Culture, Postmodernism* (Bloomington; Indianapolis: Indiana University Press, 1986), 188.

43 McHale, in *Postmodernist Fiction,* argues that modernist works sought to explore how we come to know things, while postmodern works ask ontological questions about the grounds that underpin epistemology itself: "What is a world?; What

kinds of worlds are there, how are they constituted, and how do they differ?"
(10). McHale's account has the virtue of providing what is perhaps the clearest
distinction between modernist and postmodern works, even if he emphasizes that
there are many texts which occupy a liminal space between them. But the clarity
of McHale's conception also relies on the notion that there are clearly discernable
paradigms (or "dominants") which can be used to differentiate modernism and
postmodernism—a claim that many of his contemporaries view with considerable
suspicion.

44 Linda Hutcheon, in "Beginning to Theorize Postmodernism," *A Postmodern
    Reader,* Ed. Joseph Natoli and Linda Hutcheon (Albany, NY: SUNY University
    Press, 1993), argues that "postmodernism can probably not be considered a new
    paradigm" because "it is contradictory and tends to work within the very systems
    it attempts to subvert"; nonetheless Hutcheon claims that postmodernism receives
    its most complete articulation in "historiographic metafiction," a literary subgenre
    that incorporates postmodernism's "theoretical self-awareness of history and
    fiction as human constructs," which are "made the grounds for its rethinking and
    reworking of the forms and contents of the past" (245–46).

45 Huyssen, *After the Great Divide,* 188–95. For Huyssen, postmodernism always
    generates its own content in response to its conception of modernism—which is,
    of course, also an internally generated notion that is necessarily a reification and
    attenuation of the broader practices of modernism as it historically existed. Thus,
    Huyssen argues that conceptions of postmodernism vary in relation to how they
    construe and, therefore, respond to a version of modernism, which they have
    deemed unsatisfactory. As Huyssen suggests, modernism itself was a far more
    diverse and complicated entity than is readily admitted by many antagonistic
    postmoderns—a caution echoed by both Hutcheon and McHale. At the same
    time, Huyssen argues that modernism tends toward exclusion and elitism, while
    postmodernism tends toward inclusivity and pluralism.

46 Of course, this binary is a necessary oversimplification. In reality, a much broader
    spectrum of viewpoints could be established, but, for my purposes, the difference
    between weak and strong forms of postmodernism captures the key distinction
    required to understand *Imaginative Qualities*' relationship to the postmodern.

47 Even though McHale and Huyssens' positions acknowledge the porousness of
    what might appear to be absolute distinctions, I would argue that they constitute
    "strong" accounts of postmodernism, because they posit essential differences
    between postmodernism and modernism. It's also worth noting that, based on my
    categorization, Lyotard's famous conception of postmodernism oddly appears as
    both strong and weak. On the one hand, it does depict a sharp distinction between
    the modern and the postmodern, but it does so by denying any clear form for the

latter (since, for Lyotard, the postmodern must always be inchoate). My point in raising this is to note that, while I believe the distinction between strong and weak forms of postmodernism is useful because of its explanatory power, it does not account for all of the positions taken in the postmodernism debates.

48   In McHale's account, postmodernism raises the question of ontology, which problematizes the notion of art as a distinct and autonomous form that is essentially different from other forms of discourse; postmodernist works, which McHale sees as questioning their own ontological status, are skeptical of notions of autonomy. This also pertains to Huyssens's distinction between the modernist rejection of low culture and postmodern embrace of popular forms of culture. At the heart of this distinction is a question about whether art serves a different purpose than forms of mass entertainment (as in Adorno's famous condemnation of the "culture industry") and thus can be considered autonomous. See also Frow, "What Was Postmodernism?," 63.

49   Jameson, in *Singular Modernity,* notes that postmodernism's devaluation of autonomy is not totalizing "despite its systematic and thoroughgoing rejection of all the features it could identify with high modernism and modernism proper," because it "seems utterly unable to divest itself of this final requirement of originality" (152). While postmodernism may retain this trace of autonomy, it still differs from modernism in its desire to rid itself of autonomy rather than reaffirm it.

50   Ashton, *From Modernism to Postmodernism,* 13.

51   On the distinction between romantic and modernist versions of autonomy, see Goldstone, *Fictions of Autonomy,* 12

52   Calinsecu, *Faces of Modernity,* 45.

53   Sorrentino, *Imaginative Qualities,* 169.

54   For more on the notion of heterocosm, see Brian McHale, *Postmodernist Fiction,* 215. See also Wolfgang Iser, *The Fictive and the Imaginary: Charting Literary Anthropology* (Baltimore: Johns Hopkins University Press, 1993), 78.

55   Sharon Thesen, in "in the song/of the alphabet: Gilbert Sorrentino's *Splendide Hotel,*" *The Review of Contemporary Fiction* 1.1 (1980), argues that Sorrentino substitutes art for religion, seeing "grace as the proper achievement of the artist at the same time that [he] proposes darkness and corruption as what we necessarily walk through" (57).

56   William Carlos Williams, *Imaginations* (New York: New Directions, 1970), 67.

57   M.H. Abrams, *The Mirror and the Lamp,* 47–69.

58   Jesse D. Green, "Williams' 'Kora in Hell': The Opening of the Poem as 'Field of Action,'" *Contemporary Literature* 13.3 (Summer, 1972): 297.

59   Tyrus Miller, in *Singular Examples,* argues that, unlike in the romantic model of representation, exemplified by Yeats, which presents "the poetic image's

seamless fusion of subject and object," Williams's conception of imaginative qualities "indexes a permanent 'mal-adjustment'" that constitutes "an irresolvable dissonance in the artistic process"—a tension that also appears within the work of art (163). While I agree with Miller's reading of Williams, my argument is that romantic self-reflexivity also incorporates a similar "dissonance" that anticipates, rather than conflicts with, Williams's account of representation.

60 Coleridge, *Biographia Literaria,* 297–98.

61 In this sense, Sorrentino's account of the imagination also resembles Wordsworth's formulation in "Tintern Abbey," *Lyrical Ballads* (London: J. & A. Arch, 1798), in which the senses both "half create" and half "perceive" the experience of the world (207–08).

62 Coleridge, *Biographia Literaria,* 298. Coleridge's emphasis.

63 Ibid.

64 Ibid.

65 Ibid., 296.

66 Quoted in Mary Warnock, *Imagination* (Berkeley; Los Angeles: University of California Press, 1978), 92. As Warnock points out, the word esemplastic, which Coleridge elsewhere renders as "esenoplastic" was apparently "a translation of the German '*Einbildungskraft*'" (92).

67 Coleridge, *Biographia Literaria,* 297.

68 Elin Diamond, *Unmaking Mimesis* (New York: Routledge, 1997), 65.

69 Sorrentino, *Imaginative Qualities,* 111–12.

70 Ibid., 127.

71 Ibid., 228.

72 Ibid., 169. The narrator emphasizes this point by introducing fictional characters from other novels into its text. Later in the novel, the narrator appropriates the character of Lolita from Nabokov's eponymous novel, insisting that his Lolita "is the exact Lolita that Nabokov stitched together" (193).

73 Ibid., 48.

74 Ibid., 236. It is important to note, however, that there is no ethical charge to such revelations. As the narrator notes, following this statement, "The reader will understand that this is told here not to derogate April, nor to make him feel sorry for Dick. 'I don't want your pity!' I will have Dick say" (236).

75 Sorrentino, *Something Said,* 265.

6

Conclusion: Satire and Radical Apophasis in Evan Dara's *The Easy Chain*

1 Situating avant-garde satires of the avant-garde

Over the course of the preceding chapters, I have examined the evolution of a new subgenre of self-reflexive satire, which I have termed avant-garde satires of the avant-garde. In the introduction, I noted the shared characteristics of the satires in this subgenre: their tendency to eschew any ethical or moral purpose; their use of "flat" characters for protagonists; their aversion to the description of interior psychological states; their avoidance of character development and traditional plot arcs; their (often extensive) depiction of intentionally banal dialogue; and their use of the Rabelaisian catalogue as a literary form. This unusual constellation of formal characteristics can be traced to a historical shift in the literary dominant of satire, which occurred when the ethically grounded, neoclassical paradigm of satire yielded to a romantic reenvisioning of satire as a genre whose ends are primarily aesthetic. This aesthetic potential is activated when satire self-reflexively subjects its own norms to satiric critique. By questioning the legitimacy of the rules that form the basis of satiric critique, these satires undermine their own authority and seek to problematize the relation between satirical critique and the ethical grounds that are meant to secure its meaning.

One key claim about this subgenre, which has been articulated in various ways in the course of my study of these individual texts, is that it presents a unique and illuminating perspective from which to reexamine the accepted narrative of twentieth-century literary aesthetics. Most histories of twentieth-century literature view its inaugurating event to be the appearance of modernism and the historical avant-gardes, which developed into an aesthetic dominant that retained a hegemonic hold on literary discourse until sometime after Second World War, when a new aesthetic dominant—postmodernism—appeared to signal both a break from and the exhaustion of the modernist tradition. But this subgenre contradicts this narrative in a variety of ways: by critically questioning the historical uniqueness of the modernist avant-gardes; by problematizing the notion that modernism has been exhausted; and by disputing that all forms of postmodernism constitute a radical break with modernist traditions. This critical investigation of the "standard view" resonates with a turn in modernist studies over the last decade,[1] which has broadened the investigation of modernist literature outside of its traditional periodized boundaries in order to acknowledge modernism's many links to both prior and subsequent forms of literature.

In particular, I have suggested the modernist avant-gardes owe a far greater debt to romanticism than has traditionally been acknowledged. While I do not mean to suggest that the modernist avant-gardes are simply a late romanticism, romanticism anticipates many elements of avant-gardism and creates the conditions of possibility from which the avant-gardes could arise. Acknowledging the avant-gardes' historical links to romantic aesthetics suggests the necessity for a more skeptical approach to their claims of radical novelty. But acknowledging these antecedents also opens up new ways of considering how the avant-gardes incorporated literary traditions, rather than rejecting the totality of art as an institution.

These satires also complicate and enrich typical understandings of the relation between modernism and postmodernism. One of my key assertions has been that modernism has continued to persist in important and influential forms long after its alleged demise as a cultural dominant. Avant-garde satires of the avant-garde all reaffirm a notion of aesthetic autonomy indebted to modernism, which views the work of literature as a privileged locus that is distinct from—and arguably superior to—other forms of discourse. This reaffirmation of autonomy is an essential mark of this subgenre, and, as a result, avant-garde satires of the avant-garde are incompatible with forms of postmodernism that seek to undermine or deny the autonomy of art.

While I have noted, at various points, that claims of autonomy made by specific satires have a political significance, the autonomy from ethical discourses enacted by avant-garde satires of the avant-garde entails a relation to political and social orders that is inherent in the form and development of the subgenre itself. Satire has typically been viewed as an inherently conservative genre, since its critiques are based on a set of satiric "norms" that are meant to reflect the larger norms of the group, culture, or society in which the satire is situated. Satire's didactic ethical mission serves as a means of covert social control, in which satiric targets are held to account for deviating from social norms. As a natural consequence, traditional satires—in enforcing social norms—often disproportionately focus their attacks on those who exist at the margins of society, whether due to reasons of class, race, sexual orientation, gender, levels of education, or the like.[2]

To assert satire's autonomy from ethical discourses is a political gesture because it deactivates the relationship between authority, norms, control, and ridicule that has traditionally animated satire. Following this logic, these satires' excision of their own ethical authority comprises not only a liberating gesture, but also a liberalizing gesture in a political and democratic sense: by undermining their ethical authority, these satires also resist the co-option of satire as a means of social control that supports hegemonic power through the literary scapegoating of those whose form of life differs from accepted norms. Such satires no longer accept proclamations of transcendent authority,[3] but rather must locate the basis of their authority in the display of some other quality—in this case, an aesthetic quality, which is the product of individual human labor and creative power on the part of the author, rather than a transcendent, authorizing discourse.

In suggesting that the rejection of satire's ethical grounds—which constitutes the point of departure for the subgenre of avant-garde satires of the avant-garde—corresponds with the rise of liberal democracy as mode of social and political organization, I do not mean to assert that the actual political or ideological content of these satires is necessarily democratic. Although Wyndham Lewis was influenced by radical politics from both the right and left, he was consistent in critiquing liberalism as a political orientation. In other words, while I am noting a correspondence between this subgeneric articulation of autonomy and liberal democracy, I am not simply submitting this particular regime of satire to ideology critique—a method that, in decoding aesthetics as a repressed power relation of another form, threatens to flatten out the polysemy and multiplicity of affect that characterizes the work of art in the first place. While I think the correspondence between the rejection of ethical grounds and liberalism's rejection of transcendental authority can be observed when these satires are considered together as a subgenre, it does not follow that this correspondence is determining over individual works within this subgenre. While this subgenre's claim of autonomy from ethics reflects the process of democratization, the individual satires within it must be examined in relation to their specific contexts.

I have sought to demonstrate how these satires' assertions of autonomy are entangled with contemporary social and political questions. For Lewis, for example, autonomous satire's power derives precisely from its ability to acknowledge the influence of tradition while openly resisting it; although satire, in his conception, may be autonomous from ethical grounds, it is also nothing less than the form par excellence for a new aesthetic modernity, a project that had inherently political dimensions. Sorrentino's *Imaginative Qualities,* as I have argued, asserts autonomy not to withdraw art from the world, but rather to posit, albeit apophatically, a new form of relation between art and life that does not fall back into the exhausted and interrelated paradigms of an instrumentalized art or an aestheticized approach to life. Even Gaddis's *The Recognitions*—which, in my reading, comes closest to approximating a *l'art pour l'art* conception of autonomy by producing an ambivalent sublime that results in a moment of aesthetic unity that supersedes logic—still cannot disentangle its autonomy claims from larger social and political dimensions. The novel's conception of its own "lateness," for example, is at heart a social and political problem. In drawing out the political and social implications of these autonomy claims, my analyses reflect Lisa Siraganian's insight in *Modernism's Other Work* (2012) that aesthetic autonomy's "operation was always conceived simultaneously and deliberately as an aesthetic *and* political act."[4]

I will conclude with a brief examination of Evan Dara's *The Easy Chain* (2009), a satiric novel that appropriates the form of avant-garde satires of the avant-gardes to make a pointed political critique. Moreover, *The Easy Chain* extends and intensifies the apophatic utopianism of this subgenre of satire, through an unusually oblique mode of allusion. This novel once again reiterates a modernist conception of autonomy, but this invocation of autonomy does not simply comprise a conservative desire to return to an idealized past. Instead, *The Easy Chain* uses the contemporary suspicion of both autonomy claims and the avant-garde itself to indirectly question the contemporary modes of production and exchange that characterize late capitalism. Here, autonomy functions not as a philosophical presupposition to underwrite an aestheticism hermetically sealed off from "reality," but as a provocation to think through and question (although never in an explicit or programmatic way) the relation between art and the social in an era of global capitalism.

2 "Negate negate negation": Evan Dara's *The Easy Chain*

At first glance, *The Easy Chain* by Evan Dara[5] does not appear to meet the criteria I have established for avant-garde satires of the avant-garde. There are, for example, very few mentions of art and few direct references to the avant-garde in this novel. Instead, *The Easy Chain* applies its satirical eye to Chicago's business world, ridiculing aspects of commerce and economics with a particular emphasis on the capacity of individuals and institutions with large reserves of capital or excessive personal charisma to manipulate the market for their own ends, even when it is clearly against the public good.

Although the avant-garde does not appear to be an explicit target in this novelistic satire of contemporary capitalism, the work's experimental literary techniques owe clear debts to both the modernist avant-gardes in general and the tradition of self-reflexive satire in particular. Like the other satiric novels I have examined, *The Easy Chain* is a long and "difficult" work that violates conventions of the realist novel: it prizes surface descriptions, renders long passages of banal dialogue with extreme fidelity, employs Rabelaisian catalogues, and buries major plot points behind what appear to be irrelevant digressions. It also satirizes a specific group in critiquing the cultural and economic elites in Chicago of the early 2000s. *The Easy Chain* also applies a variety of literary techniques that echo Gaddis's work, in particular: Dara uses em dashes to render dialogue (a technique Gaddis appropriated from Joyce) and the narrative is related through a panoply of constantly rotating voices, rather than an omniscient narrator or point-of-view character. The subject matter of Dara's novel—which satirizes economic elites and the speculative investments of those with large stores of capital—also owes clear debts to William Gaddis's novel *J R* (1976) in which a seven-year-old boy constructs a paper empire. As I will argue, however, *The Easy Chain* explicitly extends the category of avant-garde satires of the avant-garde through an innovative use of negation that further intensifies the apophatic gestures of these earlier satires. This intensified apophaticism reconnects the novel with the modernist avant-gardes and demonstrates how this subgenre of satire continues to manifest in new and unexpected iterations.

The Easy Chain may also seem an odd text to examine in that it is not a particularly well-known novel, and seems, at best, marginal to the cannons of contemporary literature forming in scholarly discussions and on university syllabi. I would argue, however, that the marginal status of *The Easy Chain* clarifies its relation to the other novels I have examined, all of which languished in various forms of obscurity long after their original publication. Wyndham Lewis's work interested only a few isolated scholars until the 1970s, and *The Apes of God,* in particular, only started to receive broader critical attention in the 1990s. William Gaddis's *The Recognitions* developed a devoted cult audience in the years following its publication, but he did not receive broader literary accolades until his second novel, *J R,* won the National Book Award in 1976. While significant scholarship on Gaddis's work first appeared in the early 1980s, much of this was driven by one critic, Steven Moore, though Gaddis's work now has attracted a significant body of scholarship. Gilbert Sorrentino's *Imaginative Qualities of Actual Things* only began to be discussed by literary academics in the early 2000s through a special issue in *The Review of Contemporary Fiction;* even still, Sorrentino's work occupies a peripheral position in cannons of late-twentieth-century fiction. In this sense, the marginality of Dara's work makes it of a kind with the other novels I have examined.

The first two hundred pages of *The Easy Chain* comprise a series of brief anecdotes related by a continuously revolving cast of unnamed narrators, which recount how Lincoln Selwyn, an Englishman raised in the Netherlands, climbs the social ladder in Chicago through a combination of his "skill almost inhuman at putting you at ease"[6] and shrewd advice from his public relations consultant, Auran. This narrative is interrupted when Selwyn suddenly disappears, an event that the novel mimics on a formal level by suspending the text for forty-two almost completely blank pages[7] (a somewhat infamous gesture frequently mentioned in reviews of the novel). When the text resumes, the narrative becomes increasingly fragmented, employing a radical parataxis that jumps between different speakers, settings, and even rhetorical styles with relatively few signposts for confused readers. Some of these later sections, which appear to constitute Lincoln's internal monologue, bear the influence of modernist poetry, employing line breaks and an incessant repetition that recalls authors such as Gertrude Stein:

Turn the dark the Dark corner
Into unto light's vector
Take the prison &
Strike the jailors &
Take the prison &
Strike the jailors
Deny deny them
Deny deny them
Deny deny them being
Great refusal the
Great refusal &
Negate negate negation
Negate negate negation[8]

Although these poetic monologues extrapolate on themes and plot points within the novel, they are largely hermetic and impenetrable, displaying the "difficulty" often seen as a hallmark of modernist aesthetics. *The Easy Chain* also betrays its modernist influences in undermining and complicating standard narrative practices. For example, just as it appears poised to reach its narrative climax in a terrorist attack on the Chicago Mercantile Exchange Building (making literal the novel's satiric attack on the world of finance), the narrative again ceases and is followed, instead, by an "essay" about attempts to privatize Chicago's public water supply.[9] The novel concludes with a long (and darkly comic) monologue by a man being tortured and interrogated by Selwyn, which is rendered with eccentric typography (the irregular capitalization of letters) and intentional misspellings. This conclusion—in an exemplary modernist fashion—contains layers of irony and ambiguity that raise as many questions about the narrative as they resolve. When taken together, the novel's wild experimentation with form, style, content, genre, and mode of address clearly place it in a tradition of the modernist experimental novel as exemplified by Joyce's *Ulysses* and Lewis's own *The Apes of God*.

But I will argue that the modernist avant-gardes exert an influence on *The Easy Chain* that goes beyond these stylistic and formal attributes. In particular, *The Easy Chain* employs a strategy of radical apophasis that invokes the modernist avant-gardes through a series of oblique references. Through these indirect allusions, the text signals the importance of the avant-garde to its satirical critique in a manner that indicates *The Easy Chain*'s membership in this subgenre of satire. The text first enunciates its apophatic methods—albeit somewhat ironically[10]—through the character of "El Rubio" (whose real name is Ernesto Luis de Catamarca). Having realized that his life was motivated entirely by the accumulation of material things and the attainment of instant gratification, El Rubio embarks upon a drastic plan of action with the hope of imparting greater meaning to his life:

> Whenever an option, passion, or plurality of possibilities would present itself to me, I would choose and do exactly the opposite of what my first inclination told me. Far from following my instincts, I would now refute them. First thought, worst thought, and that unto terminus. . . . And so I set up a contra fund of the mind. Whatever I was, I was against.[11]

Despite his hopes that such a plan will result in a drastic change of circumstances, El Rubio finds that "in four years, I was Senior Vice-President for Internal

Affairs of the Mazorca Insurance Co., a robust concern that holds offices in seventeen cities throughout Argentina."[12] With the failure of his original plan, El Rubio comes to a surprising conclusion: "There had been one thing I had not negated, and that negation itself. One thing I had not run contrary to, and that the contrarian posture . . . I would negate negation."[13]

This program of negating negation (which also reappears in the selection from Lincoln's monologue I reproduced earlier) recalls the recursive negation of self-reflexive satire that aligns avant-garde satires of the avant-garde with apophasis. The form of double negation enables the negative to take on a *positive* content, a fact that El Rubio himself notes, when he suggests that his program "would be inaugurating a new mode of grand approbation, one closer to a declaration of faith."[14] At the same time, it also recalls—and is likely an allusion to—another famous episode of *Seinfeld*, entitled "The Opposite," in which George Costanza states that "every decision I've ever made, in my entire life, has been wrong."[15] He decides instead to go against his natural instincts: "I will do the opposite. I used to sit here and do nothing, and regret it for the rest of the day, so now I will do the opposite, and I will do something!"[16] Like El Rubio, Costanza finds immediate success as a result of his negative method.

The Easy Chain employs the double negation of apophasis at a formal level by intentionally leaving a series of gaps, holes, and "negatives" in the novel's narrative, all of which suggest a positive content through their conspicuous absence—a gesture similar to the conception of negative space in the visual arts.[17] Lincoln Selwyn provides the best example of this deployment of the negative. Although he dominates the narrative action, Lincoln remains an absent figure in the text. Even the story of his rise to prominence is not told through his perspective, but through anecdotes, hearsay, rumor, and speculation provided by unnamed interlocutors whose reliability is dubious. The textual mirroring of Lincoln's disappearance through the use of blank pages, which I mentioned earlier, represents another such negative moment in the text. Even the later sections of poetic monologue "told" from Lincoln's point of view are emptied of subjective content through their use of heavy repetition that obscures the coherence of his inner monologue. Because of these literary techniques, Lincoln appears as an absence not unlike Pierpoint in Lewis's *The Apes of God*; as one character notes of Lincoln, "this guy is a nothing, a null set, a zero with a thousand faces."[18] In this manner, the novel's various negatives and absences take on a present character within the text, as is characteristic of apophasis.

But another even more radical apophasis occurs within the novel in relation to the modernist avant-gardes. Although there is very little explicit engagement with art or aesthetics in the novel, I would suggest this omission presents another form of apophasis and that the work of art is actually the novel's secret content—a point signaled by a series of indirect references within the text indicating that one of *The Easy Chain*'s key themes is the difficulty of creating autonomous art in a time of late capital that seeks to replace all alternate forms of value with purely economic ones.

The first hint of this hidden content can be seen in the protagonist's name, Lincoln Selwyn, which can be read in multiple ways. On one hand, it intentionally recalls Abraham Lincoln (himself a famous resident of Illinois), but on the other, it can be reduced to a series of puns. Lincoln, which can be read phonetically as a "link in," appears to refer to the novel's titular "easy chain" (itself an allusion to Philip Larkin's "Spring Warning"[19])—a description of the pathway to personal success that Lincoln charted. His last name similarly recalls verbs ("sell" and "win") that seem explicitly related to the kind of economic success he pursues. But more importantly, the name Selwyn alludes to Ezra Pound's early long poem, "Hugh Selwyn Mauberley" (1920), which suggests that the novel's interest in the iniquities caused by contemporary economics is closely linked to its concern with the work of art.

"Mauberley" is important in establishing this connection since, in this poem, Pound attempted to "expos[e] those forces that make the artist's full realization impossible in modern England," the most important of which was "commercialism and the insistence on money as an aesthetic standard."[20] Various moments in "Mauberley" more or less explicitly suggest that there is something about the pace of industrialized modernity that cannot be reconciled with art that encourages aesthetic contemplation:

> The age demanded an image
> Of its accelerated grimace,
> Something for the modern stage,
> Not, at any rate, an Attic grace;
>
> No, not certainly, the obscure reveries
> Of the inward gaze;
> Better mendacities
> Than the classics in paraphrase![21]

While it is important to note that these positions are heavily ironized throughout the poem (indeed, Mauberley's own art-for-art's sake aestheticism appears to be explicitly satirized as belonging to an exhausted nineteenth-century tradition), passages like these problematize the role of the contemporary poet in a time that increasingly appears to see value only in utility. In this sense, "Mauberley" can also be said to be a poem about the question of autonomy, since it interrogates the relation between art and the world.[22] Given *The Easy Chain*'s similar critique of late modernity as an era determined by the values of global, economic exchange, its references to "Mauberley" imply a similar view of the relation between the valorization of economic value and the increasing difficulties faced by those writers and artists who value their works in other ways (or, at least, not only in monetary terms).

At first blush, this connection may appear tenuous, but the text explicitly links its own satire to Pound's positions on art through another set of allusions, which occur in one of the novel's pivotal scenes, when Lincoln is initially introduced to Auran, the public relations consultant who will enable his meteoric rise to the status of local celebrity. During their discussion, Auran's pitch to Lincoln references two of Ezra Pound's most well-known sayings: "Anyone can get his name in the paper once. The goal is to get *back* in, regularly, all the time. To be news that stays news. Lincoln, starting right now you should view your life as a work of art, with art's sovereign goal: make it news!"[23] Auran invokes both Pound's famous claim that "literature is news that stays news"[24] and his oft-quoted phrase "Make it new,"[25] which he used as the title for a 1935 collection of his essays. In alluding to Pound at this moment, the text links its critique of economics with Pound's articulation of a modernist aesthetics, and his critique of commerce's deleterious effects on the work of art in "Mauberley" and elsewhere.[26] In this implicit linkage between *The Easy Chain*'s satire and Pound's concerns, the novel announces its connection to the subgenre of avant-garde satires of the avant-garde.

The Easy Chain can be considered an avant-garde satire of the avant-garde, but only in a radically apophatic sense: although the avant-garde is never explicitly named, it is nevertheless evoked to the extent that it becomes a palpable absence. On the one hand, this gesture would seem to be a significant departure from other forms of the genre that I have examined. On the other, it represents yet another intensification of the techniques of radical negation and apophasis, which I have associated with this subgenre of satire. In *The Easy Chain*, the traditional content of this subgenre, which is to say the avant-garde itself, is negated in ways that enable the book to comment upon the avant-garde's disappearance in late modernity. The novel presents a particular paradox, because the gesture that would seem to disqualify it as a candidate for this subgenre (its omission of the avant-garde), also signals its place in the genre, since this omission is a form of apophasis characteristic of self-reflexive satire.

In this paradoxical gesture, the novel reveals other allegiances to this subgenre. Not only does it construct its response to late modernity in reference to modernism (in this case through its allusions to Pound), in much the way that *The Apes of God, The Recognitions,* and *The Imaginative Qualities of Actual Things* have, but also, through this apophatic invocation of the autonomous work of art, the novel once again interrogates the relationship between life and art in a manner characteristic of avant-garde satires of the avant-garde. Although these satires inevitably focus on the past, since they orient themselves in relation to a notion of the modernist avant-gardes, this does not mean that the genre has been exhausted. *The Easy Chain* constitutes another extension and intensification of the apophatic utopianism of self-reflexive satire, which indicates that the subgenre continues to evolve in response to contemporary contexts. Initially, this may appear to contradict the assertion I made in my examination of Gilbert Sorrentino's *Imaginative Qualities,* in which I argue that Sorrentino's novel constitutes a "limit-Modernism" that also establishes a firm boundary on this subgenre, which is incompatible with strong forms of postmodernism. In implying such a "limit," it would seem that Sorrentino's satire presents a telos to the genre, beyond which it cannot extend. I would argue, however, that avant-garde satires of the avant-garde are still—albeit in odd forms—being produced and that this genre, which ceaselessly attacks its own normative assumptions, is still finding ways to develop and explore its apophatic and utopian assertions of modernist autonomy in a time of late capital.

The Easy Chain demonstrates the particular and enduring power of this unusual subgenre of self-reflexive satire. Avant-garde satires of the avant-garde have persisted precisely because they are able to track the complicated relation between art and its social and political contexts. In their simultaneous denial of any transcendent grounds, their assertion of their own autonomy, and their rigorous and relentless self-interrogation, they are able to register the overdetermined and frequently paradoxical or negative relationship between aesthetic claims and the various discourses, institutions, and traditions that have exerted an influence on such claims. At the same time, the subgenre's extreme self-reflexivity means that these relations never settle into a concrete form, which might threaten to found a new ground for satiric critique. In this sense, they also reveal the complexity of relations between the social and the fictional, while simultaneously refusing any closure that would reduce the work of art to its conditions of possibility. In attempting to negotiate and preserve this complexity, these satires offer a unique and privileged viewpoint from which to reconsider the manner in which Western, literary aesthetics have developed since the rise of romanticism, and how these developments continue to make themselves felt under the conditions of late modernity.

Notes

1   For one overview of the changes in modernist studies, see Douglas Mao and Rebecca L. Walkowitz, "The New Modernist Studies," *PMLA*, 123. 3 (2008): 737–48. Goldstone, in *Fictions of Autonomy*, critiques Mao and Walkowitz's position and articulates an alternate program (5).

2   Bogel, in *The Difference Satire Makes*, suggests that satiric critique resembles "social rituals of purification, casting out, and scapegoating" (46).

3   Following the logic of my argument, traditional satires that accept the transcendental authority of their ethical grounds can be seen to correlate with the political form of monarchy, which is also founded on the grounds of the transcendental authority of the monarch.

4   Siraganian, *Modernism's Other Work*, 3. My emphasis.

5   Dara first came to prominence when his debut novel, *The Lost Scrapbook* (1996), won the Fiction Collective 2's Innovative Fiction Award, which was judged in that year by the celebrated novelist William Vollmann. Notably, the name Evan Dara is a pseudonym, and the real identity of the author has never been revealed. Dara disappeared for twelve years after publishing *The Lost Scrapbook*, only resurfacing in 2008 to self-publish his second novel *The Easy Chain*. He has subsequently published his third novel, *Flee*, in July of 2013.

6   Evan Dara, *The Easy Chain* (New York; Roma: Aurora Publishers, 2008), 346.

7   Ibid., 208–49. Despite the fact that Dara's first novel was well-received by critics, *The Easy Chain* appears to have been self-published by Dara through his own press, Aurora Publishers. Although no one knows why Dara has chosen to publish via this method, I would speculate that including so many blank pages in a novel would be anathema to most publishers.

8   Dara, *The Easy Chain*, 418.

9   Ibid., 438–53.

10   Ibid., 142. Ironically, El Rubio's entire speech is a pitch for an unusual business plan: he gives money (via check) to famous people, and—once the checks have been signed, cashed, and returned—sells them at a profit to autograph collectors.

11   Ibid., 140.

12   Ibid., 141.

13 Ibid., 142.

14 Ibid.

15 Larry David and Jerry Seinfeld, "The Opposite," *Seinfeld,* season 5, episode 21, directed by Tom Cherones, aired May 19, 1994 (Culver City, CA: Sony Pictures Home Entertainment, 2005), DVD.

16 Ibid.

17 There is strong textual evidence throughout his work to suggest that Dara has thought about negative modes of representation in considerable detail. For example, in *Flee* (New York; Roma: Aurora Publishers, 2013), one character offers the following statement: "Not a de Brogliesque absence of presence but a Tertullian presence of absence" (17).

18 Dara, *The Easy Chain,* 358.

19 Philip Larkin, *Collected Poems,* Ed. Anthony Thwaite (London: Marvell Press, 1988), 237. The relevant lines in the poem read as follows:

> But there are some who mutter: "Joy
> Is for the simple or the great to feel,
> Neither of which we are." They file
> The easy chain that bound us, jeer
> At our ancestral forge . . . (237)

The poem, which Larkin wrote when he was only seventeen, appears to be an antiwar poem, and, in this sense, its connection to the plot of Dara's novel is somewhat obscure. The allusion seems undeniable, however, given the presence of a character named Larkin in *The Easy Chain.* That being said, the poem ends with a reference to those who "follow with their eye/The muffled boy, with his compelling badge,/On his serious errand riding to the gorge" (237). The observation of the young boy (presumably a soldier) seems to mirror the intense scrutiny of young Selwyn undertaken by the many nameless observers in the novel.

20 John Espey, *Ezra Pound's Mauberley: A Study in Composition* (Berkley; Los Angeles; London: University of California Press, 1955), 15. There are other links between *The Easy Chain* and "Mauberley" at a formal level, since both of them make use of parataxis and ambiguous speakers. Indeed, critics have debated whether or not Mauberley himself even speaks in any of the poems, and, if he does, which sections might be considered "his." For a good survey of these disputes, see Stephen J Adams, "Hugh Selwyn Mauberley," *The Ezra Pound Encyclopedia,* eds. Demetres P. Tryphonopoulos and Stephen J. Adams (Westport, CT: Greenwood Press, 2005), 150–51.

21 Ezra Pound, "Hugh Selwyn Mauberley" *in* Espey, *Ezra Pound's Mauberley,* 119.

22   Hugh Witemeyer, in "Early Poetry 1908–20," *The Cambridge Companion to Ezra Pound,* Ed. Ira B. Nadel (Cambridge: Cambridge University Press, 1999), argues that "*Mauberley* is an extended case study of what happens when, as Eliot put it "'the doctrine of Art for Art's sake' is challenged by the demand that art 'be instrumental to social purposes'" (55).

23   Dara, *The Easy Chain*, 63.

24   Ezra Pound, *The ABC of Reading* (New York: New Directions, 2010), 29.

25   It is an oft-noted irony, however, that this phrase was, in fact, not one of Pound's own invention. Mary Paterson Cheadle, in *Ezra Pound's Confucian Translations* (Ann Arbor: University of Michigan Press, 1997), notes that the phrase is "an injunction written on the eighteenth-century B.C. King T'ang's 'bathtub,'" which Pound rendered "AS THE SUN MAKES IT NEW/DAY BY DAY MAKE IT NEW/ YET AGAIN MAKE IT NEW" (80). James J. Wilhelm, in *Ezra Pound: The Tragic Years, 1925–72* (University Park, PA: Pennsylvania State University Press, 1994), argues that Pound's translation was actually decisively influenced by an earlier French edition, which translated the passage as "Renew thyself daily, utterly make it new, and again new, make it new" (27).

26   Dara's novel seems to take up Pound's economic critiques in a generalized fashion, without reflecting Pound's interest in Italian fascism or C.H. Douglas's theories of social credit. Kenner, in *The Pound Era*, provides an excellent summary of the basic principles of social credit economics (300–17). See also Alec Marsh, *Money and Modernity: Pound, Williams and the Spirit of Jefferson* (Tuscaloosa, Alabama: The University of Alabama Press, 1998).

Bibliography

Abrams, M. H. "English Romanticism: The Spirit of the Age." In *Romanticism Reconsidered: Selected Papers from the English Institute*, edited by Northrop Frye, 26–72. New York; London: Columbia University Press, 1963.

Abrams, M. H. *The Mirror and the Lamp: Romantic Theory and the Critical Tradition*. Oxford: Oxford University Press, 1971.

Adams, Stephen J. "Hugh Selwyn Mauberley." In *The Ezra Pound Encyclopaedia*, edited by Demetres P. Tryphonopoulos and Stephen J. Adams, 150–51. Westport, CT: Greenwood Press, 2005.

Adorno, Theodor, Benjamin, Walter, Bloch, Ernst, Brecht, Bertolt and Lukács, Georg. *Aesthetics and Politics*. London: Verso Books, 1977.

Adorno, Theodor, Benjamin, Walter, Bloch, Ernst, Brecht, Bertolt and Lukács, Georg. *Kierkegaard: Construction of the Aesthetic*. Translated by Robert Hullot-Kentor. Minneapolis: University of Minnesota Press, 1989.

Adorno, Theodor, Benjamin, Walter, Bloch, Ernst, Brecht, Bertolt and Lukács, Georg. *Aesthetic Theory*. Translated by Robert Hullot-Kentor. London: The Athlone Press Ltd., 1997.

Agamben, Giorgio. "What is a Paradigm?" In *The Signature of All Things: On Method*, translated by Luca D'Isanto and Kevin Attell, 9–32. Brooklyn, NY: Zone Books, 2009.

Agamben, Giorgio. *The Man Without Content*. Translated by Georgia Albert. Stanford: Stanford University Press, 1999.

Agamben, Giorgio. *Stanzas: Word and Phantasm in Western Culture*. Translated by Ronald L. Martinez. Minneapolis: University of Minnesota Press, 1993.

Alberti, Leon Battista. *On Painting*. Translated by Cecil Grayson. London: Penguin, 1972.

Altieri, Charles. "Why Modernist Claims for Autonomy Matter." *Journal of Modern Literature* 32.3 (Spring 2009): 1–21.

Andrews, David. "Of Love, Scorn, and Contradiction: An Interpretive Overview of Gilbert Sorrentino's *Imaginative Qualities of Actual Things*." *The Review of Contemporary Fiction* 23.1 (2003): 9–44.

Ashton, Jennifer. *From Modernism to Postmodernism: American Poetry and Theory in the Twentieth Century*. Cambridge: Cambridge University Press, 2006.

Ayers, David. *Wyndham Lewis and Western Man*. London: Macmillan, 1992.

Beasley, Rebecca. "Wyndham Lewis and Modernist Satire." In *The Cambridge Companion to the Modernist Novel*, edited by Morag Shiach, 126–36. Cambridge: Cambridge University Press, 2007.

Behler, Ernst. *Irony and the Discourse of Modernity*. Seattle; London: University of Washington Press, 1990.

Behler, Ernst. "The Theory of Irony in German Romanticism." In *Romantic Irony*, edited by Frederick Garber, 43–81. Amsterdam; Philadelphia: John Benjamins Publishing Company, 2008.

Benjamin, Walter. *Illuminations*. Translated by Harry Zohn. New York: Schocken Books, 1969.

Bennett, Andrew. *Romantic Poets and the Culture of Posterity*. Cambridge: Cambridge University Press, 1999.

Bernhard, Thomas. *Extinction*. Translated by David McLintock. New York: Vintage, 1995.

Bernstein, J.M. *Against Voluptuous Bodies: Late Modernism and the Meaning of Painting*. Stanford: Stanford University Press, 2006.

Bogel, Fredric V. *The Difference Satire Makes: Rhetoric and Reading from Jonson to Byron*. Ithaca; London: Cornell University Press, 2001.

Booth, Wayne. *The Rhetoric of Fiction*, 2nd Edition. Chicago: University of Chicago Press, 1983.

Bourdieu, Pierre. *Distinction*. Oxon: Routledge Kegan Paul, 1984.

Bourdieu, Pierre. "The Historical Genesis of a Pure Aesthetic." In *Analytic Aesthetics*, edited by Richard Shusterman, 147–60. Oxford: Basil Blackwell, 1989.

Bourdieu, Pierre. *The Rules of Art: Genesis and Structure of the Literary Field*. Translated by Susan Emanuel. Cambridge, UK: Polity Press, 1996.

Bradbury, Malcolm and McFarlane, James, eds. *Modernism: A Guide to European Literature 1890–930*. London: Penguin, 1976.

Braddock, Jeremy. *Collecting as Modernist Practice*. Baltimore, MD: Johns Hopkins University Press, 2012.

Bradshaw, David. "*The Apes of God*." In *Wyndham Lewis: A Critical Guide*, edited by Andrzej Gasiorek and Nathan Waddell, 97–111. Edinburgh: Edinburgh University Press, 2015.

Bridson, D.G. *The Filibuster: A Study of the Political Ideas of Wyndham Lewis*. London: Cassell and Co., Ltd., 1972.

Brooker, Peter. *Bohemia in London: The Social Scene of Early Modernism*. New York: Palgrave, 2004.

Brown, Nicholas. *Utopian Generations: The Political Horizon of Twentieth-Century Literature*. Princeton; Oxford: Princeton University Press, 2005.

Brown, Nicholas. "The Work of Art in the Age of Its Real Subsumption Under Capital." *Nonsite*. March 13, 2012. Retrieved at http://nonsite.org/editorial/the-work-of-art-in-the-age-of-its-real-subsumption-under-capital.

Bru, Sascha. *Democracy, Law, and the Modernist Avant-Gardes: Writing in the State of Exception*. Edinburg: Edinburgh University Press, 2009.

Buchloh, Benjamin. *Neo-Avantgarde and Culture Industry: Essays on European and American Art from 1955 to 1975*. Cambridge, MA: MIT Press, 2000.

Bürger, Peter. *Theory of the Avant-Garde*. Translated by Michael Shaw. Manchester: Manchester University Press, 1984.

Bürger, Peter. "Avant-Garde and Neo-Avant-Garde: An Attempt to Answer Certain Critics of *Theory of the Avant-Garde*," *New Literary History* 41.4 (2010): 695–715.

Burn, Stephen J. "The Collapse of Everything." In *Paper Empires: William Gaddis and the World System*, edited by Joseph Tabbi and Rhone Shavers, 46–62. Tuscaloosa: University of Alabama Press, 2007.

Butler, Marilyn. *Peacock Displayed: A Satirist in His Context*. London: Routledge, 1979.

Butler, Marilyn. *Romantics, Rebels and Reactionaries: English Literature and Its Background, 1760–1830*. New York; Oxford: Oxford University Press, 1982.

Butler, Marilyn. "Romanticisms in England." In *Romanticism in National Context*, edited by Roy Porter and Mikulas Teich, 37–67. Cambridge: Cambridge University Press, 1988.

Calinescu, Matei. *Faces of Modernity: Avant-Garde, Decadence, Kitsch*. Bloomington, Indiana: Indiana University Press, 1977.

Campbell, Joseph. *The Mythic Image*. Princeton, NJ: Princeton University Press, 1981.

Charlton, David. "Introduction to *Kreisleriana*." In *E.T.A. Hoffmann's Musical Writings: Kreisleriana, The Poet and Composer, Music Criticism*, translated by Martin Clarke, 1–22. Cambridge: Cambridge University Press, 1989.

Chartier, Roger. *The Order of Books: Readers, Authors, and Libraries in Europe Between the Fourteenth and Eighteenth Centuries*. Translated by Lydia G. Cochrane. Stanford: Stanford University Press, 1994.

Cheadle, Mary Paterson. *Ezra Pound's Confucian Translations*. Ann Arbor: University of Michigan Press, 1997.

Clemens, Justin. *The Romanticism of Contemporary Theory: Institutions, Aesthetics, Nihilism*. Aldershot, UK: Ashgate Publishing Ltd., 2003.

Colebrook, Claire. *Irony*. London; New York: Routledge, 2004.

Coleridge, Samuel T. *Biographia Literaria*. London: William Pickering, 1847.

Connery, Brian A. and Combe, Kirke, eds. *Theorizing Satire: Essays in Literary Criticism*. New York: St. Martin's Press, 1995.

Conrad, Peter. *Shandyism: The Character of Romantic Irony*. New York: Barnes and Noble Books, 1978.

Cronan, Todd. *Against Affective Formalism: Matisse, Bergson, Modernism*. Minneapolis, MN: University of Minnesota Press, 2013.

Currie, Robert. "Wyndham Lewis, E.T.A. Hoffmann, and *Tarr*." *Review of English Studies* 30.188 (1979): 169–81.

Curtis, L. Perry, Jr. *Apes and Angels: The Irishman in Victorian Caricature*. Washington, DC: Smithsonian Institution Press, 1971.

Dara, Evan. *The Lost Scrapbook*. Tuscaloosa, AL: Fiction Collective 2, 1996.

Dara, Evan. *The Easy Chain*. New York; Roma: Aurora Publishers, 2008.

Dara, Evan. *Flee*. New York; Roma: Aurora Publishers, 2013.

Dasenbrock, Reed Way. *The Literary Vorticism of Ezra Pound and Wyndham Lewis: Towards the Condition of Painting*. Baltimore: Johns Hopkins University Press, 1985.

David, Larry and Seinfeld, Jerry. "The Pitch." *Seinfeld*. Directed by Tom Cherones. Culver City, CA: Sony Pictures Home Entertainment, 2005. DVD.

David, Larry and Seinfeld, Jerry. "The Opposite." *Seinfeld*. Directed by Tom Cherones. Culver City, CA: Sony Pictures Home Entertainment, 2005. DVD.

Derrida, Jacques. "Post-Scriptum: Aporias, Ways and Voices." In *Derrida and Negative Theology*, edited Harold Coward and Toby Foshay, 283–324. Albany, NY: SUNY University Press, 1992.

Derrida, Jacques. *Aporias*. Translated by Thomas Dutoit. Stanford: Stanford University Press, 1993.

Diamond, Elin. *Unmaking Mimesis*. New York: Routledge, 1997.

Diepeveen, Leonard. *Mock Modernism: An Anthology of Parodies, Travesties, Frauds, 1910–1935*. Toronto: University of Toronto Press, 2014.

Dryden, John. *The Essays of John Dryden*, Vol. 2. Edited by William Patton Ker. Oxford: Clarendon Press, 1900.

Duve, Thierry De. *Kant After Duchamp*. Cambridge, MA: The MIT Press, 1996.

Dyer, Gary. *British Satire and the Politics of Style, 1789–832*. Cambridge, UK: Cambridge University Press, 1997.

Eagleton, Terry. *Literary Theory: An Introduction*. Minneapolis, MN: University of Minnesota Press, 2008.

Eagleton, Terry. "Unhoused," *The London Review of Books* 30.10 (May 22, 2008): 19–20.

Edwards, Paul. *Wyndham Lewis: Painter and Writer*. New Haven; London: Yale University Press, 2000.

Edwards, Paul. "*The Apes of God* and the English Classical Tradition." In *Wyndham Lewis the Radical: Essays on Literature and Modernity*, edited by Carmelo Cunchillos Jaime, 91–108. Bern, Switzerland: Peter Lang AG, 2007.

Edwards, Paul. "Lewis, Satire, and Portraiture." In *The Cambridge Companion to Wyndham Lewis*, edited by Tyrus Miller, 72–86. Cambridge: Cambridge University Press, 2015.

Egginton, William. *A Wrinkle in History: Essays on Literature and Philosophy*. Aurora, CO: The Davies Group, 2007.

Eldridge, Richard and Cohen, Paul. "Art and the Transfiguration of Social Life: Gaddis on Art and Society." In *Powerless Fictions?: Ethics, Cultural Critique and American Fiction in the Age of Postmodernism*, edited by Ricardo Miguel Alfonso, 41–52. Amsterdam: Rodopoi, 1996.

Eliot, T. S. "Tradition and the Individual Talent." In *Selected Essays*, 3–11. New York: Harcourt Brace, 1932.

Elliott, Robert C. "The Definition of Satire: A Note on Method." *Yearbook on Comparative and General Literature* 11 (1962): 22.

Elliott, Robert C. *The Power of Satire: Magic, Ritual, Art.* Princeton, NJ: Princeton University Press, 1960.

Elliott, Robert C. "The Satirist and Society." In *Satire: Modern Essays in Criticism*, edited by Ronald Paulson, 205–17. Englewood Cliffs, NJ: Prentice-Hall, 1971.

Elliott, Robert C. "'What's the Difference?': Revisiting the Concepts of Modernism and the Avant-Garde." In *Europa! Europa?: The Avant-Garde, Modernism and the Fate of a Continent*, edited by Sascha Bru, et al., 21–35. Berlin: Walter de Gruyter GmbH & Co., 2009.

Enzensberger, Hans Magus. *The Consciousness Industry: On Literature, Politics, and the Media.* New York: Seabury Press, 1974.

Espey, John. *Ezra Pound's Mauberley: A Study in Composition.* Berkley; Los Angeles; London: University of California Press, 1955.

Eysteinsson, Astradur. *The Concept of Modernism.* Ithaca, NY: Cornell University Press, 1990.

Eysteinsson, Astradur and Liska, Vivian, eds. *Modernism*, Vol. 1. Amsterdam; Philadelphia: John Benjamins Publishing Co., 2007.

Farley, David G. *Modernist Travel Writing: Intellectuals Abroad.* Columbia, MO: University of Missouri Press, 2010.

Feijo, Antonio. *Near Miss: A Study of Wyndham Lewis (1909–30).* New York: Peter Lang Publishing Inc., 1998.

Ferguson, Frances. "On the Numbers of Romanticisms." *ELH* 58.2 (Summer 1991): 471–98.

Fiedler, Leslie. "The Death of Avant-Garde Literature." In *The Collected Essays of Leslie Fiedler*, Vol. 2, 454–60. New York: Stein and Day, 1971.

Flaubert, Gustave. *The Letters of Gustave Flaubert: 1830–57.* Edited and translated by Francis Steegmuller. Cambridge, MA: Harvard University Press, 1980.

Foshay, Toby Avard. *Wyndham Lewis and the Avant-Garde: The Politics of the Intellect.* Montreal: McGill-Queen's University Press, 1992.

Foster, Hal. *The Return of the Real: The Avant-Garde at the End of the Century.* Cambridge, MA: MIT Press, 1996.

Foucault, Michel. "What is an Author?" In *The Foucault Reader*, edited by Paul Rabinow, 101–20. New York: Pantheon Books, 1984.

Fowler, Alastair. *Kinds of Literature: An Introduction to the Theory of Genres and Modes.* Cambridge, MA: Harvard University Press, 1982.

Frank, Manfred. *The Philosophical Foundations of Early German Romanticism.* Translated by Elizabeth Millan-Zaibert. Albany, NY: SUNY University Press, 2004.

Freed, Mark M. *Robert Musil and the NonModern.* New York: Continuum, 2011.

Friedberg, Anne. *The Virtual Window from Alberti to Microsoft.* Cambridge, MA: MIT Press, 2006.

Frieden, Ken. *Genius and Monologue.* Ithaca; London: Cornell University Press, 1985.

Friedman, Susan Stanford. "Definitional Excursions: The Meanings of Modern/
    Modernity/Modernism." In *Disciplining Modernism*, edited by Pamela L. Caughie,
    11–32. New York: Palgrave Macmillan, 2009.

Frow, John. *Time and Commodity Culture: Essays in Cultural Theory and Postmodernity.*
    Oxford: Oxford University Press, 1997.

Frye, Northrop. *The Anatomy of Criticism.* Princeton: Princeton University Press, 1957.

Fuchs, Miraim. "'*il miglior fabbro*': Gaddis' Debt to T.S. Eliot," In *In Recognition of
    William Gaddis*, edited by John Kuehl and Steven Moore, 93–105. Syracuse, NY:
    Syracuse University Press, 1984.

Furst, Lilian. *Fictions of Romantic Irony.* Cambridge, MA: Harvard University Press, 1984.

Gabriele, Peter De. "Clothes Make the Ape: The Satirical Animal in Rochester's Poetry."
    Early Modern Literary Studies 18.1/2 (2015): 1–15.

Gaddis, William. *The Recognitions.* New York: Penguin, 1993.

Gaddis, William. *JR.* New York: Penguin, 1993.

Gaddis, William. *A Frolic of His Own.* New York: Poseidon Press, 1994.

Gasiorek, Andrzej. *Wyndham Lewis and Modernism.* Horndon, UK: Northcote House
    Publishers, 2004.

Gasiorek, Andrzej. "Wyndham Lewis on Art, Culture and Politics in the 1930s."
    In *Wyndham Lewis and the Cultures of Modernity*, edited by Alice Reeve-Tucker,
    Andrzel Gasiorek, and Nathan Waddell, 201–22. Surrey: Ashgate, 2011.

Gay, Peter. *Modernism: The Lure of Heresy, from Baudelaire to Beckett and Beyond.* New
    York: W.W. Norton & Co., 2008.

Genter, Robert. *Late Modernism: Art, Culture, and Politics in Cold War America.*
    Philadelphia: University of Pennsylvania Press, 2010.

Gide, André. *The Counterfeiters.* Translated by Dorothy Bussy and Justin O'Brien. New
    York: Vintage, 1973.

Gill, James E., ed. *Cutting Edges: Postmodern Perspectives on Eighteenth-Century Satire.*
    Knoxville, TN: University of Tennessee Press, 1995.

Girard, René. *The Scapegoat.* Translated by Yvone Freccero. Baltimore: Johns Hopkins
    University Press, 1986.

Gluck, Mary. *Popular Bohemia: Modernism and Urban Culture in Nineteenth-Century
    Paris.* Cambridge, MA: Harvard University Press, 2005.

Goldstone, Andrew. *Fictions of Autonomy: Modernism from Wilde to de Man.* Oxford:
    Oxford University Press, 2013.

Green, Jack. *Fire the Bastards!* Normal, IL: Dalkey Archive Press, 2012.

Green, Jesse D. "Williams' 'Kora in Hell': The Opening of the Poem as 'Field of Action.'"
    Contemporary Literature 13.3 (Summer 1972): 295–314.

Greenberg, Jonathan. *Modernism, Satire, and the Novel.* Cambridge: Cambridge
    University Press, 2011.

Greenwood, Jodie. "The Crisis of the System: *Blast's* Reception." *Wyndham Lewis and
    the Cultures of Modernity*, edited by Anrzej Gasiorek, Alice Reeve-Tucker, and
    Nathan Waddell, 77–94. Surrey: Ashgate, 2011.

Griffin, Dustin. *Satire: A Critical Reintroduction*. Lexington, KY: University Press of Kentucky, 1994.

Groff, Peter. "Who is Zarathustra's Ape?" In *A Nietzschean Bestiary: Becoming Animal Beyond Docile and Brutal*, edited by Christa Davis Acampora, and Ralph R. Acampora, 17–31. Lanham, MD: Rowman & Littlefield Publishers Inc. 2004.

Guilhamet, Leon. *Satire and the Transformation of Genre*. Philadelphia: University of Pennsylvania Press, 1987.

Gurewitch, Morton. *The Comedy of Romantic Irony*. Lanham, MD: University Press of America Inc., 2002.

Guy, Josephine M. *The British Avant-Garde: The Theory and Politics of Tradition*. New York: Harvester Wheatsheaf, 1991.

Hamilton, Paul. "'A Shadow of Magnitude': The Dialectic of Romantic Aesthetics." In *Beyond Romanticism: New Approaches to Texts and Contexts 1780–832*, edited by Stephen Copley, 11–31. London; New York: Routledge, 1992.

Hamilton, Paul. "From Sublimity to Indeterminacy: New World Order or Aftermath of Romantic Ideology." In *Romanticism and Postmodernism*, edited by Edward Larrissy, 13–28. Cambridge: Cambridge University Press, 1999.

Hartman, Geoffrey. *Criticism in the Wilderness: The Study of Literature Today*. New Haven: Yale University Press, 1980.

Hassan, Ihab. "POSTmodernISM: A Paracritical Bibliography." In *Paracriticisms: Seven Speculations of the Times*, 39–62. Urbana, IL; Chicago: University of Illinois Press, 1975.

Highet, Gilbert. *The Anatomy of Satire*. Princeton: Princeton University Press, 1926.

Hindrichs, Cheryl. "Late Modernism, 1928–45: Criticism and Theory." *Literature Compass* 8.11 (2011): 840–55.

Hoffmann, E.T.A. "Report of an Educated Young Man." In *E.T.A. Hoffmann's Musical Writings: Kreisleriana, The Poet and Composer, Music Criticism*, translated by Martin Clarke, 136–43. Cambridge: Cambridge University Press, 1989.

Hoffmann, Gerhard. *From Modernism to Postmodernism: Concepts and Strategies of Postmodern American Fiction*. Amsterdam; New York: Rodopi, 2005.

Hulme, T.E. *The Collected Writings of T.E. Hulme*. Oxford: Clarendon Press, 1994.

Hutcheon, Linda. "Beginning to Theorize Postmodernism." In *A Postmodern Reader*, edited by Joseph Natoli and Linda Hutcheon, 243–72. Albany, NY: SUNY University Press, 1993.

Huyssen, Andreas. *After the Great Divide: Modernism, Mass Culture, Postmodernism*. Bloomington, IN: Indiana University Press, 1986.

Huyssen, Andreas. *Twilight Memories: Marking Time in a Culture of Amnesia*. New York: Routledge, 1995.

Isaak, Jo Anna. *The Ruin of Representation in Modernist Art and Texts*. Ann Arbor: UMI Research Press, 1986.

Iser, Wolfgang. *The Fictive and the Imaginary: Charting Literary Anthropology*. Baltimore: Johns Hopkins University Press, 1993.

Jakobson, Roman. "The Dominant." In *Selected Writings, Vol. 3: Poetry of Grammar and Grammar of Poetry*, 751–56. The Netherlands: Walter de Gruyter, 1981.

Jameson, Fredric. *Fables of Aggression: Wyndham Lewis, the Modernist as Fascist.* Berkeley: University of California Press, 1979.

Jameson, Fredric. "Postmodernism and Consumer Society." In *Postmodern Culture*, edited by Hal Foster, 111–25. London: Pluto Press, 1985.

Jameson, Fredric. *A Singular Modernity: Essay on the Ontology of the Present.* London: Verso, 2002.

Jameson, Fredric. "Postmodernism, or the Cultural Logic of Late Capitalism." *New Left Review* 1.146 (1984): 59–92.

Janson, H. W. *Apes and Ape Lore in the Middle Ages and the Renaissance.* London: The Warburg Institute, University of London, 1952.

Jencks, Charles. *Late Modern Architecture and Other Essays.* New York: Rizzoli, 1980.

Johnston, John H. *Carnival of Repetition: Gaddis's The Recognitions and Postmodern Theory.* Philadelphia: University of Pennsylvania Press, 1990.

Jones, Steven E. *Satire and Romanticism.* New York: St. Martin's Press, 2000.

Jones, Steven E., ed. *The Satiric Eye: Forms of Satire in the Romantic Period.* New York: Palgrave Macmillan, 2003.

Jones, Steven E. *British Satire, 1785–840*, 5 Vols. London: Pickering and Chatto, 2003.

Josipovici, Gabriel. *What Ever Happened to Modernism?* New Haven: Yale University Press, 2010.

Jung, Carl. *Alchemical Studies, The Collected Works of Carl Jung*, Vol. 13. Edited by Herbert Read, Michael Fordham, and Gerhard Adler. New York: Pantheon Books, 1953.

Kant, Immanuel. *Critique of Judgment.* Translated by James Creed Meredith. Edited by Nicolas Walker. Oxford: Oxford University Press, 2007.

Kenner, Hugh. *Wyndham Lewis, 1886–957.* London: Metheun, 1954.

Kenner, Hugh. *The Pound Era.* Berkeley; Los Angeles: University of California Press, 1971.

Kenner, Hugh. "The Making of the Modernist Canon." *The Chicago Review* 34.2 (Spring 1984): 49–61.

Kernan, Alvin. *The Cankered Muse: Satire of the English Renaissance.* New Haven; London: Yale University Press, 1959.

Kiernan, Robert. *Frivolity Unbound: Six Masters of the Camp Novel.* New York: Continuum, 1990.

Kiralyfalvi, Bela. *The Aesthetics of Gyorgy Lukacs.* Princeton, NJ: Princeton University Press, 1975.

Klein, Scott W. *The Fictions of James Joyce and Wyndham Lewis: Monsters of Nature and Design.* Cambridge: Cambridge University Press, 1994.

Knight, Charles A. "Satire, Speech, and Genre." *Comparative Literature* 44.1 (1992): 22–41.

Knight, Charles A. *The Literature of Satire*. Cambridge: Cambridge University Press, 2004.

Knight, Christopher J. *Hints and Guesses: William Gaddis's Fiction of Longing*. Madison: University of Wisconsin Press, 1997.

Knight, Christopher J. "Trying to Make Negative Things Do the Work of Positive Ones: Gaddis and Apophaticism." In *William Gaddis: "The Last of Something,"* edited by Crystal Alberts, Christopher Leise, and Birger Vanwesenbeeck, 51–68. Jefferson, North Carolina; London: McFarland & Company, Inc., 2010.

Knight, Christopher J. *Omissions Are Not Accidents: Modern Apophaticism from Henry James to Jacques Derrida*. Toronto: University of Toronto Press, 2010.

Kostelanetz, Richard. "Introduction: What is Avant-Garde?" In *The Avant-Garde Tradition in Literature*, 3–6. Buffalo, NY: Prometheus Books, 1982.

Krauss, Rosalind. *The Originality of the Avant-Garde and Other Modernist Myths*. Cambridge, MA: MIT Press, 1986.

Lacoue-Labarthe, Philippe and Nancy, Jean-Luc. *The Literary Absolute: The Theory of Literature in German Romanticism*. Translated by Philip Barnard and Cheryl Lester. Albany, NY: SUNY Press, 1988.

Laski, Alexander. "The Politics of Dancing – Gay Disco Music and Postmodernism." In *The Last Post: Music after Modernism*, edited by Simon Miller, 110–32. Manchester: Manchester University Press, 1993.

Latham, Sean. *The Art of Scandal: Modernism, Libel Law, and the Roman à Clef*. Oxford: Oxford University Press, 2009.

Leja, Michael. *Reframing Abstract Expressionism: Subjectivity and Painting in the 1940s*. New Haven: Yale University Press, 1993.

Lenain, Thierry. *Monkey Painting*. London: Reaktion Books, 1997.

Lewis, Wyndham. *Tarr: The 1918 Version*. Edited by Paul O'Keefe. 1918. Reprint. Santa Rosa, CA: Black Sparrow Press, 1990.

Lewis, Wyndham. *The Art of Being Ruled*. Edited by Reed Way Dasenbrock. 1926. Reprint. Santa Rosa, CA: Black Sparrow Press, 1989.

Lewis, Wyndham. *The Lion and the Fox: The Role of the Hero in the Plays of Shakespeare*. 1927. Reprint. London: Methuen & Co Ltd., 1966.

Lewis, Wyndham. *Time and Western Man*. 1927. Reprint. Boston: Beacon Press, 1957.

Lewis, Wyndham. *The Childermass*. London: Chatto and Windus, 1928.

Lewis, Wyndham. *Tarr* (Revised Edition). 1928. Reprint. Hammondsworth: Penguin, 1982.

Lewis, Wyndham. "The Diabolic Principle," In *The Enemy*, Vol. 3, edited by Wyndham Lewis, 9–85. 1929. Reprint. Santa Rosa, CA: Black Sparrow Press, 1994.

Lewis, Wyndham. *Paleface: The Philosophy of the 'Melting Pot'*. New York: Haskell House, 1929.

Lewis, Wyndham. *Apes of God*. 1930. Reprint. Santa Barbara, CA: Black Sparrow Press, 1981.

Lewis, Wyndham. *Satire and Fiction.* London: The Arthur Press, 1930.

Lewis, Wyndham. *The Diabolic Principle and the Dithyrambic Spectator.* New York: Haskell House, 1931.

Lewis, Wyndham. *Men Without Art.* Edited by Seamus Cooney. 1934. Reprint. Santa Rosa, CA: Black Sparrow Press, 1987.

Lewis, Wyndham. *The Hitler Cult.* London: Dent, 1939.

Lewis, Wyndham. *The Jews, Are They Human?* 1939. Reprint. New York: Gordon, 1972.

Lewis, Wyndham. *Wyndham Lewis the Artist: From "BLAST" to Burlington House.* New York: Haskell House Publishers Ltd., 1939.

Lewis, Wyndham. *The Demon of Progress in the Arts.* London: Methuen & Co Ltd., 1954.

Lewis, Wyndham. *Collected Poems and Plays.* Edited by Alan Munton. New York: Persea Books, 1979.

Lewis, Wyndham. *The Complete Wild Body.* Edited by Bernard Lafourcade. Santa Rosa, CA: Black Sparrow Press, 1982.

Lewis, Wyndham. *Creatures of Habit and Creatures of Change: Essays on Art, Literature, and Society 1914–1956.* Edited by Paul Edwards. Santa Rosa, CA: Black Sparrow Press, 1989.

Lewis, Wyndham. *Tarr.* Oxford: Oxford University Press, 2010.

Loesberg, Jonathan. *A Return to Aesthetics: Autonomy, Indifference, and Postmodernism.* Stanford: Stanford University Press, 2005.

Lovejoy, Arthur O. "On the Discrimination of Romanticisms." *PMLA* 39.2 (June 1924): 229–53.

Lowenstein, Andrea F. *Loathsome Jews and Engulfing Women: Metaphors of Projection in the Works of Wyndham Lewis, Charles Williams, and Graham Greene.* New York; London: New York University Press, 1993.

Lowy, Michael and Sayre, Robert. *Romanticism Against the Tide of Modernity.* Durham, NC: Duke University Press, 2001.

Luhmann, Niklas. "A Redescription of 'Romantic Art.'" *MLN* 113.3 (1996): 506–22.

Lyotard, Jean-Francois. *The Postmodern Condition: A Report on Knowledge.* Translated by Geoff Bennington and Brian Massumi. Manchester: Manchester University Press, 1979.

Lyotard, Jean-Francois. *The Postmodern Explained: Correspondence, 1982–1985.* Edited by Julian Pefanis and Morgan Thomas. Minneapolis, MN: University of Minnesota Press, 1993.

Lyotard, Jean-Francois. *Lessons on the Analytic of the Sublime.* Translated by Elizabeth Rottenberg. Stanford, CA: Stanford University Press, 1994.

Man, Paul de. "The Rhetoric of Temporality." In *Interpretation: Theory and Practice,* edited by Charles S. Singleton, 173–209. Baltimore: The Johns Hopkins Press, 1969.

Mann, Paul. *The Theory-Death of the Avant-Garde.* Bloomington, IN: Indiana University Press, 1991.

Mansfield, Elizabeth. *Too Beautiful to Picture: Zeuxis, Myth, and Mimesis.* Minneapolis, MN: University of Minnesota Press, 2007.

Mao, Douglas. *Solid Objects: Modernism and the Test of Production.* Princeton, NJ: Princeton University Press, 1998.

Mao, Douglas and Walkowitz, Rebecca L. "The New Modernist Studies." *PMLA* 123.3 (2008): 737–48.

Marcuse, Herbert. *The Aesthetic Dimension: Towards a Critique of Marxist Aesthetics.* Translated by Herbert Marcuse and Erica Sherover. Boston: Beacon Press, 1978.

Marsh, Alec. *Money and Modernity: Pound, Williams and the Spirit of Jefferson.* Tuscaloosa, Alabama: University of Alabama Press, 1998.

Marshall, Ashley. *The Practice of Satire in England: 1658–1770.* Baltimore, MD: Johns Hopkins University Press, 2013.

Marx, Karl. *The Unknown Karl Marx.* Edited by Robert Payne. London: University of London Press, 1971.

Marx, William. "The Twentieth Century: Century of the Arrière-Gardes?" In *Europa! Europa?: The Avant-Garde, Modernism and the Fate of a Continent*, edited by Sascha Bru, et al., 59–71. Berlin: Walter de Gruyter GmbH & Co., 2009.

Materer, Timothy. *Wyndham Lewis the Novelist.* Detroit: Wayne State University Press, 1976.

Matz, Aaron. "The Years of Hating Proust." *Comparative Literature* 60.4 (2008): 355–69.

Matz, Aaron. *Satire in an Age of Realism.* Cambridge: Cambridge University Press, 2010.

McHale, Brian. *Postmodernist Fiction.* New York; London: Metheun, 1987.

McMahon, Cliff. *Reframing the Theory of the Sublime: Pillars and Modes.* Lewiston, NY: Edwin Mellen Press, 2004.

Mellor, Anne K. *English Romantic Irony.* Cambridge, MA: Harvard University Press, 1980.

Mellors, Anthony. *Late Modernist Poetics: From Pound to Prynne.* Manchester, NY: Manchester University Press, 2005.

Menke, Christoph. *The Sovereignty of Art: Aesthetic Negativity in Adorno and Derrida.* Translated by Neil Solomon. Cambridge, MA: MIT Press, 1998.

Milan-Zaibert, Elizabeth. *Fredrich Schlegel and the Emergence of Romantic Philosophy.* New York: SUNY University Press, 2007.

Miller, Richard. *Bohemia: The Protoculture Then and Now.* Chicago: Nelson Hall, 1977.

Miller, Tyrus. *Late Modernism: Politics, Fiction, and Arts between the World Wars.* Berkeley: University of California Press, 1999.

Miller, Tyrus. "Fictional Truths: *Imaginative Qualities of Actual Things* between Image and Language." *Review of Contemporary Fiction* 23.1 (Spring 2003): 59–67.

Miller, Tyrus. "The Avant-Garde, Bohemia and Mainstream Culture." In *The Cambridge History of Twentieth-Century English Literature*, edited by Laura Marcus and Peter Nicholls, 100–16. Cambridge: Cambridge University Press, 2005.

Miller, Tyrus. *Singular Examples: Artistic Politics and the Neo-Avant-Garde.* Evanston, IL: Northwestern University Press, 2009.

Moore, Steven. *William Gaddis.* Boston: Twayne Publishers, 1989.

Muecke, D.C. *The Compass of Irony.* London: Methuen, 1969.

Mul, Jos De. Romantic Desire in (Post)Modern Art and Philosophy. Albany, NY: SUNY University Press, 1999.

Munton, Alan. "Introduction: Wyndham Lewis Our Contemporary." In *Wyndham Lewis the Radical,* edited by Carmello Cunchillos Jaime, 7–20. Bern: Peter Lang AG, 2007.

Munton, Alan. "Wyndham Lewis: From Proudhon to Hitler (and Back): The Strange Political Journey of Wyndham Lewis." *E-rea: Revue Electronique d'Etudes sur le Monde Anglophone* 4.2 (2006).

Murphet, Julian. "Introduction: On the Market and Uneven Development." *Affirmations* 1.1 (2013): 1–20.

Murphy, Richard. *Theorizing the Avant-Garde: Modernism, Expressionism, and the Problem of Postmodernity.* Cambridge: Cambridge University Press, 1999.

Nicol, Bran. *Postmodernism and the Contemporary Novel.* Edinburgh: Edinburgh University Press, 2002.

Nicholls, Peter. "Apes and Familiars: Modernism, Mimesis, and the Work of Wyndham Lewis." *Textual Practice* 6.3 (1992): 421–38.

Nicholls, Peter. *Modernisms: A Literary Guide.* Bassingstoke, England: Macmillan, 1995.

Nichols, James W. *Insinuation: The Tactics of English Satire.* The Hague; Paris: Mouton & Co. N.V., 1971.

Nokes, David. *Raillery and Rage: A Study of Eighteenth Century Satire.* Brighton: The Harvester Press Ltd., 1987.

Normand, Tom. *Wyndham Lewis the Artist: Holding the Mirror up to Politics.* Cambridge: Cambridge University Press, 1992.

Olster, Stacey. "Gilbert Sorrentino's Problematic Middle Child: *Imaginative Qualities of Actual Things.*" *Review of Contemporary Fiction* 23.1 (Spring 2003): 70–89.

Ortega y Gasset, José. *The Dehumanization of Art and Other Essays on Art, Culture, and Literature.* Translated by Helene Weyl. Princeton: Princeton University Press, 1968.

Owens, Craig. "The Discourse of Others: Feminists and Postmodernism." In *The Anti-Aeshtetic,* edited by Hal Foster, 57–82. New York: The New Press, 1983.

Patterson, Ian. "Apes, Bodies and Readers." In *Volcanic Heaven: Essays on Wyndham Lewis's Painting and Writing,* edited by Paul Edwards, 123–34. Santa Rosa, CA: Black Sparrow Press, 1996.

Paulson, Ronald. *The Fictions of Satire.* Baltimore: Johns Hopkins University Press, 1967.

Peacock, Thomas L. *Nightmare Abbey.* 1818. Reprint. Oxford; New York: Woodstock Books, 1992.

Peacock, Thomas L. *The Works of Thomas Love Peacock: Headlong Hall, Melincourt, Nightmare Abbey, Maid Marian.* London: George Routledge and Sons Ltd., 1905.

Peacock, Thomas L. *The Works of Thomas Love Peacock*, Vol. 6. London: Constable and Co. Ltd., 1927.

Peacock, Thomas L. *The Letters of Thomas Love Peacock* Vol. 1. Edited by Nicholas A. Joukovsky. Oxford: Clarendon Press, 2001.

Pease, Donald. "Sublime Politics." In *The American Sublime*, edited by Mary Arensberg, 21–51. Albany, NY: SUNY University Press, 1986.

Peckham, Morse. "Towards a Theory of Romanticism." *PMLA* 66.2 (March 1951): 5–23.

Poggioli, Renato. *The Theory of the Avant-Garde*. Translated by Gerald Fitzgerald. Cambridge, MA: Harvard University Press, 1968.

Pound, Ezra. *The Cantos*. New York: New Directions, 1998.

Pound, Ezra. *The ABC of Reading*. New York: New Directions, 2010.

Prance, Claude A. *The Characters in the Novels of Thomas Love Peacock 1785–1866 with Bibliographical Lists*. Lewiston, NY: The Edwin Mellen Press, 1992.

Praz, Mario. *The Romantic Agony*. Second Edition. Oxford: Oxford University Press, 1970.

Puchner, Martin. *Poetry of the Revolution: Marx, Manifestos and the Avant-Garde*. Princeton, NJ; Oxford: Princeton University Press, 2006.

Quema, Anne. *The Agon of Modernism: Wyndham Lewis's Allegories, Aesthetics, and Politics*. London: Associated University Presses, 1999.

Rainey, Lawrence. *Institutions of Modernism: Literary Elites and Public Culture*. New Haven; London: Yale University Press, 1998.

Ranciere, Jacques. *The Politics of Literature*. Translated by Julie Rose. Cambridge, UK: Polity Press, 2011.

Read, Herbert. "Surrealism and the Romantic Principle." In *Surrealism*, edited by Herbert Read, 19–91. London: Praeger, 1971.

Redfield, Marc. "Aesthetics, Theory, and the Profession of Literature: Derrida and Romanticism." *Studies in Romanticism* 46 (Summer/Fall 2007): 227–46.

Richardson, Alan. *The Neural Sublime: Cognitive Theories and Romantic Texts*. Baltimore, MD: Johns Hopkins University Press, 2010.

Roberts, Andrew Michael. "Romantic Irony and the Postmodern Sublime." In *Romanticism and Postmodernism*, edited by Edward Larrissy, 141–56. Cambridge: Cambridge University Press, 1999.

Rosenheim, Edward W., Jr. *Swift and the Satirist's Art*. Chicago; London: University of Chicago Press, 1963.

Rosenthal, Lecia. *Mourning Modernism: Literature, Catastrophe, and the Politics of Consolation*. New York: Fordham University Press, 2011.

Rudrum, David. *Stanley Cavell and the Claim of Literature*. Baltimore: Johns Hopkins University Press, 2013.

Ruthven, K.K. "The Anethical Imperative." *Wet Ink* 3 (2006): 31–3.

Saiedi, Nader. *The Birth of Social Theory: Social Thought in the Enlightenment and Romanticism*. Lanham, MD: University Press of America Inc., 1993.

Schaffner, Anna Katharina. "Inheriting the Avant-Garde: On the Reconciliation of Tradition and Invention in Concrete Poetry." In *Neo-Avant-Garde*, edited by David Hopkins, 97–117. Amsterdam; New York: Rodopi, 2006.

Schenker, Daniel. *Wyndham Lewis: Religion and Modernism*. Tuscaloosa; London: University of Alabama Press, 1992.

Scherzinger, Martin. "In Memory of a Receding Dialectic: The Political Relevance of Autonomy and Formalism in Modernist Music." In *The Pleasure of Modernist Music: Listening, Meaning, Intention, Ideology*, edited by Arved Ashby, 68–102. Rochester, NY: University of Rochester Press, 2004.

Schlegel, Friedrich. *Philosophical Fragments*. Translated by Peter Firchow. Minneapolis, MN: University of Minnesota Press.

Schmid, Thomas. *Humor and Transgression in Peacock, Shelley, and Byron: A Cold Carnival*. Lewiston, NY: The Edwin Mellen Press, 1992.

Schock, Peter. "The Marriage of Heaven and Hell: Blake's Myth of Satan and Its Cultural Matrix." *ELH* 60.2 (Summer 1993): 441–70.

Schulte-Sasse, Jochen. "Foreword: Theory of Modernism Versus Theory of the Avant-Garde." In Peter Bürger, *Theory of the Avant-Garde*, translated by Michael Shaw, vii–xvii. Manchester: Manchester University Press, 1984.

Schwank, Klaus. "From Satire to Indeterminacy: Thomas Love Peacock's *Nightmare* Abbey." In *Beyond the Suburbs of the Mind: Exploring English Romanticism*, edited by Michael Gassenmeier and Norbert H. Platz, 151–62. Essen: Verlag Die Blaue Eule, 1987.

Seidel, Michael. *The Satiric Inheritance: Rabelais to Stern*. Princeton: Princeton University Press, 1979.

Sicari, Stephen. *Modernist Humanism and the Men of 1914*. Columbia, SC: University of South Carolina Press, 2011.

Siebers, Tobin. "Allegory and the Aesthetic Ideology." In *Interpretation and the Allegory: Antiquity to the Modern Period*, edited by John Whitman, 469–86. Leiden; Boston: Brill, 2000.

Simpson, David. *Irony and Authority in Romantic Poetry*. London: Macmillan, 1979.

Simpson, David. *The Academic Postmodern: A Report on Half-Knowledge*. Chicago; London: University of Chicago Press, 1995.

Simpson, Paul. *On the Discourse of Satire: Towards a Stylistic Model of Satirical Humour*. Amsterdam; Philadelphia: John Benjamins Publishing Co., 2003.

Siraganian, Lisa. *Modernism's Other Work: The Art Object's Political Life*. Oxford; New York: Oxford University Press, 2012.

Snyder, John. *Prospects of Power: Tragedy, Satire, the Essay, and the Theory of Genre*. Lexington, KY: University Press of Kentucky, 1991.

Sontag, Susan. *Against Interpretation and Other Essays*. New York: Farrar, Straus, and Giroux, 1966.

Sorrentino, Gilbert. *The Imaginative Qualities of Actual Things*. 1971. Reprint. Normal, Il: Dalkey Archive Press, 1991.

Sorrentino, Gilbert. *Mulligan Stew.* New York: Grove Press, 1979.

Sorrentino, Gilbert. "Post-Modernism Explained." *Mississippi Review* 8.1 (Winter/ Spring 1979): 36.

Sorrentino, Gilbert. *Something Said: Essays.* San Francisco: North Point Press, 1984.

Sorrentino, Gilbert. "Interview with Alexander Laurence," *The Write Stuff: Interviews,* http://www.altx.com/int2/gilber.sorrentino.html, accessed November 8, 2011.

Sorrentino, Gilbert. "A Conversation with Gilbert Sorrentino by John O'Brien," Dalkey Archive Press, http://www.dalkeyarchive.com/a-conversation-with-gilbert-sorrentino-by-john-obrien/, accessed December 3, 2013.

Southey, Robert. *A Vision of Judgment.* London: Longman, Hurst, Rees, Orme, and Brown, 1821.

Speaight, Robert. *Francois Mauriac: A Study of the Writer and the Man.* London: Chatto & Windus, 1976.

Tabbi, Joseph. "Matter into Imagination: The Cognitive Realism of Gilbert Sorrentino's *Imaginative Qualities of Actual Things.*" *Review of Contemporary Fiction* 23.1 (Spring 2003): 90–107.

Test, George A. *Satire: Spirit and Art.* Tampa: University of South Florida Press, 1991.

"The Philosophy of Melancholy: A Poem in Four Parts." *The New Review, or Monthly Analysis of General Literature* 1.2 (February 1813): 147–49.

Thesen, Sharon. "In the song/of the alphabet: Gilbert Sorrentino's *Splendide Hotel.*" *The Review of Contemporary Fiction* 1.1 (1980): 56–61.

Trotter, David. *Paranoid Modernism.* Oxford: Oxford University Press, 2001.

Waddell, Nathan. *Modernist Nowheres: Politics and Utopia in Early Modernist Writing, 1900–1920.* London: Palgrave Macmillan, 2012.

Waddell, Nathan. "Providing Ridicule: Wyndham Lewis and Satire in the 'Postwar-to-end-war' World." In *Utopianism, Modernism, and Literature in the Twentieth Century*, edited by Alice Reeve-Tucker and Nathan Waddell, 56–73. London: Palgrave Macmillan, 2013.

Wagner, Geoffrey. *Wyndham Lewis: A Portrait of the Artist as the Enemy.* London: Routledge & Kegan Paul, 1957.

Walker, Keith. "Lord Rochester's Monkey (Again)." In *That Second Bottle: Essays on the Earl of Rochester*, edited by Nicholas Fisher, 81–88. Manchester: Manchester University Press, 2000.

Wallace, Jeff. "Modernists on the Art of Fiction." In *The Cambridge Companion to the Modernist Novel*, edited by Morag Shiach, 15–31. Cambridge: Cambridge University Press, 2007.

Warnock, Mary. *Imagination.* Berkeley; Los Angeles: University of California Press, 1978.

Weinberg, Kurt. *On Gide's* Prométhée: *Private Myth and Public Mystification.* Princeton, NJ: Princeton University Press, 1972.

Weisenburger, Steven. *Fables of Subversion: Satire and the American Novel, 1930–1980.* Athens, GA: University of Georgia Press, 1995.

Weiskel, Thomas. *The Romantic Sublime: Studies in the Structure and Psychology of Transcendence.* Baltimore, MD: Johns Hopkins University Press, 1976.

Wellbery, David. *The Specular Moment: Goethe's Early Lyric and the Beginnings of Romanticism.* Stanford: Stanford University Press, 1996.

Wellek, Rene. "The Concept of 'Romanticism.'" *Comparative Literature* 1.2 (Spring 1949): 147–72.

Wilde, Oscar. "The Decay of Lying." In *Intentions: The Works of Oscar Wilde*, edited by Jules Barbey d'Aurevilly, Lady Wilde, 7–65. London: Lamb, 1909.

Wilhelm, James J. *Ezra Pound: The Tragic Years, 1925–1972.* University Park, PA: Pennsylvania State University Press, 1994.

Williams, Orlo. "The Parisian Prototype." In *On Bohemia: The Code of the Self-Exiled*, edited by Cesar Grana and Marigay Grana, 58–68. London: Transaction Publishers, 1990.

Williams, William Carlos. *Imaginations.* New York: New Directions, 1970.

Wimsatt, William K., Jr. and Brooks, Cleanth. *Literary Criticism: A Short History.* New York: Knopf, 1957.

Wimsatt, William K. and Beardsley, Monroe. "The Intentional Fallacy." *The Sewanee Review* 54.3 (July–September 1946): 468–88.

Winchell, Mark Royden. *Cleanth Brooks and the Rise of Modern Criticism.* Charlottesville, VA: The University Press of Virginia, 1996.

Witemeyer, Hugh. "Early Poetry 1908–1920." In *The Cambridge Companion to Ezra Pound*, edited by Ira B. Nadel, 43–58. Cambridge: Cambridge University Press, 1999.

Wood, Jamie. "Lewis, Satire, and Literature." In *Wyndham Lewis: A Critical Guide*, edited by Andrzej Gasiorek and Nathan Waddell, 82–96. Edinburgh: Edinburgh University Press, 2015.

Woolf, Virginia. "How It Strikes a Contemporary." In *Selected Essays*, edited by David Bradshaw, 23–31. Oxford; New York: Oxford University Press, 2008.

Wordsworth, William and Coleridge, Samuel T. *Lyrical Ballads.* London: J. & A. Arch, 1798.

Wragg, David. *Wyndham Lewis and the Philosophy of Art in Early Modernist Britain.* Lewiston, NY: Edwin Mellen Press, 2006.

Wyatt, David. *Secret Histories: Reading Twentieth-Century American Literature.* Baltimore: Johns Hopkins University Press, 2010.

Yu, Christopher. *Nothing to Admire: The Politics of Poetic Satire from Dryden to Merrill.* Oxford: Oxford University Press, 2003.

Zimbardo, Rose A. *At Zero Point: Discourse, Culture, and Satire in Restoration England.* Lexingtion, KY: The University Press of Kentucky, 1998.

Index

9 781501 348082